EXPORT PROMOTION

A Decision Support Model Approach

**LUDO CUYVERS &
WILMA VIVIERS**

EDITORS

SUN PRESS

Export Promotion:
A Decision Support Model Approach

Published by SUN MeDIA MeTRO under the SUN PReSS imprint

ISBN 978-0-9870096-3-0

Cover & text design by Maryke Venter
Page layout by Christine van Deventer
Set in 9/14 Humnst777 BT

Academic, professional and reference works are published under this imprint in print and electronic format. This publication may be ordered directly from www.sun-e-shop.co.za.

www.africansunmedia.co.za/www.sun-e-shop.co.za

Contents

List of figures

List of tables

Annexures

Abbreviations

ASEAN: Association of Southeast Asian Nations

AU: African Union

AWEX: Agence wallonne à l'Exportation et aux Investissements Etrangers

B2B: Business-to-business

BDBH: Belgiesche Dienst voor de Buitenlandse Handel

BGA: Bundesverband des Deutschen- und Aussenhandels (e.v.)

BI: Business Intelligence

BIS: Business, Innovation and Skills

BLEU: Belgium-Luxembourg Economic Union

BRIC: Brazil, Russia, India and China

BSTC: Bilateral Scientific and Technological Co-operation

CBI: Centre for the Promotion of Imports from Developing Countries

CDC: Consultancy Development Centre

CEEC: Central and Eastern European Countries

CI: Competitive Intelligence

CV: Critical Value

DFA: Department of Foreign Affairs

DSM: Decision Support Model

DTI: Department of Trade and Industry

EBOPS: Extended Balance of Payments for Services

EMIA: Export Market and Investment Assistance

EPO: Export promotion organisation

EPRG: Export promotion research group

EPS: Export promotion strategies

EU: European Union

FAO: Food and Agriculture Organisation

FAS: Foreign Agricultural Service

FDI: Foreign Direct Investment

FER: Foreign Economic Representatives

FIT: Flanders Investment and Trade

FWO: Fonds Wetenschappelijk Onderzoek

GATS: General Agreement on Trade in Services

GATT: General Agreement on Tariffs and Trade

GDP: Gross Domestic Product

GNI: Gross National Income

GNP: Gross National Product

HS: Harmonised System

ICTSD: International Centre for Trade and Sustainable Development

IMF: International Monetary Fund

ITC: International Trade Centre

ITED: International Trade and Economic Development

ITPC: Investment and Trade Policy Centre

JCSA: Jewellery Council of South Africa

LPI: Logistics Performance Index

MA: Market Accessibility

MNC: Multi-national Company

NEPAD: New Partnership for Africa's Development

NIC: New Industrialising Countries

NRF: National Research Foundation

NTB: Non-tariff Barriers

NWU: North-West University

OECD: Organisation for Economic Co-operation and Development

ONDD: Office National du Ducroire

OSI: Openness for Services Imports

REO: Realistic Export Opportunity

RCA: Revealed Comparative Advantage

SACEEC: South African Capital Equipment Export Council

SACU: Southern African Customs Union

SADC: Southern African Development Community

SAMAC: South African Macadamias Growers' Association

SARB: South African Reserve Bank

SD: Services Demanded

SI: Specialisation Index

SITC: Standard International Trade Classification

SME: Small- and Medium-sized Enterprises

SO: Sectoral Organisation

SP: Services Produced

SSAS: Sector-Specific Assistance Scheme

STATSSA: Statistics South Africa

TISA: Trade and Investment South Africa

TOM: Trade Opportunity Matrix

TPSF: Trade Policy Strategy Framework

UN: United Nations

UNCTAD: United Nations Conference on Trade and Development

VDBH: Vlaamse Dienst voor de Buitenlandse Handel

WTO: World Trade Organisation

Contributors

LUDO CUYVERS is emeritus professor of the University of Antwerp, Belgium, where he is still Director of the Centre for ASEAN Studies, and extraordinary professor at the North-West University (Potchefstroom campus), South Africa. He received his PhD degree in 1977 from the Faculty of Applied Economics, University of Antwerp, Belgium. Between 1989 and 2009 Ludo Cuyvers was a member of the Board of Directors of Office National du Ducroire (Brussels), the Belgian federal credit insurance company, and since 1991 he is member of Flanders Investment & Trade, the export and investment promotion organsation of the Flemish region of Belgium.

WILMA VIVIERS is a professor and the director of the School of Economics in the Faculty of Economic and Management Sciences at the North-West University (Potchefstroom campus). She received her PhD in 1988 from the former Potchefstroom University of CHE. She received the ITRISA fellowship award for her contribution to the promotion of South African exports, the "Women in Research" award from the South African Association of Women Graduates as well as the NRF rating for established researchers. In 2011 she received the Department of Science and Technology's 'Distinguished Women in Science' runner-up award for her outstanding contribution to building South Africa's scientific and research knowledge base.

ERMIE ANNELIES STEENKAMP is a senior lecturer at the School of Economics in the Faculty of Economic and Management Sciences at the North-West University (Potchefstroom campus). She has recently (2011) finished her PhD on identifying export opportunities for South Africa with special reference to Africa. Her research mainly focuses on export promotion in South Africa and the measurement of market accessibility for South Africa in different countries around the world. She is currently part of a project team for the North-West University to identify realistic export opportunities for South Africa on HS 6 digit level, using a Decision Support Model (DSM).

SONJA GRATER has been a lecturer in the School of Economics at the North-West University since 2008. She completed her PhD in International Trade at the North-West University (Potchefstroom campus) in 2011 on international trade in services. She has published an article from her Master's thesis and a book chapter on her current work on services trade. She has also been involved in several conference presentations. She gained practical experience in the logistical environment while working in the freight forwarding industry for four years.

MARIÉ-LUCE KÜHN is a director and co-founder of IBIS. She has a distinguished career in competitive intelligence (CI) and knowledge building. Marié-Luce has widely published on CI. She participated in international research teams into the CI practices in various countries and is member of the Export Promotion Research Group of the North-West University (NWU). At present she is involved in CI training and developing CI capabilities in companies including tracking and scanning competitive forces for a variety of companies in various industries. Marié-Luce holds a PhD in International Trade from the NWU (Potchefstroom campus).

RIAAN ROSSOUW is a micro-economist with more than eight years of consulting, research and teaching experience. He has wide-ranging experience in most sectors and overall economic and development issues. His research interests include social and economic dimensions of inequality and applied general equilibrium modelling, particularly as applied to the African (and South African) context, with a special focus on regional disparities, decision support systems, development planning and international trade. He has partaken in consultancy work for various industries (both local and international) from governmental departments, financial institutions, private companies, international organisations, through to real economy institutions such as freight transport companies and utility providers. He has experience in teaching both students and development practitioners in the field.

MICHEL DUMONT taught International Economics and International Economic Organizations at the Faculty of Applied Economics, University of Antwerp (Belgium). He was assistant professor in Economics of Innovation at Delft University of Technology (The Netherlands) in 2007, before joining the Federal Planning Bureau of Belgium where he is currently involved in research on R&D, innovation and productivity.

NOLEEN SITHOLE-PISA is a PhD student in the School of Economics at the North-West University (Potchefstroom campus). Her PhD studies is in International Trade focusing on industrial clusters in the North-West province of South Africa. She completed her Masters degree in 2010 on the export promotion of South African edible nuts to Germany. She has published an article from her Master's thesis. She has also been involved in several conference presentations.

Foreword

The research, which is reported in the present volume, is the result of a long collaboration between the editors, going back to 2000, with a comparative study of competitive intelligence of South African and Belgian exporters, funded under the Flemish government's research programme for Bilateral Scientific and Technological Cooperation (BSTC) between Flanders and seven priority countries that included South Africa.

It was a little step from competitive intelligence and the involvement of export supporting organisations, to the broader theme of export promotion. This step was also a natural one for two reasons: Prof. Ludo Cuyvers, since the inception of the Flemish export promotion organisation member of the Board of Directors, had designed a decision support model, in collaboration with Proff. Patrick De Pelsmacker, Glenn Rayp and Irene Roozen, as far back as 1991, and Prof. Wilma Viviers had set up at the North-West University in South Africa an Export Promotion Research Group in 2006, where South African export promotion priorities were discussed.

In 2005, the DSM was mentioned in the "Draft National Export Strategy 2006-2009" of the Department of Trade and Industry (DTI) as one of the two pillars on which South Africa aimed to build its export strategy. In 2006, when Prof. Viviers approached senior officials of Trade and Investment, South Africa (TISA) and the Department of Trade and Industry (DTI) to apply the DSM in South Africa, her proposal evidently met with much interest, which started a close cooperation between the NWU and the DTI. The DSM's methodology was revised and tailored to meet South Africa's unique trade circumstances. It was applied in South Africa in 2007, 2009 and 2010. The endeavour resulted in many research publications and presentations, and the consolidation of the Export Promotion Research Group (EPRG) at NWU, with researchers from Belgium and South Africa being led by Proff. Wilma Viviers and Ludo Cuyvers. Most of the contributions to this publication/book have their origins in the work the EPRG has undertaken since 2006.

As the DSM had been applied to Belgium in the early and mid 1990s, and to Thailand and the Philippines afterwards, during which the methodology had been occasionally modified, a need was arising to take stock of the newest developments of the DSM, as well as to further investigate the many uses of the DSM results. From these the idea of writing the present volume arose.

Following several requests to present the results of the DSM to various government organisations, and as more postgraduate students became interested in undertaking graduate research into export promotion, it was decided the EPRG's research would have greater value if it were to be published. Fellow researchers were invited to contribute to the publication; the final result being a publication dealing in various topical aspects relating to the development of the DSM, the identification of export opportunities, the application of the model in diverse countries, and the strategic application of results in both public and private sector export promotion activities.

Two of the contributors had already published extended versions of their chapters, or related work, in peer-review journals, and they agreed to re-publication of this work in the book.[1] Some chapters also drew on the work of three doctoral (PhD) theses, completed during the course of the research project.[2]

1   Cuyvers, L. & Dumont, M. 2008. The assessment of public export activities using DSM results: the case of Belgium. *Review of Business and Economics*, 53(1): 69-92.

    Steenkamp, E.A., Rossouw, R., Viviers, W. & Cuyvers, L. 2009. Export market selection methods and the identification of realistic export opportunities for South Africa using a decision support model. [Online.] Available from: http://www.sadctrade.org/node/281.

2   Kuhn, M-L. 2010. *Exporters' information requirements: The role of Comptetive Intelligence in the export promotion of extruders*. Published PhD thesis. Potchefstroom: NWU.

    Grater, S. 2011. *The development of an export opportunities model for South African services*. Unpublished PhD thesis. Potchefstroom: NWU.

    Steenkamp, E.A. 2011. *The identification of export opportunities for South African products with special reference to Africa*. Unpublished PhD thesis. Potchefstroom: NWU.

Acknowledgements

A book like this would not be possible without the assistance and contributions of many researchers and colleagues who have shaped the field and our ideas in it. The DSM was originally designed by Ludo Cuyvers, Patrick De Pelsmacker, Glenn Rayp and Irene Roozen, and without their seminal intellectual input the output in this volume would not have been possible. The DSM and its applications were also presented and thoroughly discussed at a number of international conferences, as well as at workshops both in Belgium and South Africa, from which we all benefited greatly.

In addition to contributing to this publication, a number of people and institutions have added to the success of the continued export promotion research project. They are:

- The Flemish Government and the Flemish Foreign Trade Organisation (presently Flanders Investment and Trade) for its initial financial investment in the development and first applications of the DSM;

- WorkWell Research Unit and the newly-established TRADE Research Niche Area, both within the Faculty of Economic and Management Sciences of the North-West University (Potchefstroom campus), for their generous sponsorships in making this publication possible.

- The National Research Foundation (NRF) of South Africa for financial assistance;

- The Department of Trade and Industry (the DTI) for its financial support during the application of the DSM in South Africa in 2007, 2009 and 2010. In particular, gratitude must be afforded to Mr Riaan le Roux, Chief Operating Officer (COO) of Trade and Investment (TISA), a division of the DTI (Department of Trade and Industry), who, over many years, provided outstanding assistance and expert advice in refining and updating the DSM specifically for South African circumstances;

- The University of Antwerp and the Fonds Wetenschappelijk Onderzoek – Vlaanderen (FWO-Vlaanderen) for granting Prof. Ludo Cuyvers sabbatical leave for one year, and the NWU, specifically the Faculty of Economic and Management Sciences, for granting Prof. Wilma Viviers sabbatical leave for six months; such leave making it possible for the two editors to complete many chapters;

- The members of the Export Promotion Research Group (EPRG) who, since 2006, through their postgraduate studies have contributed ideas to and participated in the development of this publication. In alphabetical order, they are Sonja Grater (PhD student, 2011), Adelia Jansen van Rensburg (PhD student, 2009), Marié-Luce Kühn (Masters student, 2004 and PhD student 2010), Jacyntha Maclennan (Masters student, 2010), Joseph Pearson (PhD student, 2007), Professor Riaan Rossouw (researcher and developer of the DSM Dashboard), Noleen Sithole-Pisa (Masters student, 2010, and research assistant, 2009-2011), and Ermie Steenkamp (PhD student, 2011);

- Drs Sonja Grater and Ermie Steenkamp, who provided valuable and enthusiastic assistance in the final editing of chapters, and Danielle le Clus for her technical assistance in the final stages of the book;

- All other authors who submitted contributions to this book and, in doing so, assisted both in taking the discussion further and in developing the ideas and insights into an area that could contribute to continuing debate; and

- SUN MeDIA MeTRO, who generously agreed to assist in publishing an extremely interesting, but probably not very profitable book. Our warm and heartfelt gratitude extends to them all, and in particular, to Wilna Killian.

Ludo Cuyvers
University of Antwerpen, Belgium
ludo.cuyvers@ua.ac.be

Wilma Viviers
North-West University, Potchefstroom,
South Africa
wilma.viviers@nwu.ac.za

Chapter 1

Introduction

Ludo Cuyvers & Wilma Viviers

Export promotion is often regarded as a public good and is, therefore, in many countries supplied, wholly or partially, by the public sector. Export promotion organisations (EPOs)[1] are, however, increasingly facing diminishing returns in the use of export promotion instruments, particularly the more traditional and most widely-used instruments, such as the participation in trade missions, the participation in trade fairs and exhibitions, etc. Empirical support for this assumption can be found in studies such as Alvarez (2004), De Wulf (2001), and others, including for the existence of diminishing returns to scale of the export promotion budgets (see e.g. Lederman, Olarreaga & Payton, 2006).

On the other hand, with the success of the export strategies of a number of Newly Industrialising Countries (NICs) and emerging exporting countries, public export promotion organisations in both the developed and the developing countries are facing an urgent need of enhancing the efficiency of their export promotion activities, the more so as many of these EPOs are confronted with constraints in the available financial and other resources.

From this it follows that EPOs are in need of criteria to prioritise their activities to the markets and products that are offering the most promising export results for the countries which they represent, and to develop the most appropriate export promotion strategies for the products and the markets which they prioritised. Therefore, governments and organisations that want to stimulate their countries' exports, have to identify a smaller number of realistic

---

1   Many alternative terms are used in the literature, such as public export promotion agencies (PEPAs), export promotion agencies (EPAs), trade promotion agencies (TPAs) and trade promotion organisations (TPOs). However, for the purpose of consistency, the term export promotion organisation (EPO) will be used throughout this publication.

export opportunities from the vast number of possible opportunities that exist as only a limited number of export opportunities can be explored due to scarce resources (people and finance).

Therefore, as governments and organisations are operating with these scarce resources, a subsequent selection of opportune markets and product groups (product-country combinations) has to be made. Furthermore, the development of an export promotion strategy or the analysis of the effectiveness of existing export promotion programmes has to rely on hard quantitative data on foreign markets.

In order to assist export promotion organisations to better and more efficiently design export promotion programmes, geared to the continuously changing international environment, a decision support model was developed by Cuyvers *et al.* (see Cuyvers, De Pelsmacker, Rayp & Roozen, 1995). It was first applied to Belgium in 1992, 1993 and 1995 for the Flemish EPO (Cuyvers *et al.*, 1995) and for academic purposes in 1996, 2003 and 2008, and to Thailand (Cuyvers, 1996; 2004) and the Philippines. After that the methodology was revised and refined to suit better the South African situation in 2007, 2009 and 2010 (Viviers & Pearson, 2007; Pearson, Viviers, Cuyvers & Naudé, 2010; Viviers, Rossouw & Steenkamp, 2009; Viviers, Steenkamp, Rossouw & Cuyvers, 2010).

This model endeavours to make a selection of possible export markets, which are potentially profitable, from the set of all possible worldwide product-country combinations. Using macroeconomic data and international trade statistics, the selection process of the model consists of four consecutive filters, such that results from a previous filter are used as input and starting point in the next filter (for a detailed description of the DSM methodology, see Chapter 4).

In the course of the years also the nature of the international trade data used changed from SITC 2-digits in 1992, to SITC 4-digits data in the 1995 Belgian DSM run, as well as the subsequent runs for Belgium, Thailand and the Philippines, with a last run for Belgium-based on SITC 4-digit data in 2008.

Although in the first application of the DSM to South Africa of 2007 also SITC 4-digit data had been used, it was decided for the subsequent applications to South Africa, Belgium and Thailand, to rather use HS 6-digit data. The rationale for this change was as follows. The export opportunities detected on the basis of the DSM approach are taking the form of product-country combinations and are to be used by export promotion organisations and exporters. These users, however, are not familiar with SITC product categories, but rather with the product codes that are appropriate to perform export and import customs procedures, which are these of the Harmonised System (HS). The drawback of using HS

6-digit international trade data, unfortunately, is that the results are very hard to compare with these from previous applications. Moreover, from the point of view of export promotion the number of detailed export opportunity leads to follow up is staggering and require to be further narrowed down. One of the aims of the present volume is to find better ways to do so and to assist EPOs to prioritise their activities.

Part I of this book focuses on the political circumstances in which the applications of the DSM in Belgium took place, international market selection methods and the development of the decision support model (DSM).

Public export promotion involves a number of "players", such as the EPO, but also the political authorities, sectoral organisations, the business community, individual exporters, etc. It goes without saying that the material and organisational interests of these players are mostly not the same. An analytical tool as the DSM easily leads to a list of export opportunities and priorities, which in its details is at odds with some of these interests. Therefore, the results of the DSM are often met with opposition from some of the "players". Chapter 2 is an attempt to make a public choice analysis of export promotion and which motivates the DSM as an objective tool to counter lobby pressures on export promotion. As a tool for assisting export promotion organisations, the DSM was originally developed for the EPO of the Flemish region of Belgium. In Chapter 2, the subsequent events following its first applications are interpreted from a political economy point of view. Although the chapter starts with a simple game theoretical approach to public export promotion, it is shown that, based on the historical experience with the DSM, in the real world much more "players" and more complicated interactions are involved. Yet, some conclusions are drawn which, we hope, are relevant both for the theory and the practice of public export promotion.

In Chapter 3, the vast literature on market selection methods is reviewed and the DSM approach is assessed within this literature. From this assessment it appears that for the purposes of the prioritising, planning and designing of public export promotion activities, the DSM conforms to the prerequisites that all possible world-wide product-country combinations must be considered and that a limited list of the product-country combinations with the highest export potential for the exporting country should be produced in order for an export promotion organisation to use their resources optimally. The assessment based on the literature review also clearly reveals that, in contrast to other market selection methods, the DSM seems to be capable of handling a large array of possible product-country combinations due to the filtering process used, and finally provide a list of priority products in each country and, vice versa, a list of priority countries for each product.

The DSM methodology, as such, is explained in detail in Chapter 4. As the DSM was developed in 1992 and applied on a number of occasions, also since then a number of changes were introduced, based on experience. In 1993, for example, a scaling factor for export growth at product level was introduced, in order to correctly assess negative growth rates. Or else, as another example, when the ONDD, the organisation the political and commercial country scores of which are used in Filter 1 of the DSM, changed its risk scoring scales, this required for a subsequent minor revision of the selection procedure of that filter. Instead of asking the reader to go back to the original publications and integrate these changes for himself, Chapter 4 lays out the DSM methodology as it is at present, and as it is applied in the subsequent chapters, in a concise and coherent way.

Part II focuses on applications of the methodology of the DSM. This part consists of three chapters: a discussion of the DSM results for Belgium and, where possible, a comparison which previous results (Chapter 5), the comparison of the most recent DSM results for Belgium, South Africa and Thailand (Chapter 6) and the identification of export opportunities for South African products in the rest of the African continent (Chapter 7).

In Chapter 5, the DSM methodology as explained in Chapter 4 is illustrated in detail and concretely, by following step-by-step its application for Belgium. The present application is using 2003-2007 HS 6-digit international trade data. This should allow the reader to fully understand how the analysis is performed, in the first place, but it also allows some comparison with previous DSM results. This leads to a first and tentative assessment of the robustness of DSM results and some challenging conclusions about the scope for public export promotion in a rapidly changing international economic environment.

Next, in Chapter 6, the DSM results derived for Belgium, Thailand and South Africa as respective exporting country are compared. In addition, in order to allow a better prioritisation of the realistic export opportunities detected, the analysis in that chapter also concentrates on these opportunities for which the respective exporting countries have already acquired a sufficient degree of comparative advantage, thus allowing an analysis and comparison of the opportunities that in principle can be tapped immediately. The comparison of the results of the three countries reveals important differences.

As said and fully explained in Chapter 4, the logic of the DSM is to be applied to identify export opportunities in the world at large. In Chapter 7, the geographical coverage of the DSM analysis for South Africa is restricted to the African continent. The reason for this restriction is that, although by itself leading to instructive information, the results of an unrestricted application for exporting developing countries might on a number of occasions and for a large number of export opportunities, be unpractical, due to geographical and cultural distance from the far-away markets. Moreover, the neighbouring countries might be engaged in a regional integration process, such that the political authority of the exporting country for economic or other strategic reasons prefers to deepen the international trade links with these neighbours. It should be clear that as a matter of principle we are not advocating such restricted geographical coverage of the analysis of the DSM, as there is a serious risk that the exporters' objective interests and potentials of exporting to the most promising markets might be sacrificed to the wishes and interests of the political authorities and their bureaucracy. However, we concede that for a number of reasons it should be accepted, as is the case for South Africa and its prioritising of the African market.

Part III focuses on some further applications of the DSM methodology and the strategic use of the DSM results. This part consists of four chapters: an assessment of public export activities using the DSM results of Belgium (Chapter 8), the development of strategies for export promotion using the DSM (Chapter 9), the development of a DSM for the identification of export opportunities for services (Chapter 10), and the use of Competitive Intelligence (CI) as an instrument to serve exporters' information requirements regarding concrete realistic export opportunities (Chapter 11).

Although the DSM has been developed and used for the identification of the export opportunities of countries, and therefore as a tool to design and plan export promotion activities at the level of the product and importing country, it can also be used as tool *post factum* to assess the export promotion activities actually planned and executed. What is required for this purpose is to translate these activities in product-country combinations, after which these can be compared with the list of realistic export opportunities in the same period. This is done for Belgium in Chapter 8, be it for 2000-2003, thus referring to a previous application of the DSM for Belgium, as the one reported at length in Chapter 5.

Following a hint in Cuyvers, De Pelsmacker, Rayp & Roozen (1995) on public export promotion strategies based on the characteristics of the realistic export opportunities detected using the DSM, Chapter 9 further elaborates on such strategies as combinations of specific export promotion instruments. The strategies are categorised into offensive market exploration, offensive market expansion and defensive market maintenance strategies, based on the market presence in the importing country achieved by the exporting country. They, in turn, are further categorised according to the import market characteristics for the product at issue. This categorisation is illustrated by developing three concrete studies of export promotion strategy for South African products, corresponding with three of its many realistic export opportunities. It is shown that the broad categorisation of the export promotion strategies proposed is leading to specific combinations of export promotion instruments, but that for the concrete elaboration of the strategies more detailed information, both qualitative and quantitative, on the many aspects of international marketing are required.

The nature of the data used in previous DSM applications limited its use to the detection of export opportunities of products for the exporting country. However, the logic of the DSM could also be applied to identify export opportunities for services. At the time the DSM was developed, the international data on services were scant, to say the least. This situation changed dramatically during the past couple of years, and allowed to rethink the DSM methodology, with due regard of the nature of the available data on international trade in services, to be applied to services. This innovative attempt was made for South Africa and is reported in Chapter 10.

Many firms regard exporting as a means to counter and monitor growing foreign competition, enlarge their market base, and augment profitability. However, despite the financial implications of selling to foreign markets, the process is uncertain and has many potential pitfalls. Exporting requires detailed knowledge of various factors (e.g. foreign business practices, cultures, competition) that could affect a small firm's ability to be successful in foreign markets (Belich & Dubinsky, 1999:45). It is, therefore, clear that if an increasing number of firms move into export operations, gathering and processing the right information will be of critical importance. Chapter 11 firstly examines exporters' need for information, the types of information considered important by exporters and the sources consulted for gathering information. Finally, this chapter considers the manner in which EPOs and exporters associations can use CI as an instrument to assist exporters in identifying the information they need to collect from the available sources and eventually making strategic business decisions based on the results of the CI process. The results from the DSM studies can be an important source of information for the EPOs in order to assist exporters in their decision-making regarding export opportunities for their products as well as identified potential markets.

In Chapter 12, the main conclusions on the DSM methodology and its use are listed. In addition, present limitations are mentioned and an agenda for future research formulated.

References

Alvarez, R. 2004. Sources of export success in small- and medium-sized enterprises: The Impact of Public Programs. *International Business Review*, 13: 383-400.

Belich, T.J. & Dubinsky, A.J. 1999. Information processing among exporters: an empirical examination of small firms. *Journal of Marketing Theory and Practice*, 7(4): 45-59.

Cuyvers, L., De Pelsmacker, P., Rayp, G. & Roozen, I.T.M. 1995. A decision support model for the planning and assessment of export promotion activities by government promotion institutions: the Belgian case. *International Journal of Research in Marketing*, 12(2): 173-186.

Cuyvers, L. 1996. Export opportunities of Thailand: a decision support model approach. *Journal of Euro-Asian Management*, 2(2): 71-97.

Cuyvers, L. 2004. Identifying export opportunities: the case of Thailand. *International Marketing Review*, 21(3): 255-278.

De Wulf, L. 2001. Why have trade organization failed, and how they can be revitalized? PREM Notes #56, World Bank.

Lederman, D., Olarreaga, M. & Payton, L. 2006. Export promotion organisations: what works and what does not. *Trade Note 30*, World Bank group, Washington D.C.

Pearson, J.J.A., Viviers, W., Cuyvers, L. & Naudé, W. 2010. Identifying export opportunities for South Africa in the southern engines: a DSM approach. *International Business Review*, 19(4): 345-359.

Viviers, W. & Pearson, J.J.A. 2007. The construction of a decision support model for evaluating and identifying realistic export opportunities in South Africa. Unpublished report prepared for the Department of Trade and Industry, South Africa, May. 92 p.

Viviers, W., Rossouw, R. & Steenkamp, E.A. 2009. The sustainability of the DSM for identifying realistic export opportunities for South-Africa: 2007-2008. Unpublished report prepared for the Department of Trade and Industry, South Africa, February. 105 p.

Viviers, W., Steenkamp, E.A., Rossouw, R. & Cuyvers, L. 2010. Identifying realistic export opportunities for South Africa: application of a decision support model (DSM) using HS 6-digit level product data. Unpublished report prepared for the Department of Trade and Industry, South Africa, September. 57 p.

Part I

The development of a decision support model
for export promotion

Chapter 2

The political economy of public export promotion: the case of the Flemish region, Belgium

Ludo Cuyvers[1]

2.1 Introduction

Public export promotion involves the use of a number of policy instruments, the impact of which is well-documented in the literature, such as that of exchange rate manipulation or subsidies. Other instruments are much less rigorously analysed. Moreover, not only the impact of these instruments is relevant, but in order to understand their existence, an analysis of the working of the policy formulation and implementation process is even more required.

Why export subsidies, or subsidies in general, for instance, are granted has been analysed using game theory. Political economy models mostly assume that governments want to maximise their political following (e.g. Hillman & Ursprung, 1988). Mathematically, the function that determines the political following reflects the welfare gains of the interest groups due to specific policy measures (e.g. export subsidies) and the welfare losses of others (e.g. the loss of consumer surplus due to higher prices). In the Grossman-Helpman model (Grossman & Helpman, 1994) the interests of economic sectors are represented by lobbyists who are paying contributions to the political decision-makers that depend on the trade policy measures taken. In this model, the government will select the set of trade policy

1   The author is member of the Board of Directors of Flanders Invest & Trade (FIT). However, the opinions expressed in this chapter are not reflecting these of FIT, and he is assuming sole responsibility. Comments by Jan Bouckaert and Michel Dumont on an earlier draft are gratefully acknowledged.

measures (among which subsidies), which is maximising the weighted sum of aggregate social welfare and the lobbyists' contributions.

Apart from imperfect competition, strategic trade policy is prompted by market imperfections related to imperfect knowledge or economies of scale internal and external to the company (see e.g. Brander & Spencer, 1985). Due to the imperfect competition situation, these other market imperfections make it possible to influence the volume of output and therefore the cost of production of the exporting firms by subsidising production, marketing, access to information, research, etc. Export subsidies, therefore, are very diverse and can take subtle forms.

Indirect subsidisation often takes place through the government financially supporting or otherwise the organisation of seminars and workshops on business in well-identified foreign markets, official trade missions abroad, the participation in trade fairs and exhibitions, the presence of commercial attachés at embassies, etc. In fact, these are just of few instruments the use of which is to overcome, or at least counteract, information market imperfections. Their use being a long-standing tradition, however, they are mostly lacking innovation. No country can avoid them, but they have to be increasingly supplemented by other and newer instruments. Yet, their use and rationale can only be explained by the presence of imperfections in the market of information and knowledge, and the economies of scale, both internal and external to the company, or by the welfare gains associated with co-operation and co-ordination.

The decades of use of the traditional instrument of public export promotion, as well as the ever-increasing number of countries using them, rendered them less effective, not to say made them blunt. Evidence indicates that export promotion activities are showing diminishing returns (e.g. Czinkota, 2002; Lederman, Olarreaga & Payton, 2006) and it, therefore, can readily be assumed that for instance each new trade mission to a foreign market, all other factors and instruments remaining the same, will show a smaller contribution to the exports of the organising country. In addition, the available financial and other resources for public export promotion are becoming increasingly scarce, in contrast to the expenses to be made. More than ever before, an optimal use of the scarce resources – given the set of instruments of public export promotion – is, therefore, of paramount importance, which implies that in designing strategies for the export promotion of related goods and services in the world market, the best combination of instruments has to be considered, which will lead to the highest return in terms of exports growth.

This optimisation requires a scientific approach which identifies the important potential export opportunities, using hard statistical data and state-of-the-art analytical tools, and which allows to design the most suitable and sufficiently focused export promotion strategies. Observation learns, however, that this optimisation is often hampered by the interaction of the relevant "players", such as private sector lobbyists, politicians, bureaucrats within or outside the public export promotion organisation, to mention a few. Therefore, a good understanding of the strategic moves of the players, which would lead to the optimal outcome, is required.

2.2   A simple game theoretic illustration of export promotion

Assume that two players are determining the number of international trade missions to be organised: the export promotion organisation (EPO) and a sectoral organisation (SO). The trade missions are, however, organised separately, but are catering to the needs of the "fish pond" of exporters who will benefit from it. The trade missions organised separately by each of the players is influenced by these organised by the other. The total exports generated by export promotion by the respective players can, therefore, be written as:

$$E_{EPO} = a_1 + b_1 M_{EPO} + c_1 M_{SO}$$

$$E_{SO} = a_2 + b_2 M_{EPO} + c_2 M_{SO}$$

with E_{EPO} and E_{SO} standing for exports generated by the Fs' and SOs' trade missions respectively, M_{EPO} and M_{SO} for the trade missions organised by the EPOs and the SOs, and the parameters a_1, a_2, b_1, b_2, c_1 and c_2 for the "spill-over effects" between the export promotion activities of the two players.[2] From this their respective reaction curves can be derived. If $M_{SO} = 0$, $E_{EPO} = a_1 + b_1 M_{EPO}$ and thus $M_{EPO} = (E_{EPO} - a_1)/b_1$. Similarly M_{SO} can be derived for $M_{EPO} = 0$. The reaction curves R_{EPO} and R_{SO} thus show how the number of trade missions that each player wants to organise decreases for increases in the number organised by the other, according to the equations for R_{EPO} and R_{SO}:

$$M_{EPO} = (E_{EPO} - c_1 M_{SO} - a_1)/b_1$$

$$M_{SO} = (E_{SO} - c_2 M_{EPO} - a_2)/b_2$$

These reaction curves are depicted in Figure 2.1. They are intersecting at N, the Nash equilibrium, which is the situation where the missions organised by the EPO are inciting the SO to organise a number of missions itself, which, in turn, would trigger the EPO to act as it is doing now, and the other way round.

The players consider the exports generated by their actions as the gain for the exporters, from which they deduct the efforts and costs expended to organise the trade missions,

---

2   Alternatively the variables can represent "shocks" in which case they are deviations from the present (or average) values.

which also are showing diminishing returns. The net welfare gains can be expressed in mathematical terms as:

$$W_{EPO} = E_{EPO} - e_1 M_{EPO}{}^{-2}$$

$$W_{SO} = E_{SO} - e_2 M_{SO}{}^{-2}$$

Figure 2.1. Game between EPO and SO about the organisation of international trade missions.

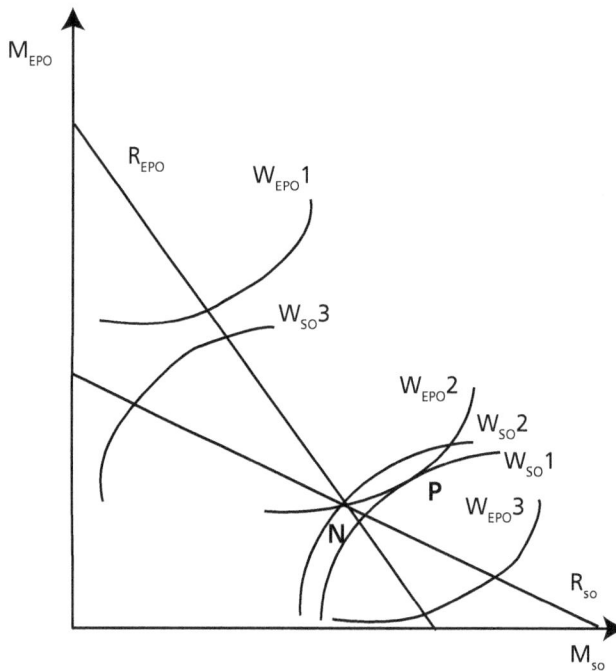

Each player attempts to maximise its W by designing and organising an appropriate number of trade missions. The EPO will attempt to increase its W, moving from $W_{EPO}1$ to $W_{EPO}2$ and $W_{EPO}3$. Likewise the SO will attempt to reach the highest W by moving from $W_{SO}1$ to $W_{SO}2$ and $W_{SO}3$. In doing so each is moving up its reaction curve until N is reached.

From Figure 2.1 it also will appear that when the EPO and the SO are cooperating and designing a cooperative strategy, they will maximise a joint $W = uW_{EPO} + (1-u)W_{SO}$ at P, the Pareto equilibrium, where their respective W's are tangent.

The picture becomes more complicated if the SO is contributing financially, from its membership fees, to the operations of the EPO, and when the EPO is partially subsidising the international trade missions organised by the SO, but the game played is essentially the same, although involving now more and other interactions. Thus, other factors may enter the W-functions, such as the financial contributions and subsidies, or the number of exporters reached, or even the bureaucratic impact of the two organisations (e.g. proxied by their respective budgets).

We can also consider another, but similar game, which is played between the EPO and the political authorities, with the political authorities being influenced by the amount of taxes generated directly and indirectly by the exports (net of the financial contribution to the EPO), and the EPO's welfare W, apart from the exports generated, influenced by e.g. its budget, the number of employees and the exposure of its international network of attachés. Also in such a game a Nash equilibrium will be reached in the end, although the strategic moves will be somewhat more complicated.

Consider for instance the following game, where both the EPO and the political authorities are organising trade missions, which through their interactions are generating exports, as follows:

$$E_{EPO} = a_1 + b_1 M_{EPO} + c_1 M_P$$

$$E_P = a_2 + b_2 M_{EPO} + c_2 M_P$$

The welfare function of the EPO and P, which each will maximise, is assumed to be:

$$W_{EPO} = g_1 \tau m(E_{EPO} + E_P) - e_1 M_{TPA}^{-2}$$

$$W_P = (1-g_1) \tau m(E_{EPO} + E_P) - e_1 M_P^{-2}$$

with τ the average income tax rate, m the income multiplier and g_1 the share of taxes generated by the income from the exports. It can be seen that the Nash equilibrium of this game between EPO and P is reached in essentially the same way as depicted in Figure 2.1.[3]

The existing political economy models of international trade have not incorporated the subtler and more widely used public export promotion activities in their analysis. The present chapter endeavours to show the need to do so, by providing concrete factual insight into the major "players" in the game of designing and planning public export promotion activities, as well as into their not always economical, let alone welfare maximising behaviour. As will become clear below, even the scientific or other tools used in this game are a game by itself.

---

3   Michel Dumont has suggested that the interrelationship between EPO and SO can also be considered as a duopoly with both EPO and SO attempting to maximise the number of participants to their activities. In addition, the negotiations between EPO and P can be modelled as a situation with both maximising the number of participants to their respective missions, but with the budget of the EPO, as a function of the number of participants, being a subsidy for the EPO and a cost for P.

Not surprisingly, EPOs have been incited by important or large exporters and influential lobbyists with privileged contacts, to take specific initiatives and/or organise specific activities. More than often, this influence was also exercised by political authorities themselves, the more so as these authorities are the prime movers in organising activities such as diplomatically supported official trade missions, in which they are represented as well. Moreover, the political class and the political authorities were (and are) the potential supporters of the EPO, within their sphere of influence, which also have the power to curb its activities. In the past, the relationship between political authorities and EPO was often *quasi feudal*.

However, many EPOs evolved new instruments of export promotion, such as the provision of tailor-made support services for exporters, the organisation of media campaigns in target markets, the development of a network of personal contacts with decision-makers in the foreign markets, the provision of better focused, more specialised and more detailed information and intelligence, etc. This allowed them to wrestle themselves free, at least partly, from undue political influence and to better use own expertise and networks, as well as to better respond to the new opportunities of the "information society".[4]

The aim of this chapter is to look into the factors and parties/players that are, in an interactive way, influencing public export promotion, based on own experience since the late 1980s and early 1990s with the development and application of a decision support model (DSM) for the Flemish EPO in Belgium. The results of the DSM would allow a scientifically based follow-up of realistic export opportunities and better defined and focused export promotion strategies by the EPO. In this way we will identify the players that became involved and their motives. We hope not only to contribute in this way to the history of Belgian public export promotion, but also to show that the export promotion game is much more complicated than political economy theories have been able to model. Yet, such formal political economy modelling, even partially, would be an important and path-breaking contribution, as it would lead to a much better insight into the alternative outcomes of the game and the way to these. This is, however, beyond the scope of this chapter.

---

4   The previous methods of information dissemination to exporters about foreign markets are largely outdated due to the exporters' enhanced capacities and possibilities to gather this information themselves on the Internet. Many EPOs, therefore, have abandoned their traditional role of information providers and are focusing increasingly on the provision of tailor-made information and supporting services.

2.3 Export promotion in the Flemish region of Belgium: political and economic considerations

Until 1990, the main government organisation responsible for export promotion in Belgium was the *Belgiesche Dienst voor de Buitenlandse Handel (BDBH)*. The law of 8 August 1988, which amended the special law of 8 August 1980 regarding institutional reform, transferred part of its former competences to the Belgian regions Flanders, Wallonia and Brussels Capital Region. This regionalisation had been negotiated politically and aimed at bringing export promotion closer to the needs of the small- and medium-sized exporters. It was the outcome of an unfinished process of political and economic regionalisation of the country, of which it was also part. As a result, a major slice of the political powers over international trade promotion came into the hands of the newly established regional governments of Belgium.

Somewhat schematising a complicated political compromise, this regionalisation implied that general export promotion and general information collection, including the updating of the exporters database, remained at the federal level, but that the regions became responsible for the more company-oriented export promotion services, such as coaching and supporting companies in exporting to new markets, the subsidising of the companies' participation in international trade fairs and exhibitions, etc. The BDBH became largely a coordinator of the export promotion initiatives of the regions, although also organising trade missions abroad presided by the Crown Prince. In addition, by the special law of 16 January 1989 on the financing of Communities and Regions, 444.5 million Belgian francs (ca. 11 million euro) were transferred from the federal BDBH budget to the regions, of which Flanders received 58%, Wallonia 33% and Brussels Capital Region 9%. The responsibilities of the BDBH were curbed further by the law of 24 June 1997, but it remained responsible for interregional coordination and consultation. The revision of the Belgian constitution of 2001 contained provisions to reduce overlap of competences between the federal and regional level by the creation of a special agency for interregional coordination and consultation and the dissolution of the BDBH (Law of 13 July 2001, Art. 3).

The Belgian situation of the 1970s and 1980s is a case in point to illustrate the political economy of public export promotion. Facing the new responsibilities regarding international trade promotion transferred from the Belgian federal level to the Flemish region, the author of these lines was commissioned by the then Flemish vice-president and minister of economy, Norbert De Batselier, to provide a policy advice on the needs and requirements of a regional Flemish policy of public export promotion and acquisition. In our policy advice to the vice-president (Cuyvers, 1989b), we proposed the creation of the *Vlaamse Dienst voor de Buitenlandse Handel (VDBH)*, which happened in 1991 (since 2005: *Flanders Investment & Trade*), and outlined its organisational structure. We also emphasised the need to categorically abandon the old practice of the BDBH to compose an annual programme of activities, mostly by simply compiling the proposals from the various industries as ventilated by the representatives of the sectoral organisations.

With due regard to the need to provide more focused and tailor-made activities, and to tackle public export promotion in a more innovative, professional and scientific way, the transfer of the former federal export promotion mandate to the Belgian regions, allowed the Flemish EPO to live up to the slogan of its regional political authorities: "What we do ourselves, we do better!" Contrary to the BDBH, the *Vlaamse Dienst voor de Buitenlandse Handel (VDBH)* discussed its proposal for the annual activities programme with sectoral representatives in its Advisory Board. This procedure was abandoned, however, in the mid-1990s, when the daily management of the *Vlaamse Dienst* was granted more autonomy.

In order to assist the *Vlaamse Dienst* in designing and planning the most suitable export promotion activities, we were commissioned in October 1991 by the Flemish vice-president and minister of economy to construct a decision support tool allowing the identification of the most promising realistic export opportunities, which in turn would help the *Vlaamse Dienst* in its annual activities programme. The research was conducted by a team of researchers at the University of Antwerp. The results of the Decision Support Model (DSM), which was constructed, were presented to the *Vlaamse Dienst* in September 1992, and thoroughly discussed with the sectoral representatives in its Advisory Board.

Our recollection today of these discussions is that the management of VDBH had rather mixed feelings about the DSM. On the one hand, it seems that they liked being provided a powerful analytical tool that was also new and innovative. Moreover, this tool would allow them to use the results piecemeal and selectively, and thus to silence public criticism (which on occasions was even voiced in the Flemish Parliament) that some of their activities were badly or wrongly targeted or could not sufficiently be justified. On the other hand, we are convinced that the management of the VDBH, and possibly also the political authorities, felt constrained by the results, when these were at odds with their ideas and priorities.[5] It

5   The management of the VDBH at that time consisted of a triumvirate with one director-general and two under-director-generals. Their political affiliations differed and their appointment was the result of a politically negotiated deal. One of the under-director-generals was very much supportive and in favour of the DSM, while the director-general clearly was in favour in as much as he could "bend" the results where they suited his own ideas and priorities. The powers of the management were constrained by the Board of Directors, which often created frustrating situations of wrangling. This was changed in 1995 when the VDBH was reformed into *Export Vlaanderen* with one managing director responsible for the daily management, working in close contact and consultation with the Cabinet of the Minister, and in which the Board largely was restricted to play a supervisory role. Therefore, although formally being granted more autonomy, in reality the *quasi-feudal* relationship with the competent Minister and his Cabinet had become stronger. Today, *Flanders Investment & Trade (FIT)*, which succeeded *Export Vlaanderen* in 2005, is managed by a managing director and the Board of Directors. The operations and management of FIT are assessed by "key performance

is not surprising that they objectively became allies of the sectoral organisations, which felt threatened by the results of the DSM, as the export promotion activities of these organisations were often based on demands from within the sectors or on the *Fingerspitzengefühl* of the top of these organisations or their representatives. A temporary compromise was reached in the Board of Directors of the VDBH that the DSM results would be used together with these of an annual survey of the commercial attachés abroad about priorities.

To be fair, the DSM was a new, but also a complicated analytical tool and its operation time consuming. The model largely built on techniques discussed in the literature on international market selection (see Chapter 3). Quantitative and statistical information on all the countries in the world (not only those to which Belgium was exporting) and their imports at disaggregated level (instead of investigating Belgium's export performance at product level, which often was the practice) were "filtered", finally leading to a list of "realistic export opportunities" (see Cuyvers, De Pelsmacker, Rayp & Roozen, 1995). In 1993, for the preparation of the annual activities programme of 1994, an update was made in close collaboration with a staff member of VDBH. However, no further policy supporting research based on the DSM was done and as policy instrument for the VDBH the DSM met a silent death.

Admittedly, apart from being complicated and requiring a solid statistical background for all who wanted to apply it, the DSM was afflicted with other apparent shortcomings. The DSM might give the impression of a "push-button" device; in fact it certainly is not. A major stumbling block in its operation is the derivation of some thresholds in its "filters", e.g. for imports growth or import market concentration, which is intricate and needs insight and research expertise, unfortunately lacking in the VDBH. The international trade data used were according to the Standard International Trade Classification (SITC) at 2 digits, and later at 4 digits, which does not allow identifying the products for exporters in a sufficiently detailed way. Rather, product groups were identified as offering realistic export opportunities in individual foreign markets. Moreover, this data that were "filtered" through the model, although the most recent available, were mostly two years old. However, the main reasons for the demise of the DSM as policy instrument have to be found elsewhere.

In 1992, a switch in ministerial responsibilities took place. It is well known that each new minister is at pains of differentiating himself from his predecessor. The DSM was a "child" of a previous minister and was soon considered by the new minister as a nasty legacy of a political opponent. Moreover, the politicians in power and their entourage have not much inclination, if at all, to justify their actions by having to refer to hard statistical data and analysis by academics.

indicators" laid down in a five-year management contract with the Flemish government.

As suggested before, also the representative sectoral organisations were not very amused that the output of the model often could force them to direct their attention to other markets than these that were traditionally looked at, and that it limited their impact on the annual activities programme of the EPO.

Apart from political rivalry and the mixed feelings about the DSM both inside the VDBH and in the sectoral organisations, due to their own agendas and priorities, also purely political reasons can be listed to explain the fate of the DSM in Flanders. These political reasons are going back to the 1988 "breaking in" of the Socialist Party into the then centre-right wing Flemish government and the coming of political "heavy weight" and outspoken ideologically driven socialist Norbert De Batselier in the Flemish executive as vice-president and regional minister of economy. Lacking a smooth working administration and good regional statistics, he would commission during the first 18 months of his mandate, 21 policy supporting researches, among which our advice on how to organise the just regionalised public export promotion mandate. He would incorporate our advice entirely in his Policy Letter to the Flemish Council of March 1990, and later entrust to us the construction of a decision support tool, which would assist the VDBH in identifying priority markets and designing its annual activities programme accordingly.

Combining sharp intellectual insight and vision with pragmatism, De Batselier met with open hostility and caustic opposition from the Liberal Party and some fractions of the Christian-Democrats, as well as from the *Vlaams Economisch Verbond*, the Flemish private sector organisation (Hellinck, 2010:175-178). Not surprisingly, the DSM was ludicrously portrayed by a number of political opponents and private sector representatives, both inside and outside the Board of Directors of VDBH, as an instrument that would introduce government dirigisme, if not right away socialist economic planning, in public export promotion, which traditionally was the realm of the exporters' organisations and their lobbyists.

De Batselier was also confronted with obstinacy, including from top-ranked civil servants. His biographer Bart Hellinck writes:

> The man, who in accordance with the agreement within the political majority, was appointed as head of the VDBH was constantly and publicly – as a civil servant – questioning his ministerial decisions, hired his daughter and acquaintances without entrance exam, wanted to focus on non-priority markets ... On the occasion of the solemn installation ceremony of the Board of Directors and the Advisory Board of VDBH, De Batselier had declared that they would not suffer from his dirigisme, in as much as they would work quickly, correctly and efficiently. When the funny pranks of the director-general became apparent, he attempted to stick to this intention. In internal notes circulating in his Cabinet he wrote that he did not want to interfere patronisingly: it was the business of the VDBH board members when they were 'crazy enough' to follow the personal foreign policy of the leading official. Rapidly

things got out of hand and a flaming letter from De Batselier and Gaston Geens (the Regional President – L.C.) came in response to 'this nonsense' (Hellinck, 2010:184, our translation).

Like the other traditional political parties, the Socialist Party suffered a severe election defeat in November 1991. The Christian-Democratic Party strengthened its grip on the Flemish Executive and their new Flemish president of the council also became responsible for economy, which regularly led to an undermining of the former policies of De Batselier, who remained vice-president, but now had become the minister of environment.

There can be no doubt that the association of the DSM with the previous regional minister of economy, contributed to its silent disappearance as instrument for preparing and assessing export promotion in Flanders. Both political opposition as well as opposition from the major lobby groups of the private sector against De Batselier's policy stance had accumulated during the legislature, such that soon after he had taken up other responsibilities, also the political weight of the DSM results waned dramatically.

From the cenacles of power we occasionally heard some disconcerting rumours:

(i)   As the author of these lines was since its establishment a member of the Board of Direc-
        tors of the VDBH, further commissioning research to him and his team at the University
        of Antwerp, would create a conflict of interest;

(ii)   Lacking time, people and expertise, the DSM research could not be conducted by the
        VDBH internally; and

(iii)   The research on the DSM in the past had given one university team a monopoly – how
        about cooperating with others?

As a consequence, for the next ten years, public export promotion in Flanders as organised by its EPO was largely based on a rather rudimentary or even incorrect use of limited statistical data.[6]

The Flemish avenue being blocked, we occasionally set out applying the DSM for purely academic purposes to identify and analyse the realistic export opportunities of Belgium again, or these of other countries such as Thailand and the Philippines, about which we were doing research (see e.g. Cuyvers, 1996; Cuyvers, 2004). But the DSM finally "rose from its ashes" in South Africa, where it was first mentioned in the 2005 "Export Promotion Strategy" of the government (DTI, 2005) as one of the two policy instruments in the years to come, after which the South African Department of Trade and Industry (DTI) commissioned research using the DSM, directed and supervised by Prof. W. Viviers (North-West University,

---

6   "Incorrect" means that even if international trade data were used, the Belgian export statistics
     were mostly looked at. It is evidently the foreign import data that contain the relevant information,
     rather than the Belgian export data, as the possibility cannot be ruled out that Belgium, or Flanders
     for that matter, is leaving import markets for specific products insufficiently tapped.

Potchefstroom Campus). Where required the model was improved and adapted to the South African situation.[7] The DSM output, consisting of the list of South Africa's realistic export opportunities, based on the latest statistical data, soon was used by the DTI to programme and conduct a number of well-targeted export promotion activities[8] (see Chapter 6 for a comparison of the DSM results for Belgium, South Africa and Thailand).

In contrast to Flanders in the 1991-1994 period, where it had been intended to finally have the model run and used within the EPO, South Africa opted from the outset for the research being conducted by external, and therefore, independent researchers. This seems to be the best option, in spite of some subtle attempts by the EPO and its staff to try the results to their own ends. Luckily some quick successes in concrete export promotion actions in the field created sufficient credibility with the DTI management to limit intentional or unintentional attempts to "direct" the results of the model.[9]

2.4 The DSM researcher as communicator in the export promotion game

The issue whether methodological and statistical research of export markets and export opportunities can best be conducted by the EPO, or else by independent researchers, shows a number of facets that need clarification and careful consideration. External research evidently offers a much larger probability of independence and objectivity, while internal research by the EPO can be easily influenced and directed. Moreover, with external research, the EPO can focus fully on the translation of the research results in policy measures. External policy supporting research of the kind at issue is, however, by definition not a "one-shot" activity, but structural and repeated, which in turn implies that the external researchers and their research funding become dependent on the "goodwill" of the decision-makers within the EPO. We have here another indefinitely repeated game between the external research team and the EPO. It thus remains to be seen how independent the researcher will remain.

The problem is not easier when looked from the EPO's perspective. External research is making the EPO dependent on the researchers, which can lead to a research monopoly. It

---

7   Belgium and Thailand have neighbouring countries at a similar level of economic development, the competitive position in specific foreign markets of which, therefore, can be used as "benchmark". South Africa's neighbours are too dissimilar for this purpose.

8   For the first results we refer to Pearson (2007). An analysis of South Africa's opportunities in the BRIC countries was published separately as Pearson, Viviers, Cuyvers and Naudé (2010). The final results are in Viviers, Steenkamp, Rossouw and Cuyvers (2010).

9   This observation is given with the required reservation as it is based only on the attempts that were brought to our notice. It remains to be seen whether these were attempts to "direct", or rather originate from insufficient insight in the DSM and its results. For instance requests by the EPO for further research on well-identified, but apparently non-existing export opportunities can be interpreted both ways.

will be remembered that this was argued against the continuation of the DSM research for the VDBH in 1994 and afterwards. Attempts by the EPO to break out of this situation can easily create an acute conflict between the need to have the policies permanently based on research that follows the same methodology, and the intellectual property of methodology and research results if the research is entrusted to external researchers. The relationship between external researchers and EPO is clearly one of dancing on a tightrope.

The external research team should be considered as a communicator in the export promotion game. By providing output from statistical analysis, informational input is provided to the players of the game. In a sense, the external research team is behaving in this capacity as international economic organisations are doing when involved in a game of international economic policy coordination (see e.g. Cuyvers, 1989a). In contrast to these international organisations, such as the IMF or the OECD, the research team is not in a position to provide information to the players about each other's targets and strategies. Neither – again in contrast to the role played by international economic organisations in games of international policy coordination – can it act as supervisor of the repeated cooperative game of identifying target countries and products. But by providing the list of realistic export opportunities and other information on relevant import market characteristics, the team will give input to the players' own strategy formulation and therefore will make the game more transparent. By further comparing, during the game, the probable outcomes in terms of export performance of the country of alternative public export promotion activities and export promotion strategies, and feeding this back to the players, it will also thoroughly perform its function of facilitator and communicator.

2.5   Some conclusions

Public export promotion today is facing the urgent need to innovate and diversify its instruments. The traditional instruments, such as the organisation of international trade missions and of a network of commercial attachés abroad, participation in international trade fairs and exhibitions, the provision of general information on "doing business with …" etc. have been used extensively and are showing rapidly decreasing returns. Tailor-made and better-focused export promotion activities have to be designed, requiring a scientific approach rather than the eclectic pragmatism, which is often applied by EPOs.

In this chapter we have indicated that the EPO is only one of the players who impact export promotion activities, as the outcome of an indefinitely repeated game. The political economy models of international trade policy can provide useful insight into the strategic moves of the main players in this game at the national level. However, as the tribulations of the use of the DSM as a policy instrument in Flanders show, other players and other relevant factors have to be taken into account to understand and analyse the strategic moves, their interactions and their final outcomes.

Among the players mention should be made of the political class, the government administration, specialised government agencies (such as the EPO, if any) and the representative private sector organisations. Moreover, in contrast with the present-day political economy models, the political class as player in this game is far from homogeneous and the role of differences in ideology of the political parties and their representatives, as well as the role of simple rivalry and behavioural rules of thumb, which are rather within the realm of social psychology and sociology, was acknowledged and has to be introduced in the analysis.

Each of these players aims at maximising its objective function, which contains a number of non-economic variables. Given the number of players and their objective functions, this is certainly difficult to model mathematically, but it seems fruitful to explore well-defined aspects in isolation.

We illustrated the game and its major players by looking into the issue of the introduction of a decision support model (DSM) for the planning and assessment of export promotion activities and its use in the Flemish Region of Belgium, in the 1991-1994 period, immediately after the 1988 transfer of public export promotion from the federal authorities to the regional governments. We attempted to show that not so much direct economic considerations, but rather political and ideological motives, as well as economic interests, were driving the major players in the export promotion game about the application of the DSM and the implementation of its results.

From a normative point of view, the role of an institutional communicator and independent provider of information about the future and the expected outcomes of the game played should be stressed. At a national level, this role is to some extent similar (be it not in all respects) to that of international organisations involved in a cooperative game of international economic policy coordination, such as the IMF, the WTO or the OECD in the international arena. However, from the above, it will be clear that this role cannot possibly be assigned to the EPO, who is a major player itself. We have endeavoured to show that the specialised research institute or team should rather become involved such that a better economic outcome can be expected from the strategic interactions between the players of the game of public export promotion. Although the involvement of such research institutes or teams, so it seems, is at least a sub-game, we think that it contributes substantially to the benefits and welfare gains obtained from the export promotion actions, which result from the game played.

References

Branders, J.A. & Spencer, B.J. 1985. Export subsidies and international market-share rivalry, *Journal of International Economics*, 18(1-2): 83-100.

Cuyvers, L. 1989a. Beschouwingen over internationale coördinatie van macro-economische politieken en het belang van internationale economische organisaties, *Economisch en Sociaal Tijdschrift*, 43(5): 585-601.

Cuyvers, L. 1989b. *Een Vlaams export-en acquisitiebeleid in een geregionaliseerd België*. Onderzoek in opdracht van de Vice-Voorzitter en Regionale Minister voor Economie, Antwerpen: Rijksuniversitair Centrum Antwerpen, October 1989, 93 pp.

Cuyvers, L., De Pelsmacker, P., Rayp, G. & Roozen, I.T.M. 1995. A decision support model for the planning and assessment of export promotion activities by government promotion institutions: the Belgian case. *International Journal of Research in Marketing*, 12(2): 173-186.

Cuyvers, L. 1996. Export opportunities of Thailand: a decision support model approach. *Journal of Euro-Asian Management*, 2(2): 71-97.

Cuyvers, L. 2004. Identifying export opportunities: the case of Thailand. *International Marketing Review*, 21(3): 255-278.

Czinkota, M. 2002. National export promotion: A statement of issues, changes, and opportunities. In: Kotabe, M. and Aulakh, P. (eds). *Emerging issues in international business research*. Cheltenham, UK: Edward Elgar.

DTI see South Africa. Department of Trade and Industry.

Grossman, G.M. & Helpman, E. 1994. Protection for sale. *American Economic Review*, 84(4): 833-850.

Hellinck, B. 2010. *Norbert De Batselier, een leven in de politiek.* Antwerpen: Manteau.

Hillman, A. & Ursprung, H.W. 1988. Domestic politics, foreign interests, and international trade policy. *American Economic Review*, 78(4): 729-745.

Lederman, D., Olarreaga, M. & Payton, L. 2006. Export promotion agencies: what works and what does not. *Trade Note 30*, World Bank group, Washington D.C.

Pearson, J.J.A. 2007. A decision support model to indentify realistic export opportunities for South Africa. Unpublished doctoral thesis. Faculty of Economic and Business Sciences, Potchefstroom, North-West University.

Pearson, J.J.A., Viviers, W., Cuyvers, L. & Naudé, W. 2010. Identifying export opportunities for South Africa in the southern engines: a DSM approach. *International Business Review*, 19(4): 345-359.

South Africa. 2005. *Draft National Export Strategy 2006-2009*. Pretoria.

Viviers, W., Steenkamp, E., Rossouw, R. & Cuyvers, L. 2010. *Identifying realistic export opportunities for South Africa: application of a decision support model (DSM) using HS 6-digit level product data*. Final report prepared for the Department of Trade and Industry, South Africa, September 2010, 56 pp.

Chapter 3

Overview of international market selection methods[1]

Ermie Steenkamp, Wilma Viviers & Ludo Cuyvers

3.1 Introduction

Governments and individual firms that want to stimulate growth through export development must distinguish between vast numbers of export combinations due to the fact that in most circumstances a large number of export opportunities exist, and only a limited number of these can be explored because of scarce resources (Papadopoulos & Denis, 1988:38).

The process of evaluating worldwide export opportunities is, however, complicated for a number of reasons. These include the difficulty to examine all possible export opportunities to all the countries of the world and the availability and reliability of data on specific consumers, businesses or governments (Jeannet & Hennessey, 1988:137; Brewer, 2000:155). Numerous attempts to formulate appropriate international market selection processes have been made in the literature (see section 3.2). In this chapter an overview of different market selection methods will be given.

3.2 Categorisation of international market selection methods

Papadopoulos and Denis (1988:38-51) summarised and categorised the literature on international market selection methods up until the late 1980s. They firstly identified

1   Part of this chapter was published as a working paper (Steenkamp, Rossouw, Viviers & Cuyvers, 2009) and the financial assistance received from TIPS and AusAid is hereby acknowledged.

two broad types of approaches, namely qualitative and quantitative, and then divided quantitative approaches into market grouping and market estimation methods. After considering the more recent literature on international market selection (1989 to 2010), the market estimation methods were divided into firm-level and country-level methods for the purposes of this study. The above-mentioned categorisation is illustrated in Figure 3.1 and discussed in more detail in the rest of this section.

Figure 3.1. Categorisation of the international market selection literature.

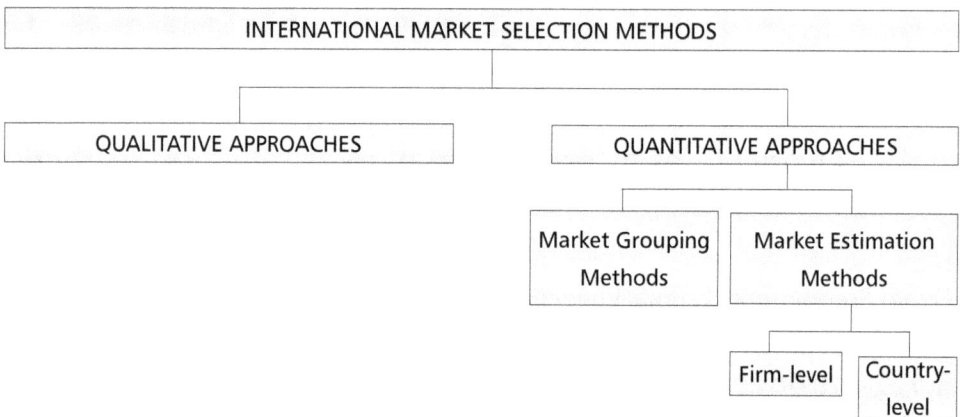

Source: Own figure based on Papadopoulos & Denis, 1988:38-51.

Most "qualitative approaches" typically start with identifying a short list of countries for further consideration. Secondly, objectives and constraints for exporting a specific product to each country under consideration are established (Papadopoulos & Denis, 1988:39). Typical sources of qualitative information used in these studies include government agencies, chambers of commerce, banks, distributors, customers, international experts and foreign market visits (Pezeshkpur, 1979). Due to the fact that most qualitative information is based on perceptions, Papadopoulos and Denis (1988:39) consider qualitative approaches to international market selection biased and largely inaccurate.[2]

"Quantitative approaches" to international market selection, on the other hand, involve analysing and comparing secondary trade data of a large number of countries. Papadopoulos and Denis (1988:39) divided quantitative approaches into two categories, namely "market grouping" methods and "market estimation" methods. Market grouping methods cluster

---

2   Although qualitative approaches are criticised for being based on perceptions, this information still has a place in the market selection process. After selecting markets on a quantitative basis, qualitative information into specific markets can be very valuable to provide market-specific information that is not always quantifiable. Qualitative and quantitative approaches should, therefore, be used together to complement one another and it is not necessary to choose the one or the other.

countries on the basis of similarity, while market estimation models evaluate market potential at firm or country level (see Figure 3.1).

Studies undertaken to attempt "market grouping" have been summarised by Papadopoulos and Denis (1988:39-41), Steenkamp and Ter Hofstede (2002:185-213) and Shankarmahesh et al. (2005:204-206). These methods are based on the assumption that the most attractive markets for a firm are the ones that most closely resemble the markets it has already penetrated successfully (Papadopoulos & Denis, 1988:41). By providing insight into structural similarities, these methods enable firms to standardise their offerings and marketing strategies across markets (Sakarya, Eckman & Hyllegard, 2007:213). Countries are clustered based on similarities in social, economic and political indicators. The demand levels of countries are mostly not taken into account (Sakarya et al., 2007:212). Market grouping methods are mostly criticised for relying exclusively on general country indicators rather than product-specific market indicators, as macro or country indicators may not reflect market demand for a product (Sakarya et al., 2007:212; Kumar, Stam & Joachimsthaler, 1993:31; Papadopoulos & Denis, 1988:41). Studies that attempted to include more product-specific information face the problem of insufficient data, are limited to the product ranges of a particular firm and cannot be applied for all possible product groups (Papadopoulos & Denis, 1988:41, 47). Sakarya et al. (2007:212) also argued that grouping methods fail to take into account similarities among groups of consumers across national boundaries. Furthermore, only focusing on countries with similar characteristics to markets already penetrated may hold the risk of overlooking lucrative opportunities in countries with other characteristics (Kumar et al., 1993:32).

"Market estimation models" evaluate foreign markets on the basis of several criteria that measure market potential and attractiveness (Sakarya et al., 2007:212; Papadopoulos & Denis, 1988:41). The criteria vary across methods and often include market wealth, size, growth, competition and access indicators (Sakarya et al., 2007:212). For the purpose of this study, the literature on market estimation methods is categorised into "firm-level" and "country-level" methods (see Figure 3.1).

"Firm-level" market estimation methods are applied by firms to identify markets for their limited product ranges. These methods usually include an analysis of the firm's objectives, profitability, managers' experience and knowledge, customer standards and attitudes and product adaptation requirements when identifying potential export markets. Apart from the older studies summarised by Papadopoulos and Denis (1988:40-47), firm-level market estimation methods include the studies of Ayal and Zif (1978), Davidson (1983), Cavusgil (1985)[3], Kumar et al. (1993), Hoffman (1997), Andersen and Strandskov (1998), Brewer

---

3   Although these are older references, they were not included in Papadopoulos and Denis's (1988) summary of the international market selection literature and are, therefore, included here.

(2000), Andersen and Buvik (2002), Rahman (2003), Alon (2004), Ozorhon, Dikmen and Birgonul (2006) and more. Most of these studies are based on the following three-stage process of evaluating the export potential of foreign markets:

(i)   a preliminary screening to select more attractive countries to investigate in detail, based on countries' demographic, political, economic and social environment;

(ii) an in-depth screening in which these products' potential (market size and growth), competitors, market access and other market factors for the countries selected in stage one are analysed; and

(iii) a final selection that involves the analysis of company sales potential, profitability and possible product adaptation.

Although country-level market selection methods might include similar variables and screening stages, the main difference between firm-level and country-level market selection methods is that firm-level methods focus on only a limited range of products and consider firm-specific issues like firm objectives, profitability, managers' experience and knowledge, customer standards and attitudes and product adaptation requirements. "Country-level" market estimation methods, on the other hand, can be more generally applied and focus on selecting export opportunities for a specific exporting country and not only a firm. These methods are, therefore, applicable to evaluate a wider range of product-country combinations than only the products a specific firm would offer. The country-level approaches could also be used by export promotion organisations of different countries to plan and assess their export promotion activities. Variables typically used in country-level market selection models may include market size and growth, indicators of economic development, domestic consumption, factors of production, tariff and non-tariff barriers, exchange rates, distances between countries and current international trade data.

In section 3.3, the ten methods that can be classified as country-level, quantitative, market estimation methods, will be discussed and assessed for the purposes of government export promotion.

3.3   Country-level market estimation methods

Ten country-level market estimation methods were identified in the literature. The main criterion for a market selection method to be classified into this category is that it should be capable of screening a wide range of product-country combinations to select export markets with realistic potential for a specific exporting country.

The methods that comply with this criterion include the decision support model (DSM) of Cuyvers *et al.* (1995, 2004), the shift-share model of Green and Allaway (1985), the global-screening model of Russow and Okoroafo (1996), the trade-off model of Papadopoulos,

Chen and Thomans (2002), the multiple criteria method of the International Trade Centre (ITC) (Freudenberg & Paulmier, 2005a, 2005b; Freudenberg, Paulmier, Ikezuki & Conte, 2007, 2008), the assessments of export opportunities in emerging markets by Cavusgil (1997:87-91), Arnold and Quelsh (1998:7-20) and Sakarya et al. (2007:208-238), the gravity model and the trade opportunity matrix (TOM) of Export Development Canada (Verno, 2008).

The above-mentioned methods will be summarised in sections 3.3.1 to 3.3.8.

3.3.1 Decision support model (DSM)

The basic ideas of Walvoord (see section 4.2) were used by Cuyvers et al. (1995:173-186) to construct a decision support model for a Belgian government export promotion organisation, namely VDBH, to provide a limited list of realistic export opportunities to which they could devote their limited financial resources (see Chapter 2).

The decision support model starts from the assumption that all world markets hold potential export opportunities for a particular country and, therefore, all possible product-country combinations (markets) enter the filtering process (Cuyvers, 2004:256). After every filter, a number of markets are rendered unrealistic and are not considered in subsequent filters.

In Filter 1, countries that hold too high a political and/or commercial risk are firstly eliminated. A second elimination of countries is done based on macro-economic size and growth. The rationale for this is that, with all the countries of the world as a starting point, Filter 1 enables the researchers to quickly eliminate countries with relatively low general market potential in order to concentrate in detail on a more limited set of possible export opportunities.

In Filter 2, a more specific assessment of the various product groups for the remaining countries is done to identify the market potential of each possible product-country combination (market). The main purpose of this filter is, therefore, to eliminate markets that do not show sufficient size and growth in demand. The main criteria that are used in this filter are the growth rate of imports of a given product group by a given country (import growth) and the value of imports of a given product group by a given country (import market size). Three variables are calculated for each market, namely short-term import growth, long-term import growth and import market size. Short-term import growth is considered to be the most recent year's growth rate in imports, while long-term growth is calculated as the average annual percentage growth in imports over a period of five years. Finally, the relative import market size is calculated as the ratio of imports of country i for product group j and the total imports of all countries that entered Filter 2 of product group j (Cuyvers et al., 1995:178; Cuyvers, 2004:259-260).

In Filter 3, trade restrictions and other barriers to entry are considered to further screen the remaining possible export opportunities. Two categories of barriers are considered in this filter, namely the degree of market concentration (competitor analysis) and trade restrictions (market accessibility).

In the last stage of the analysis (Filter 4), the export opportunities (product-country combinations) that were identified in Filter 1 to 3 are categorised according to two criteria, namely their relative market importance and their relative market size and growth (Cuyvers, 2004:267).

One of the main benefits of the DSM is that it provides a tool to assist export promotion organisations to decide how to allocate their scarce resources to export promotion activities in various markets. It also provides information on export markets that are useful to derive appropriate export promotion actions in the different markets (Cuyvers *et al.*, 1995:174). The DSM further provides export promotion organisations with a limited list of export promotion priorities, based on measurable and objective economic data and draws the attention to markets that have not previously been recognised as potential export markets (Cuyvers *et al.*, 1995:174).

Despite the above-mentioned benefits of using the DSM to identify realistic export opportunities in a country, Cuyvers *et al.* (1995:174) warn that it would be unwise to rest all export promotion decisions upon the results of the model alone. Other considerations such as feedback from foreign trade offices (on the demand side of exports) and export councils (on the supply side), should also be taken into consideration. Diplomatic and political issues would also lead to government supporting exports to a particular country, even though it might not be identified by the DSM as an economically promising market (Cuyvers *et al.*, 1995:175). Export promotion is, furthermore, an activity that is very often only effective in the long run, and since the DSM's scope is more short term and based on historical data, some export opportunities that are considered by the model as suboptimal, might be good opportunities in the long run (Cuyvers *et al.*, 1995:174). Therefore, basing export promotion decisions only on the results of the DSM, could also lead to missed opportunities. Cuyvers *et al.* (1995:174) also state that it is important to keep in mind that the purpose of the model is not to provide a ranking of export opportunities, but rather to provide a list of choices of interesting markets, grouped into categories reflecting market size, market growth and market importance.

3.3.2   Green and Allaway's shift-share model[4]

Green and Allaway's (1985) shift-share approach to identify export opportunities was described by Douglas and Craig (1992) as the only new approach to international market selection that had been proposed up until the early 1990s.

Shift-share analysis identifies growth differentials based on the changes that have occurred in market shares over time. It requires import data of the countries under investigation for the products in question at the beginning and end of the period of analysis. An expected growth figure is calculated for each product-country combination (market) based on the average growth of all combinations included in the analysis. The difference between each market's actual and expected growth is called the net shift and will be positive for markets that gained market share over the period of analysis and negative for those who lost market share. The net shift is, therefore, the difference between a market's actual performance and the performance it would have had if its growth rate had been equal to the average growth of the entire group of markets included in the analysis (Green & Allaway, 1985:84).

Furthermore, the percentage net shift is calculated by dividing the net shift of each market under investigation by the total net shift of all the markets included in the analysis and multiplying it by 100 (Green & Allaway, 1985:85). This figure provides the total gain or loss of market share accounted for by each market under investigation[5].

Green and Allaway (1985:85) applied the shift-share analysis to identify export opportunities for the USA for 51 high-technology products (SITC 4-digit level) in 20 OECD countries during the period 1974 to 1979.

Green and Allaway (1985:87) identified a few shortcomings in their analysis. These include that the timeframe of the analysis was only based on two points in time, the shift-share analyses identify only relative opportunities and the lack of greater product-specificy.

Papadopoulos *et al.* (2002:168-169) specifically reviewed Green and Allaway's (1985) shift-share model, as it seemed to address all the shortcomings of the international market selection models that they have reviewed in their study. According to Papadopoulos *et al.* (2002:168), the core strength of the shift-share approach is that it is simple and industry-specific while the main weakness, on first review, is that it is limited to import-only measures. When Papadopoulos *et al.* (2002:168) investigated the theoretical foundations of the shift-

---

4   Green and Allaway's shift-share approach was intended for firms to identify export opportunities. However, no firm-specific indicators are used in this approach and are therefore considered to be applicable to identify export opportunities for a country as well.

5   For a step-wise mathematical description of the shift-share methodology, see Papadopoulos *et al.* (2002:186-190) and Huff & Scherr (1967).

share approach, they found that other authors that applied the shift-share approach in the field of marketing found the results to be biased depending on the base years chosen, and fluctuating greatly due to outliers. Papadopoulos *et al.* (2002:168-169) subsequently tested the shift-share approach themselves by performing it for three products and 50 importing countries. They found that one country might perform very promising at one time and very poorly in subsequent years. They also found that the rankings identified by the model are volatile and that simple growth model rankings were highly correlated to the shift-share rankings. Papadopoulos *et al.* (2002:169) concluded that the shift-share approach lacked predictive power and that it is redundant due to the high correlation with the simple growth model.

In response to Russow and Okoroafo's (1996) (see section 3.3.3) comment that global screening models should be subjected to inferential statistical analyses to establish the importance of the independent variables used in these models, Williamson, Kshetri, Heijwegen and Schiopu (2006:72) examined the significance of three variables typically used in the export market selection process. These variables are

(i)   a measure of import market potential (such as the net shift in import growth as used by Green & Allaway);

(ii)   a measure of import market competitiveness; and

(iii)   a measure of barriers-to-imports.

To test the role of each variable's influence on the outcomes of the export market identification process, the relationship between the above-mentioned three explanatory variables and the dependent variable was evaluated (Williamson *et al.*, 2006:80-81). The dependent variable was defined as the change in an importing country's share in the exporting country's exports for a particular product. Williamson *et al.* (2006:80-81) argued that if this is a positive change, exporters of the product would have shortlisted this market as a potential export opportunity. The dependent variable, therefore, determines the real-world outcome of the export identification process to which the explanatory variables can be related. Williamson *et al.* (2006:88) found a negative relationship between import market potential and the dependent variable for the two exporting countries and products they used in their analysis. They also found that the import market competitiveness and barriers-to-imports variables have no independent effect on the dependent variable. Only when all three variables are used together, the dependent variable is better explained. This indicates that the variables should be used together rather than separately. According to Williamson *et al.* (2006:72), the import market potential, import market competitiveness and barriers-to-imports variables can be incorporated together into a shift-share model to identify export markets for a specific exporting country and product. Williamson *et al.* (2006), however, did not implement these changes to the shift-share model, but only tested the importance of these variables in export market selection. They discredited a shift-share framework that only uses one explanatory variable (such as Green & Allaway's shift-share model).

3.3.3 Russow and Okoroafo's global screening model

From the international business theory and market screening and assessment literature, Russow and Okoroafo (1996:50) identified three criteria to screen markets and identify export opportunities for a particular exporting country. These criteria are

(i)   product-specific market size and growth;

(ii)   factors of production; and

(iii)   economic development of the importing country.

The variables used to measure "market size" and "growth" include domestic production, imports, exports, the shift-share of domestic production, the shift-share of imports and the shift-share of exports of a specific product. The cost and availability of "factors of production" are measured by gross fixed capital formation, money supply, total international reserves, population, percentage unemployment, average hourly wages in manufacturing and surface and density. The level of "economic development" is measured by gross domestic product, gross domestic product per capita, agriculture as a percentage of GDP, manufacturing industries as a percentage of GDP, construction as a percentage of GDP, wholesale and retail trade as a percentage of GDP and transportation and communication as a percentage of GDP (Russow & Okoroafo, 1996:52).

Russow and Okoroafo (1996:52) used six randomly selected products and 192 possible importing countries around the world in their analysis to identify possible export markets for the USA. A principal components analysis was used for every product separately to determine whether the 21 variables mentioned above are interrelated. After performing the principal components analysis for the product "calculators" (as an example), seven factors were identified to use in the screening model. A cluster analysis was consequently conducted to group countries with similar market potential for a specific product. Each country group was then classified as having a high, medium or low market potential for the product in question (Russow & Okoroafo, 1996:55-58).

Russow and Okoroafo (1996:62) state that their method can assist managers to select potential markets objectively and efficiently, and distinguish markets with high export potential from those that hold little or no potential. This decreases the risk involved when venturing into new markets.

According to Russow and Okoroafo (1996:60), limitations to their study include that no sub-national opportunities are identified and, on the other hand, no export potential to country groupings (e.g. North American Free Trade Area or the European Union) are identified. Also, this screening technique is considered a starting point to identify the location of potential demand, and a full assessment of the identified markets should follow. This assessment would include a customer profile as well as determining the specific sub-national location of the opportunity and a possible grouping of the results into trade blocs.

3.3.4   Papadopoulos *et al.*'s trade-off model

According to Papadopoulos *et al.* (2002:169), the international market selection theory suggests that both the pluses and minuses of the countries under review must be considered in order to make effective market selection decisions. They identified these trade-offs as the "demand potential" (plus/positive) and "trade barriers" (minus/negative) in the countries under review. They state that many researchers identify trade barriers as the most important deterrent of exports, but most have not accounted for it in their international market selection models. This is probably due to the difficulty in quantifying non-tariff barriers, and most authors assume that non-tariff barriers would be dealt with in later stages of the internationalisation process where in-depth market analyses are conducted (Papadopoulos *et al.*, 2002:170). Papadopoulos *et al.*'s trade-off model is illustrated in Figure 3.2.

Figure 3.2. Papadopoulos *et al.*'s (2002) trade-off model.

Source: Papadopoulos *et al.* (2002:170).

Four variables were used for each of the two main constructs (demand potential and trade barriers). These variables were chosen based on relevance, frequency of use in past research

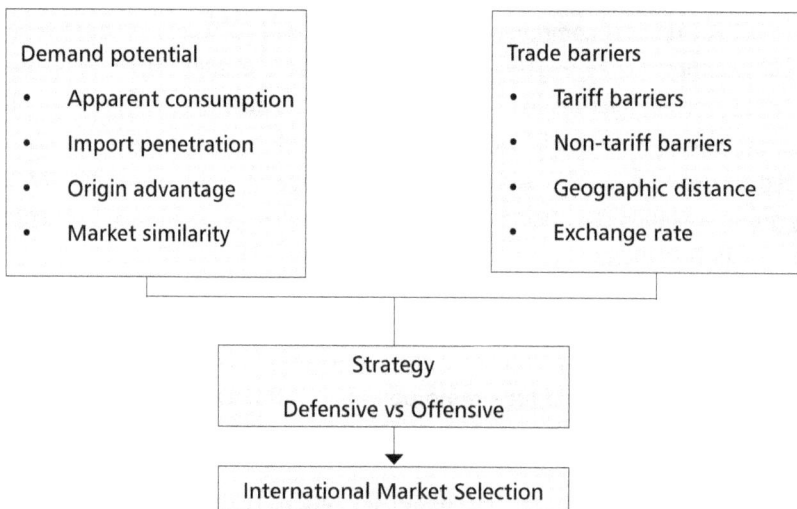

and data availability, reliability and comparability (Papadopoulos *et al.*, 2002:170-171). The variables and their measures are summarised in Table 3.1.

Table 3.1. Papadopoulos *et al.*'s (2002) trade-off model.

Demand potential	Trade barriers
Variable 1: Apparent Consumption = *Domestic production plus imports minus exports* Import data do not portray the total available market. This measure for apparent consumption is considered to be the appropriate reflection of true market size in a given industry.	**Variable 1: Tariff Barriers =** *Weighted mean annual tariff rate over the study period.* Tariffs have a direct effect on the exporter's prices and pricing strategy discretion.
Variable 2: Import Penetration = *Imports as % of apparent consumption.* This measure is widely used in industry-specific analyses. A high ratio means import market openness and low-domestic producer competitiveness, signalling an attractive market.	**Variable 2: Non-tariff barriers =** *Composite quantitative index of 20 barrier items.* Non-tariff restrictions are often a more important obstacle to exporting than tariffs are. Papadopoulos *et al.* (2002:172) developed an index consisting of all 20 barrier items in the World Trade Organisation's Trade Policy Review. Each item was weighted based on its frequency of occurrence in the target countries. WTO data was used.
Variable 3: Origin Advantage = *Exporting country's share in target market's total imports.* A high overall share indicates that the exporting country has the benefits of critical mass, favourable image in the importing market and strong trade relations between the importing and exporting countries.	**Variable 3: Geographic Distance =** *Mileage distance between exporting and target countries.* According to Papadopoulos *et al.* (2002:171), distance is directly related to transport costs and affects export price. Distance between countries' main ports was used (if no port, the capital or next closest major city was used).

Demand potential	Trade barriers
Variable 4: Market Similarity = *Overall score of four indicators, namely health and education, personal consumption, production and transportation and trade.*	**Variable 4: Exchange Rate** = *Percent change in official exchange rate vs previous year.*
According to Papadopoulos *et al.* (2002:171), demand tends to be higher in markets similar to where a product was initially developed.	According to Papadopoulos *et al.* (2002:171), volatile exchange rates between the exporting and importing countries' currencies are a major risk element in exporting and can have a big impact on pricing and strategy.
Sethi (1971) proposed 29 indicators of market similarity that were grouped in the above-mentioned four categories. Papadopoulos *et al.* (2002:171) used the indicator in each group with the highest correlation to the others in the group to measure the four indicators in their market similarity score. These were: (i) for health and education: life expectancy; (ii) for personal consumption: GNP per capita; (iii) for production and transportation: electricity production; and (iv) for trade: imports-to-GDP ratio.	

Source: Summary of Papadopoulos *et al.* (2002:170-171).

The data for each variable indicated in Table 3.1 was scaled by subtracting the lowest country value from the highest and dividing the difference by 10. Therefore, 10 equal scale intervals were formed and each country could be assigned a score from 0 to 10. Averages were calculated for the variables measuring the plusses (demand potential) and minuses (trade barriers) of each country. A score could therefore be assigned to each of the demand potential and trade barriers dimensions. High scores represented high demand potential and low trade barriers. Countries were subsequently plotted in a two-dimensional matrix illustrated in Figure 3.3.

Figure 3.3. Two-dimensional matrix for plotting countries in Papadopoulos *et al.*'s (2002) trade-off model.

High demand potential/ High trade barriers	**High demand potential/ Low trade barriers**
Low demand potential/ High trade barriers	Low demand potential/ Low trade barriers

Source: Papadopoulos *et al.* (2002:174).

Target markets in the upper right quadrant (high demand potential/low trade barriers) would offer the best export opportunities.

As many users would prefer to rank countries on a single overall score, Papadopoulos *et al.* (2002:174-175) assigned weights based on firm strategy to develop total score country attractiveness scales that combine the two dimensions. If a firm has a defensive strategy[6], it would focus more on markets that are easier to penetrate and high trade barriers would carry a bigger weight. On the other hand, if a firm has an offensive strategy[7], it would focus on markets with high demand potential, even if it may take more effort to penetrate those markets. Weighted scores for each of the two dimensions were then added to generate an overall score for each country (also see sections 3.2.4, 5.4 and 6.7 for more information on export promotion strategies).

Papadopoulos *et al.* (2002:184) stated that their model provides a significant improvement on earlier market selection models due to the fact that it captures total rather than import-only demand; it is industry-specific and was tested using three products (namely aircraft (representing industrial goods), furniture (representing consumer durables) and beverages (representing consumer non-durables)), 17 importing countries (OECD countries) and two very different exporting countries namely Canada (highly developed country and an experienced exporter) and China (world's largest population and in its earlier stages of internationalisation) (Papadopoulos *et al.*, 2002:184)).

Papadopoulos *et al.* (2002:183) identified a few limitations to their model. These include deficiencies of secondary data, unavailability, unreliability and ageing of data for some countries (particularly less-developed countries) and the lack of greater product-specificity.

6   According to Papadopoulos *et al.* (2002:171,175), a firm with a defensive export promotion strategy will focus on preventing competitors from threatening their market share.

7   A firm with an offensive export promotion strategy will seek growth at their competitors' expense and value demand potential more than being concerned about trade barriers (Papadopoulos *et al.* 2002:171,175).

3.3.5   The International Trade Centre's multiple criteria method

One of the aims of the International Trade Centre (ITC) is to assist developing countries that want to effectively focus their trade promotion efforts and extend/diversify their exports (Freudenberg, 2006). The ITC does this by using a multiple criteria method to assess the export potential of a specific exporting country (Freudenberg, 2006).

The ITC identifies priority sectors and markets for export promotion by using both quantitative and qualitative analyses. The "quantitative analysis" involves the calculation of composite indicators[8] to measure the export potential of different sectors and markets. The quantitative information required to calculate these indices includes trade statistics and market access data obtained from the ITC's "Market Access Map" and "Trade Map" databases respectively. These are online databases of global trade flows and market access barriers providing detailed and up-to-date export and import profiles and trends for over 5,300 products in 200 countries at HS two-, four-, six-, eight- and 10-digit levels (Freudenberg *et al.*, 2008:12). The databases include official data reported by countries to the United Nations Statistics Department (UN Comtrade Database).

The "qualitative analysis" includes an assessment of relevant literature and information collected from surveys and interviews with enterprises and business associations in the exporting country (Freudenberg & Paulmier, 2005a:11). Quantitative analyses usually include assessments of "domestic supply conditions" such as product quality, unit labour costs, production cost, process technology, infrastructure cost, up-/down-stream linkages between industries and competitiveness prospects in their export potential assessment. The projected "socio-economic impact" resulting from an increase in exports of the different sectors or markets is also often added to the qualitative analysis. These include projected full-time employment equivalents, poverty reduction, foreign currency generation and contribution to industrialisation and environmental sustainability (ITC, 2011).

Due to the focus of this section on quantitative market selection methods, the ITC's "quantitative assessment" of export potential will be discussed in more detail.

The following indicators are used to quantitatively evaluate the export potential of different sectors and markets (Freudenberg & Paulmier, 2005a:10-11; Freudenberg & Paulmier, 2005b:8, Freudenberg *et al.*, 2007:2; Freudenberg *et al.*, 2008:11-12, ITC, 2011):

(i)   the current export performance of the exporting country (export performance index), evaluated by current export size (exported value and world market share), export

8   A composite index is formed when individual indicators are compiled into a single index (ITC, 2011).

dynamism (export growth and relative growth[9]) and the trade balance (the absolute trade balance (exports minus imports) and the relative trade balance (absolute trade balance divided by total trade); and

(ii)   the characteristics of the international environment (world demand index/market attractiveness index[10]), evaluated by market size (imported value), market dynamism (import growth and relative growth[11]), and ease of market access conditions (average *ad valorem* tariff applied to the exporting country and the average ad valorem tariff applied to the top five competitors minus the tariff applied to the exporting country).

A composite export potential index is ultimately calculated for each sector and/or market under investigation, using the above-mentioned indices and sub-indices. The different variables are first standardised (due to the fact that it is measured in different units) before they are aggregated into the respective indices. To standardise the variables, the following formula is used (Freudenberg & Paulmier, 2005a:34; ITC, 2011):

$$100 \times (\text{Value} - \text{Lower limit})/(\text{Upper limit} - \text{Lower limit})$$

This will provide an index value ranging from 0 (weak performance) to 100 (best performance) for each variable. The 5% best-performing products define the upper limit and the 5% weakest-performing products define the lower limit for each variable. The weighting of the different sub-indices to arrive at the composite index is determined on a theoretical basis or in consultation with an advisory council of knowledgeable people in the field.

Depending on the requirements of the client (exporting country/exporter), the export potential of sectors/products/specific markets (product-country combinations) can be assessed by following the ITC method described above. For a particular country, the sectors with the highest export potential can be identified. Also, after identifying the sectors with the highest export potential for a specific country, the export potential for the products within a selected sector (e.g. fruits) can be assessed by also calculating a composite export potential index per product. If required, a product with high export potential (e.g. fresh grapes) can be selected and the countries with the highest export potential can be identified

---

9   Difference between the country's export growth and world export growth.
10   The world demand index is used when the overall potential of sectors or products needs to be assessed and is calculated by using the world import value, world import growth, share of attractive markets in world imports, average tariff advantage and world market prospects. The market attractiveness index is used when prioritising between importing countries for a specific export product. Here indicators such as country *i*'s import value, import growth and applied tariff to product *j* are used (ITC, 2011).
11   Difference between market growth and world import growth.

by calculating the market attractiveness index[12] for all possible importing countries (ITC, 2011).

The limitations of the ITC's quantitative analysis of export potential include that composite indices only measure what can be quantified and for which there are data available and the selected variables only give a snapshot at one moment in time. Furthermore, growth variables are backwards looking; weighting of the different variables is difficult to establish and rankings should be interpreted with caution, especially when differences between the respective indices for products are small (Freudenberg & Paulmier, 2005a:36; ITC, 2011).

3.3.6 Assessment of export opportunities in emerging markets

As mentioned earlier, Cavusgil (1997:87-91), Arnold and Quelsh (1998:7-20) and Sakarya *et al.* (2007:208-238) all attempted to assess export opportunities specifically in emerging markets. They argue that traditional market selection analyses fail to account for emerging markets' dynamism and future potential (Sakarya *et al.*, 2007:208)[13]. Cavusgil (1997:87-91) attempted to rank the total market potential of 25 emerging countries. Cavusgil only used country-level indicators and no product specificity was introduced.

Arnold and Quelsh (1998:7-20) proposed a foreign market assessment framework that includes three elements, namely assessing long-term market potential (using population and GDP, thus country-level measures), identifying business prospects (product-level assessment; companies must identify their own indicators for assessing demand for their product) and predicting potential profits (assessing concentration of population in urban centres versus rural villages, the distribution of wealth, telecommunications infrastructure, penetration of key consumer durables such as telephones, televisions or cars, etc.). Arnold and Quelsh's model uses only macro-level indicators to assess market potential and then concentrates on a firm-level assessment (which is mostly situation specific and qualitative) of export opportunities.

Sakarya *et al.* (2007:209) introduced long-term market potential (from Arnold & Quelsh's model), cultural distance, competitive strength of the industry and customer receptiveness as criteria for assessing emerging markets as candidates for international expansion. Their proposed model was applied for the United States as the exporting country, Turkey as the importing country and "apparel" as product/industry. Sakarya *et al.*'s (2007) model includes

---

12 In the case of identifying the sectors and products in a specific exporting country with the highest export potential, the export performance index and world demand indices are used. When the export potential for a specific product within different importing countries is assessed, only the market attractiveness index is used.

13 Although these studies only focus on identifying export opportunities in emerging markets, it can still be classified as country-level market estimation methods.

an in-depth, situation-specific assessment of each particular product-country combination under consideration that requires information that is not readily available for a large array of product-country combinations. This information includes social and moral values of consumers, wages in the industry, consumer choice opportunities, product quality, appeal of sales promotions and level of customer service.

3.3.7 The gravity model

The gravity model has been widely used over the last four decades to explain international trade flows (Kepaptsoglou, Karlaftis & Tsamboulas, 2010:1-3). Since the gravity model was first introduced by Tinbergen (1962) and Linneman (1966), it has been applied and refined by many authors attempting to analyse trade flows between regions, analyse bilateral trade flows of specific products, examine the effects of regional trade agreements, examine the factors affecting trade and estimate trade potential (see Kepaptsoglou *et al.*, 2010:1-13 for a summary of 55 empirical studies published on the gravity model in the last decade). The main idea behind the gravity model originates from Newton's gravity theory in physics (Kepaptsoglou *et al.*, 2010:2). Trade flows are regarded a result of two countries being attracted based on the "masses" (sizes) of their economies. Therefore, the larger the countries, the larger the trade among them will be. Restrictions/resistance to trade such as distance, tariffs, border controls and quantity restrictions are, however, also considered (DTI, 2004).

In its most general formulation, the gravity model explains a flow of goods between two areas i and j (F_{ij}) as a function of the characteristics of the origin (O_i) and the destination (D_j) and some measure of restrictions on this flow of goods (R_{ij}) (Kepaptsoglou *et al.*, 2010:1-3):

$$F_{ij} = O_i \cdot D_j \cdot R_{ij} \quad \text{... (1)}$$

Equation (1) can be translated into a linear function:

$$\text{Log } F_{ij} = \beta X + \varepsilon \quad \text{.. (2)}$$

where:

X: vector containing the logs of the explanatory variables;

β: vector of parameters to be estimated; and

ε: Error term.

Equation (2) indicates that trade flows (bilateral trade flows, imports or exports) can be explained by a number of explanatory variables. These explanatory variables normally include factors affecting demand and supply of the countries trading with one another and factors restricting the trade flows between countries. Variables often used to proxy demand and supply include measures of a country's size such as GDP, GDP per capita, population and area size. Variables used to measure restrictions on trade include distance, transportation costs, tariffs, quality of infrastructure and common language (Kepaptsoglou et al., 2010:3, 9, 11).

As mentioned earlier, the gravity model is often used to estimate trade flows. A specific application of the gravity model to estimate potential exports for South Africa was undertaken by the Investment and Trade Policy Centre (ITPC) of the Department of Economics at the University of Pretoria[14] together with the Department of Trade and Industry in 2004 (henceforth referred to as the South African trade potential gravity model). The main aim of this application of the gravity model was to analyse the trade potential of South Africa by predicting what trade flows ought to be, and to determine priority export markets for South Africa (DTI, 2004). Potential export values were estimated and compared with actual exports to identify priority markets in which South Africa is not utilising its export potential to a satisfactory level. Due to the similarity of the objectives of this chapter and the South African trade potential gravity model, the remainder of this section will focus on this application of the gravity model.

In the South African trade potential gravity model, a sample of the 50 countries to which South Africa has exported the most in US dollars since 2000, was used. These countries are considered the countries to which trade is supposed to have reached its potential (DTI, 2004). A gravity equation was henceforth estimated explaining bilateral exports within the sample. This equation was used to simulate bilateral exports from South Africa to any other country (given the availability of data on distance, GDP and population figures) and the simulated (potential) exports were compared with actual exports to identify export potential for South Africa (DTI, 2004). This methodology was applied to both total exports[15] as well as the five priority sectors of the DTI[16], namely textiles, transport, chemicals, minerals and agriculture (DTI, 2004). Total potential exports from South Africa as well as potential exports of South African textiles, transportation products, chemicals, minerals and agricultural products (as a whole) to different countries around the world could, therefore, be simulated and compared with actual exports (DTI, 2004).

---

14 We acknowledge the research of prof. André Jordaan on the South African trade potential gravity model.

15 Total export data for the period 1980 to 2000 were used.

16 Sectoral export data for the period 1988 to 2000 were used.

By following a panel estimation approach[17], South Africa's exports can be explained by the following equation (DTI, 2004):

$$\text{Log } X_{ijt} = C_0 + \beta_1 \text{log } EX_{jt} + \beta_2 \text{Dist}_{jt} + \beta_3 PCY_{jt} + \beta_4 \text{Prodl}_{jt} + \beta_5 \text{Infra}_{jt} + \beta_6 ERP_i + \varepsilon_i + \eta_t$$

where:

X_{ijt}: exports from South Africa to country j. The subscript i refers to the specific sector where applicable;

C_0: common intercept;

EX_{jt}: exchange rate between South Africa and country j;

Dist_{jt}: the distance in miles between South Africa and country j;

PCY_{jt}: GDP per capita of country j;

Prodl_{jt}: GDP of country j divided by the area of country j;

Infra_{jt}: an index containing a comprehensive rating of the infrastructure of country j;

ERP_i: the effective rate of protection for exports in sector i (measured mainly by tariffs);

ε_i: the country specific random effect; and

η_t: the white noise residual.

Separate estimations were performed for total exports and each of the priority sectors. The model was found to be well specified and robust in all cases. The factors used in the estimation are also considered as the core factors determining trade (DTI, 2004).

To summarise, the South African trade potential gravity model simulates the determinants of exports based on historical export data and uses this estimated model to calculate export potentials for different countries and industries. Markets in which the export potential is not adequately utilised in actual exports are then identified as priority markets.

---

17 South Africa's total or sectoral exports to 50 countries over 21 years for total exports and 13 years for sectoral exports.

3.3.8 Export Development Canada's Trade Opportunity Matrix

Based on the overload of contradicting information available to exporters and the fact that exporters mainly use generic economic information such as GDP, GDP growth and population size, which provides very little industry-specific information to make market selection decisions, Export Development Canada has developed a Trade Opportunity Matrix (TOM) (Verno, 2008).

The TOM is a forward-looking analysis in which 69 countries are ranked for business in 44 industries (ISIC 2-digit level) based on the greatest potential for new business (Verno, 2008). It ranks the countries and industries in which Canadian exporters are most likely to increase export sales.

The TOM uses historical and forecasted data to estimate models of the drivers of Canadian exports. Hereby, the size and significance of each of these drivers of Canadian exports are determined and the latest available data are fed into the estimated models in order to rank the best countries per industry or the best industries per country (Verno, 2008).

Firstly, to rank the "best countries per industry", a fixed-effects and random-effects model was estimated for each one of the 44 manufacturing industries included in the panel of data. The unrestricted models for the determinants of Canadian exports by industry are as follows (Verno, 2008):

Fixed-effects model:

$$cx_{i,t+1} = \alpha + \alpha_i + \beta_1 gdp_{i,t+1} + \beta_2 gdp_{i,t} + \beta_3 cdia_{i,t} + \beta_4 ca_{i,t} + \beta_5 mkt_{i,t+1} + \beta_6 mkt_{i,t} + \beta_7 er_{i,t+1} + \beta_8 er_{i,t} + \beta_9 CR_{i,t+1} + \beta_{10} CR_{i,t} + \varepsilon_{i,t} \quad \text{..} \quad (3)$$

Random-effects model:

$$cx_{i,t+1} = \alpha + \beta_1 gdp_{i,t+1} + \beta_2 gdp_{i,t} + \beta_3 cdia_{i,t} + \beta_4 ca_{i,t} + \beta_5 mkt_{i,t+1} + \beta_6 mkt_{i,t} + \beta_7 er_{i,t+1} + \beta_8 er_{i,t} + \beta_9 CR_{i,t+1} + \beta_{10} CR_{i,t} + \omega_{i,t} + \lambda_t + \mu_i \quad \text{..} \quad (4)$$

where:

α is the common intercept, α_i is the individual country intercept, $\varepsilon_{i,t}$ and $\omega_{i,t}$ are the error terms, λ_t is the time error term and μ_i is the individual error term;

$CX_{i,t+1}$: future Canadian exports of goods produced in sector j to country i. $cx_{i,t+1} = CX_{i,t+1} / \Sigma_i CX_{i,t+1}$;

$gdp_{i,t}$: country i's percentage change in real GDP;

$CDIA_{i,t}$: current level of Canadian Direct Investment Abroad. $cdia_i = CDIA_{i,t} / \Sigma_i \, CDIA_{i,t}$;

$ca_{i,t}$: proxy measuring Canada's current comparative advantage in producing sector j goods relative to country i and foreign competitors with presence in county i. $ca_{i,t} = CX_i / MKT_{i,t}^2$;

MKT_j: market size of sector j in country i given by domestic production of product j plus net imports. $mkt_{i,t+1} = MKT_{i, t+1} / \Sigma_i MKT_{i,t+1}$;

$er_{i,t}$: percentage change in the cross-exchange rate between the Canadian dollar and country i's currency; and

$CR_{i,t}$: proxy for country risk computed by using Export Development Canada's economic and political ratings as well as the political ratings of International Country Risk Guide.

Verno (2008) estimated models (1) and (2) for each of the 44 industries in the data panel. He determined which model best fitted each industry by running various statistical tests. Therefore, for every industry the variables retained and the coefficients for each variable differ. In order to rank the 69 countries for each industry, a score is calculated for each country by multiplying all the estimated coefficients with the actual explanatory variables corresponding to them, and adding all these multiplied terms. The higher the score, the better the country's ranking.

In order to rank the "best industries per country", a different model needed to be estimated. This model includes only industry data and does not include any macroeconomic data due to the fact that the country is assumed to be already regarded a priority. The model also had to be adapted to include dynamic effects and compensate for statistical problems (see Verno, 2008). The final model for determining the best industries per country is the following (Verno, 2008):

$$\Delta cx_{j,t+1} = \delta \Delta cx_{j,t} + \beta_1 \Delta mkt_{j,t+1} + \beta_2 \Delta mkt_{j,t} + \beta_3 \Delta ca_{j,t+1} + \beta_4 \Delta ca_{j,t} + \varepsilon_{j,t} \quad \text{............................} \quad (5)$$

where:

j: Agriculture, ..., Jewellery (44 industries);

t: 1994, ..., 2003.

Equation (5) was estimated by using aggregated data for Canada and the world (Verno, 2008) across all 44 industries. In other words, Canada's share in world exports for industry j ($cx_{j,t}$); world spending on goods of industry j ($mkt_{j,t}$) and Canada's world comparative advantage in industry j ($ca_{j,t}$) are used as the explanatory variables. Only one model needed to be estimated across all industries. A ranking of industries per country was again established by calculating a score for each industry per country. This was done by multiplying the coefficient estimates of each of the explanatory variables with the actual industry data corresponding to it and adding the multiplied terms.

Verno (2008) regards the TOM as a tool for Canadian exporters and trade commissioners to quickly find the best country and industry export opportunities. He also notes that the TOM is relatively easy to update and, therefore, recent developments in a country or industry will quickly reflect in the TOM rankings.

The limitations of the TOM include that, like all statistical models, it uses some assumptions and generalisations and is limited by data availability and reliability (Verno, 2008). Also, industry data are broadly aggregated and one industry includes a wide variety of products. Verno (2008), therefore, recommends that the TOM results be complemented with more in-depth analyses and sector-specific knowledge.

3.4   Assessment of country-level market estimation methods

After assessment of the advantages and disadvantages of the ten country-level market estimation methods, it appears that, for the purposes of the prioritising and planning of export promotion organisations (EPOs), the DSM, that starts the market selection process with all products and countries, is particularly useful for export promotion organisations to prioritise their product- and country-level export promotion activities. A limited list of product-country combinations with the highest export potential for the exporting country can be identified in order for an export promotion organisation to use their resources optimally.

3.5   Conclusion

In this chapter, the international market selection literature was classified into various categories of methodologies (see Figure 3.1). Ten country-level market estimation models were identified in the literature and have been discussed in sections 3.3.1 to 3.3.8.

For the purposes of this volume, it was decided to select the unique DSM as it seems to be capable of handling a large array of possible product-country combinations due to the filtering process and finally identify a list of priority products in each country and vice versa, a list of priority countries for each product. With the limited list of export opportunities, the EPO can focus its limited resources for export promotion activities. Furthermore, the DSM was specifically designed for the planning and assessment of export promotion activities by government and export promotion organisations (see Chapter 2).

A detailed description of the methodology of the DSM as well as other studies that support the use of the different variables used in the filters of the DSM, follows in Chapter 4.

References

Alon, I. 2004. International market selection for a small enterprise: a case study in international entrepreneurship. *SAM Advanced Management Journal*, 69(1): 25-33.

Andersen, O. & Buvik, A. 2002. Firms' internationalisation and alternative approaches to the international customer/market selection. *International Business Review*, 11(3): 347-363.

Andersen, P.H. & Strandskov, J. 1998. International market selection: a cognitive mapping perspective. *Journal of Global Marketing*, 11(3): 65-84.

Arnold, D.J. & Quelsh, J.A. 1998. New strategies in emerging markets. *Sloan Management Review*, 40(1): 7-20.

Anal, I. & Ziff, J. 1978. Competitive market choice strategies in multinational marketing. *Columbia Journal of World Business*, 13(3): 72-81.

Brewer, P. 2000. International market selection: developing a model from Australian case studies. *International Business Review*, 10(2): 155-174.

Cavusgil, S.T. 1985. Guidelines for export market research. *Business Horizons*, 28(6): 27-33.

Cavusgil, S.T. 1997. Measuring the potential of emerging markets: an indexing approach. *Business Horizons*, 40(1): 87-91.

Cuyvers, L. 1997. Export opportunities of Thailand: a decision support model approach. *CAS discussion paper, no. 9*. [Online.] Available from: http://webhost.ua.ac.be/cas/PDF/CAS09.pdf. Accessed 17 January 2008.

Cuyvers, L. 2004. Identifying export opportunities: the case of Thailand. *International Marketing Review*, 21(3): 255-278.

Cuyvers, L., De Pelsmacker, P., Rayp, G. & Roozen, I.T.M. 1995. A decision support model for the planning and assessment of export promotion activities by government export promotion institutions: the Belgian case. *International Journal of Research in Marketing*, 12(2): 173-186.

Davidson, W.H. 1983. Market similarity and market selection: implications for international marketing strategy. *Journal of Business Research*, 11(4): 439-456.

DTI. *see* South Africa. Department of Trade and Industry.

Douglas, S.P. & Craig, C.S. 1992. Advances in international marketing. *International Journal of Research in Marketing*, 9(4): 291-318.

Freudenberg, M. 2006. Export potential assessment: identifying priority sectors for export promotion. Unpublished report of the International Trade Centre UNCTAD/WTO, Market Analysis Section.

Freudenberg, M. & Paulmier, T. 2005a. Export potential assessment in Vietnam. Unpublished report of the International Trade Centre, Market Analysis Section.

Freudenberg, M. & Paulmier, T. 2005b. Export potential assessment in Lao PDR. Unpublished report of the International Trade Centre, Market Analysis Section.

Freudenberg, M., Paulmier, T., Bijl, B. & Ikezuki, T. 2007. Export potential assessment in Nepal. Unpublished report of the International Trade Centre, Market Analysis Section.

Freudenberg, M., Paulmier, T., Ikezuki, T. & Conte, K. 2008. Export opportunity scan for Jordan: second draft. Unpublished report of the International Trade Centre, Market Analysis Section.

Green, R.T. & Allaway, A.W. 1985. Identification of export opportunities: a shift-share approach. *Journal of Marketing*, 49(1): 83-88.

Hoffmann, J.J. 1997. A two-stage model for the introduction of products into international markets. *Journal of Global Marketing*, 11(1): 67-86.

Huff, D.L. & Scherr, L.A. 1967. Measure for determining differential growth rates of markets. *Journal of Marketing Research*, 4(4): 391-395.

ITC (International Trade Centre). 2011. Training programme on export market analysis for the South African Department of Agriculture, Forestry and Fisheries, September 2010 – March 2011. (Unpublished)

Jeannet, J.P. & Hennessey, H.D. 1998. *International marketing management: strategies and cases*. Boston: Houghton Mifflin.

Kepaptsoglou, K., Karlaftis, M.G. & Tsamboula, D. 2010. The gravity model specification for modelling international trade flows and free trade agreement effects: a 10-year review of empirical studies. *Open Economics Journal*, 3: 1-13. [Online.] Available from: http://benthamscience.com/open/toeconsj/articles/V003/1TOECONSJ.pdf. Accessed 20 January 2011.

Kumar, V., Stam, A. & Joachimsthaler, E.A. 1993. An interactive multi-criteria approach to identifying potential foreign markets. *Journal of International Marketing*, 2(1): 29-52.

Linneman, H. 1966. *An econometric study of world trade flows*. Amsterdam: North-Holland Publishing.

Ozorhon, B., Dikmen, I. & Birgonul, M.T. 2006. Case-based reasoning model for international market selection. *Journal of Construction Engineering and Management*, 132(9): 940-947.

Papadopoulos, N. & Denis, J.E. 1988. Inventory, taxonomy and assessment of methods for international market selection. *International Marketing Review*, 5(3): 38-51.

Papadopoulos, N., Chen, H. & Thomans, D.R. 2002. Toward a trade-off model for international market selection. *International Business Review*, 11(2): 165-192.

Pezeshkpur, C. 1979. Systematic approach to finding export opportunities. *Harvard Business Review*, 57(5): 182-196.

Rahman, S.H. 2003. Modelling of international market selection process: a qualitative study of successful Australian international businesses. *Qualitative Market Research: An International Journal*, 6(2): 119-132.

Russow, L.C. & Okaroafo, S.C. 1996. On the way towards developing a global screening model. *International Marketing Review*, 13(1): 46-64.

Sakarya, S., Eckman, M. & Hyllegard, K.H. 2007. Market selection for international expansion: assessing opportunities in emerging markets. *International Marketing Review*, 24(2): 208-238.

Shankarmahesh, M.N., Olsen, H.W. & Honeycutt, E.D. 2005. A dominant product-dominant country framework of industrial export segmentation. *Industrial Marketing Management*, 34(3): 203-210.

South Africa. Department of Trade and Industry. (2004). A gravity model for the determination and analysis of trade potential for South Africa. [Online.] Available from: http://www.dti.gov.za/stats/gravity.pdf. Accessed 15 January 2011.

Steenkamp, E.A., Rossouw, R., Viviers, W. & Cuyvers, L. 2009. Export market selection methods and the identification of realistic export opportunities for South Africa using a decision support model. [Online.] Available from: http://www.sadctrade.org/node/281. Accessed 17 December 2009.

Steenkamp, J.E.M. & Ter Hofstede, F. 2002. International market segmentations: issues and perspectives. *International Journal of Research in Marketing*, 19(3): 185-213.

Tinbergen, J. 1962. *Shaping the world economy*. New York, NY: Twentieth Century Fund.

Verno, C. 2008. The trade opportunity matrix (TOM): an overview of Canadian export opportunities. [Online.] Available from: http://www.edc.ca/english/docs/TOM_Final_Report_Dec2008_e.pdf. Accessed 24 January 2010.

Viviers, W. & Pearson, J.J.A.P. 2007. The construction of a decision support model for evaluating and identifying realistic export opportunities in South Africa. Unpublished report prepared for the Department of Trade and Industry, South Africa, May. 92 p.

Viviers, W., Rossouw, R. & Steenkamp, E.A. 2009. The sustainability of the DSM for identifying realistic export opportunities for South-Africa: 2007-2008. Unpublished report prepared for the Department of Trade and Industry, South Africa, February. 105 p.

Viviers, W., Steenkamp, E.A., Rossouw, R. & Cuyvers, L. 2010. Identification realistic export opportunities for South Africa: application of a decision support model (DSM) using HS 6-digit level product data. Unpublished report prepared for the Department of Trade and Industry, South Africa, September. 57 p.

Williamson, N.C., Kshetri, N., Heijwegen, T. & Schiopu, A. 2006. An exploratory study of the functional forms of export market identification variables. *Journal of International Marketing*, 14(1):71-97.

Chapter 4

The methodology of the decision support model (DSM)

Ludo Cuyvers, Ermie Steenkamp & Wilma Viviers

4.1   Introduction

In Chapter 3 it was concluded that the DSM methodology is unique and specifically useful to guide export promotion organisations (EPOs) in more effective country-level export promotion activities. Therefore, in this chapter, a detailed description of the methodology of the DSM as well as other studies that support the use of the different variables used in the filters of the DSM, will be described.

4.2   The Walvoord fundamental framework of the DSM

The fundamental framework of the DSM was based on Walvoord's 1980 model for selecting foreign markets (Walvoord as in Jeannet & Hennessy, 1998:137-140, see also Chapter 3.3.1). The basic idea of Walvoord's model was that a screening/filtering process be used to assess international market opportunities. This process involves gathering relevant information on each market under investigation and filtering out less desirable markets. The screening process includes four filters in which uninteresting countries are quickly eliminated on the basis of general macro-indicators in the first filter in order to concentrate in detail on a more limited set of export opportunities in subsequent filters. Walvoord's model is illustrated graphically in Figure 4.1:

Figure 4.1. Walvoord's model for selecting foreign markets.

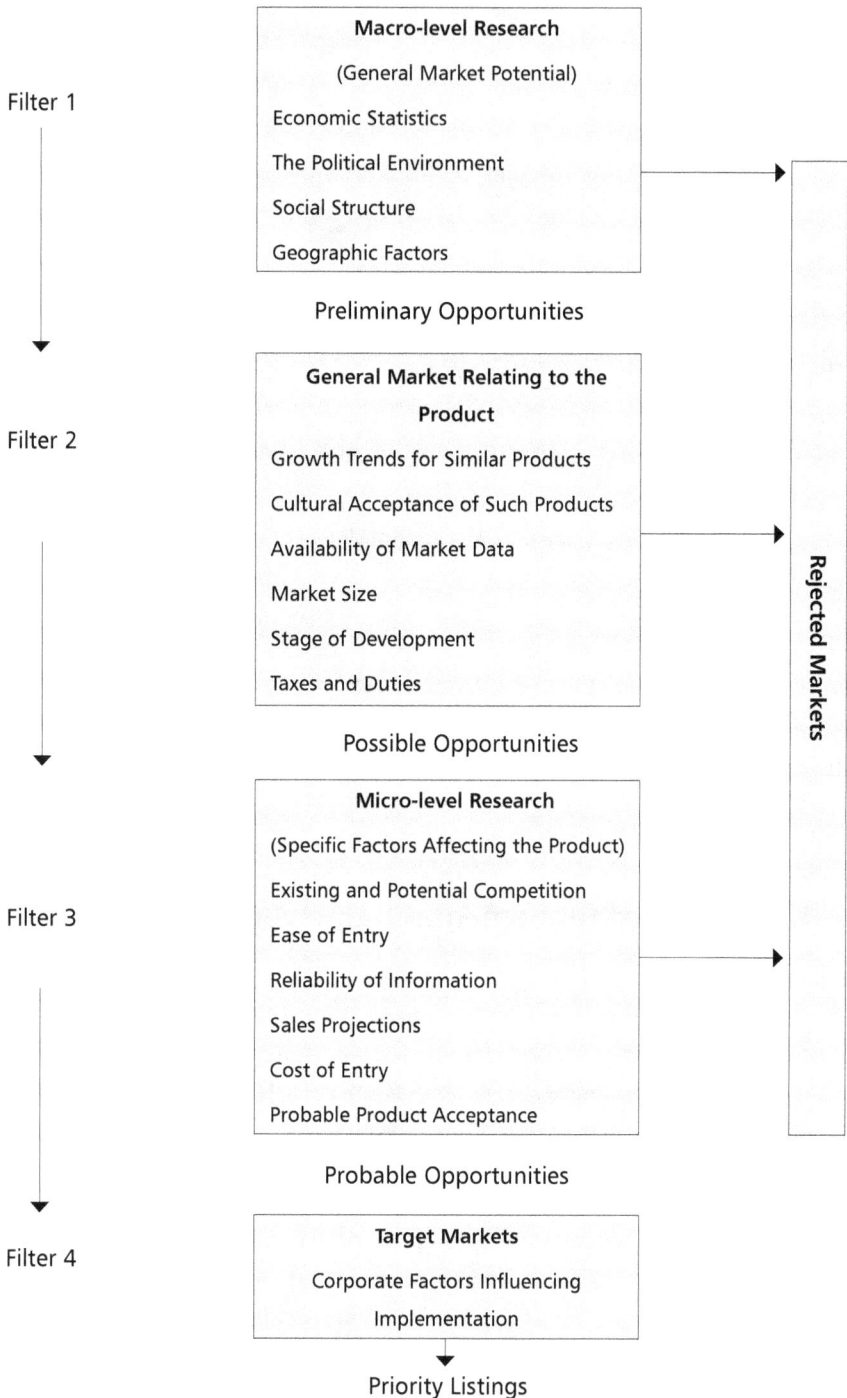

Filter 1

Macro-level Research

(General Market Potential)

Economic Statistics

The Political Environment

Social Structure

Geographic Factors

Preliminary Opportunities

Filter 2

General Market Relating to the Product

Growth Trends for Similar Products

Cultural Acceptance of Such Products

Availability of Market Data

Market Size

Stage of Development

Taxes and Duties

Possible Opportunities

Filter 3

Micro-level Research

(Specific Factors Affecting the Product)

Existing and Potential Competition

Ease of Entry

Reliability of Information

Sales Projections

Cost of Entry

Probable Product Acceptance

Probable Opportunities

Filter 4

Target Markets

Corporate Factors Influencing

Implementation

Priority Listings

Rejected Markets

Source: Jeannet & Hennessey, 1988:139.

Filter 1 entails macro-level research to assess the general market potential of each of the countries under investigation in order to identify a set of preliminary opportunities. Macro-economic statistics such as GDP and GDP per capita are used in this filter to be able to assess the size of the different markets. The political environment, social structure and geographic factors of the different countries under investigation are also assessed in this first filter (Jeannet & Hennessey, 1998:137-140).

In Filter 2 product-related criteria are assessed in order to eliminate markets (product-country combinations) that do not show adequate size and growth. Cultural acceptance of products, the stage of development of the product and taxes and duties applied to the product in the various importing countries are also considered in this filter (Jeannet & Hennessey, 1998:137-140).

In Filter 3 micro-level research is conducted to investigate specific factors that might affect the marketing and sales of a product. Existing and potential competition, cost and ease of entry, reliability of information, sales projections, probable product acceptance and profit potential for each product-country combination under consideration are taken into consideration in this filter. It is argued that micro-level factors will influence the export success or failure of a specific product in a country and that marketers should assess only a small number of product-country combinations in this filter to make it feasible to get more detailed, up-to-date information (Jeannet & Hennessey, 1998:137-140).

In Filter 4 the factors that may affect market entry into the selected countries, for the specific company for which the model is applied, are taken into consideration. An evaluation and ranking of the potential markets are, therefore, based on the specific company's resources, objectives and strategies (Jeannet & Hennessey, 1988:137-140).

No example of an application of Walvoord's model could be found in the literature. It is, therefore, assumed that the model serves as a theoretical framework to be used as a guideline for the selection of foreign markets.

Although Walvoord's model focuses on selecting foreign markets for a "firm", Cuyvers et al. (1995:173-186) used its basic framework to construct a country-level market selection model specifically designed to support the planning and assessment of export promotion activities by government export promotion institutions. They called this a decision support model (DSM) to identify realistic export opportunities for a specific exporting "country". As mentioned in Chapter 1, the DSM was applied for Belgium (Cuyvers et al., 1995), Thailand (Cuyvers, 1997; 2004) and South Africa (Viviers & Pearson, 2007; Viviers et al., 2009; 2010). Although Cuyvers et al. (1995:173-186) used Walvoord's model as a framework for the DSM, many of the variables proposed in the Walvoord model could not be used in DSM because of its firm-specific nature and the non-availability of data for the large number of product-country combinations assessed in the DSM. Examples of such variables include the stage of development of the product, sales projections, probable product acceptance and profit potential. An overview of the filters of the DSM will be subsequently provided.

4.3   The sequential filtering process of the DSM

The decision support model (DSM) starts with the assumption that all world markets hold potential export opportunities for a particular exporting country and, therefore, all possible product-country combinations enter the filtering process (Cuyvers, 2004:256). After every filter, a number of opportunities is rendered uninteresting and is not considered in subsequent filters. The sequence of the filters is illustrated in Figure 4.2.

4.3.1   Filter 1: Identifying preliminary market opportunities

In Filter 1 of the DSM, countries are eliminated that hold too high a political and/or commercial risk to the exporting country (Filter 1.1) and do not show adequate macro-economic size or growth (Filter 1.2). The rationale for this is that, with all the countries of the world as a starting point, Filter 1 enables the researchers to eliminate uninteresting countries in order to concentrate in detail on a more limited set of product-country combinations in the consecutive filters. Countries that lack general potential are, therefore, eliminated in this filter.

4.3.1.1 Filter 1.1: Political and commercial risk assessment

The first criterion that is considered in Filter 1 is the "political and commercial risk" that exporters would face in doing business with the foreign countries under investigation.

Commercial risk can be defined as the risk resulting from the deterioration of the importer's financial situation, leading to the impossibility to pay for a consignment (ONDD, 2011). Indicators that are used to measure the overall commercial risk of a country include:

(i)   "economic and financial indicators" that affect all companies' corporate results and balance sheets (e.g. devaluation of the currency, real interest rates, GDP growth and inflation);

(ii)   indicators reflecting the country's "payment experience" (the ONDD and other credit providers' past experience with the country); and

(iii)   indicators characterising the "institutional context" in which local companies operate (e.g. corruption index, transition economy) (ONDD, 2011).

Figure 4.2. Sequence of filters in the DSM.

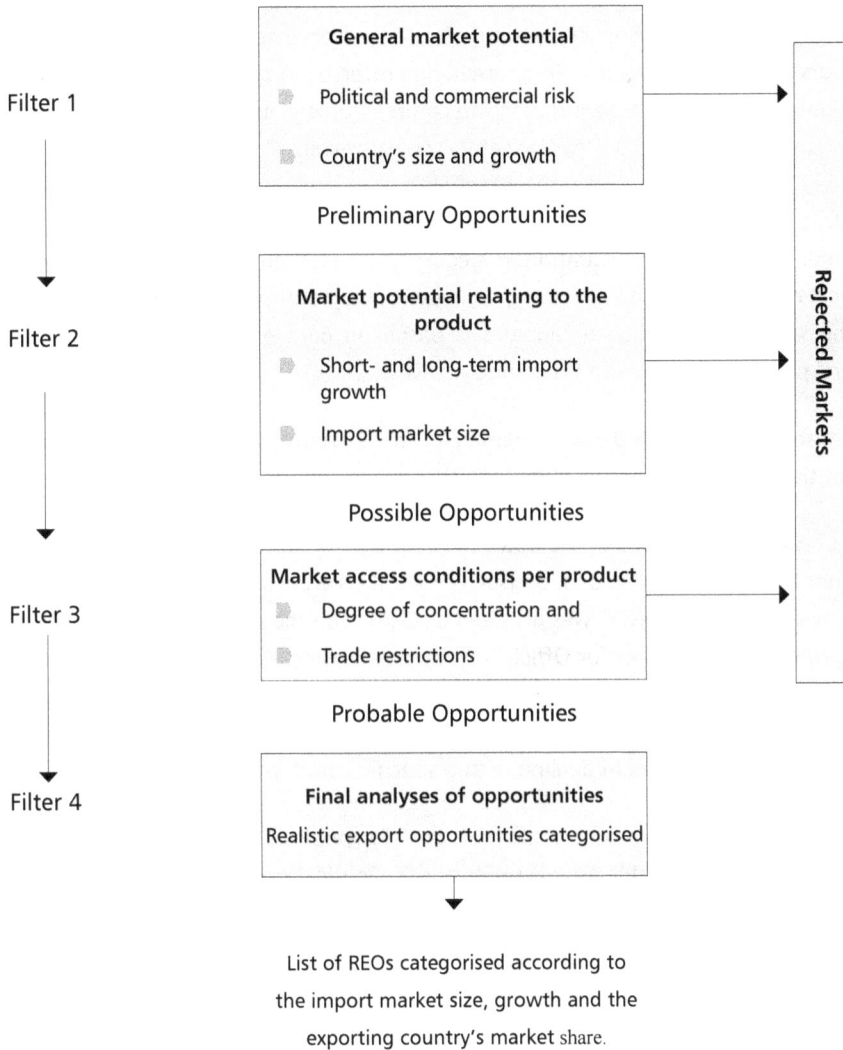

Source: Own figure constructed from Jeannet & Hennessey, 1988:139.

Political risk is defined as any event occurring in the importing country assuming the nature of *force majeure* for the importer, such as wars, revolutions, natural disasters, currency shortages and government action (ONDD, 2011). Indicators that are used to measure the political risk of a country include,

(i)   an assessment of the "economic and financial situation";

(ii)   an assessment of the "political situation"; and

(iii)   a "payment experience" analysis.

The assessment of the "financial situation" is based on external debt ratios and liquidity indicators such as the level of foreign exchange reserves. A country's "economic situation" is evaluated by using three sets of indicators, namely indicators of economic policy performance (e.g. fiscal policy, monetary policy, external balance, structural reforms), indicators of the country's growth potential (e.g. income level, savings, investments) and indicators of external vulnerability (e.g. export diversification and aid dependency). The assessment of the political situation in a country is based on a quantitative analysis of the "political risks" associated with doing business in the country (not specified by the ONDD) and the "payment experience" analysis is based on data of the ONDD and other credit insurers' past encounters with the country (ONDD, 2011).

Many academic, private and government institutions around the world rate countries on the basis of the political and commercial risks that an exporter in these countries would face[1].

In the previous applications of the DSM, the country risk ratings of the Belgian public credit insurance agency, Office National du Ducroire (ONDD) were used in this part of Filter 1. The rating methodology of ONDD was adopted by OECD and the ratings conform to the OECD's Arrangement on Guidelines for Officially Supported Export Credits[2] and are not conducted from the point of view of a specific exporting country. These ratings can readily be consulted at the ONDD website[3]. They can, therefore, be used by any exporter that wants to establish the degree of risk involved in dealing with a specific country.

The ONDD rates countries on a scale of 1 to 7 for political risk, where 1 indicates a low political risk and 7 indicates a high political risk. Political risk ratings are provided for the short, medium, and long term. The commercial risk rating is presented as either an "A", "B", or "C", where an "A" indicates low commercial risk and a "C" indicates high commercial risk (ONDD, 2011). The three political risk ratings for each country under investigation are transformed from a 1 to 7 scale to a 1 to 10 scale, whereas the commercial risk country rating is transformed in such a manner that a score of 3.33 is assigned to an "A" rating, a score of 6.67 is assigned to a "B" rating and a score of 10 is assigned to a "C" rating. This transformation is necessary to construct an overall country risk score. Firstly, an average political risk score (simple average of the three political risk scores) is calculated for each country under investigation. Secondly, the average political risk score and the commercial risk score are weighted equally to calculate an overall country risk score for each country under investigation. This country risk score is used to determine a critical value to eliminate

1   See http://www.countryrisk.com.
2   For more information see Cutts & West, 1998:12-14; Moravcsik, 1989:173-205.
3   http://www.delcredere.be.

less interesting countries from the analysis. Countries are eliminated if they belong to the two highest credit-risk groups of the ONDD, namely 6 C and 7 C.

To illustrate the process, consider country X with the following political and commercial risk ratings as an example.

Table 4.1. Country X's risk ratings.

	Political Risk: short term	Political Risk: medium term	Political Risk: long term	Commercial Risk
Country X	4	5	3	C

In order to construct the country risk score, the country risk ratings should be transformed as discussed in the previous paragraph. The transformed risk ratings for country X are given as:

Table 4.2. Country X's transformed risk ratings.

	Political Risk: short term	Political Risk: medium term	Political Risk: long term	Commercial Risk
Country X	5.71	7.14	4.29	10

By following the method described above, country X's average risk score is 7.86.[4]

When a particular country's risk score exceeds the critical value of 9.286 (short, medium and long-term political risk score equals 6 and commercial risk is rated as C), this country is excluded from further analysis of potential export opportunities. Country X in Table 4.2 would therefore be included in the further analysis of potential export markets, because its average risk score of 7.86 is below 9.286.

4.3.1.2 Filter 1.2: Macro-economic size and growth

The second criterion that is used to screen the remaining countries in Filter 1 of the DSM is a "country's macro-economic size" measured by GNP and GNP per capita (Cuyvers, 1997:4; 2004:256). Data on GNP and GNP per capita for each country for a specified period are gathered from the World Economic Outlook (IMF, 2010) and World Development Indicators (World Bank, 2010) databases and a cut-off point is identified in order to eliminate countries that do not show large enough overall potential (Cuyvers, 1997:4; 2004:258). Cuyvers *et al.* (1995:177) warned that a cut-off point should be determined in a conservative way to avoid

4   The average political risk score is calculated by [(5.71 + 7.14 + 4.29) / 3] and equal to 5.71. The average of the average political risk score and the commercial risk score is then calculated by (5.71 + 10)/2 and equal to 7.86.

eliminating too many countries. The cut-off point or critical value (*CV*) for the GNP and GNP per capita values is defined as:

$$CV = \bar{X} - \alpha\,\sigma_x$$

where X is the average of X (GNP or GNP per capita) and σ_x is the standard deviation of X (Cuyvers, 1997:4; 2004:258). α is a factor which is determined in such a way that a marginal change would cause a dramatic drop in the number of countries selected, or when a comparable number of countries is eliminated for both GNP and GNP per capita within a small range of α-values. A sensitivity analysis is, therefore, carried out, starting from $\alpha = 0.1$ and increasing it consecutively by 0.001, where the number of countries eliminated for each value of α is monitored (Cuyvers, 2004:258). It is clear that if $\alpha = 0$, the cut-off point would be the average, in which case half of the countries included in Filter 1 would be eliminated (if the data are distributed normally) (Cuyvers, 2004:256). When the α-value is increased, the number of countries eliminated will decrease gradually and the α-value that is selected would be the last one before there is a clear break in the number of countries eliminated (Cuyvers, 2004:256).

Countries are selected if:

$$X_j \geq CV$$

for at least two consecutive years of the most recent three-year period for which data are available, where X_j is the GNP or GNP per capita for country *j* (Cuyvers, 1997:4; 2004:258). If a country, for instance, has sufficient GNP or GNP per capita values for two subsequent years, but not for a third year, it will still pass the first filter. This ensures that countries that do not meet the requirements for only one year would not be eliminated for subsequent analysis (Cuyvers *et al.*, 1995:178).

4.3.2   Filter 2: Identifying possible opportunities

In Filter 2 an assessment of the various product categories for the remaining countries is done to identify product-country combinations (markets) that show adequate import size and growth.

Two criteria are used in this filter, namely "import growth" and "import market size". Import data were gathered from the World Trade Analyzer database of the International Trade division of Statistics Canada (SITC 4-digit) and the United Nations Comtrade Database (HS 6-digit)[5] (UNCTAD, 2010). The short- and long-term growth rate and the size of imports of

---

5   Given the objectives of the DSM and intended use of the results for government export promotion purposes, the databases used in the DSM should be sufficiently reliable and the use of the data

the different product-country combinations that entered Filter 2 are assessed (Cuyvers *et al.*, 1995:178; Cuyvers, 1997:5; 2004:257).

Three variables are, therefore, calculated for each product-country combination, namely "short-term import growth", "long-term import growth" and "import market size". "Short-term import growth" is considered to be the most recent available simple annual growth rate in imports. "Long-term growth" is calculated as the compounded annual percentage growth in imports over a period of five years. Finally, the relative "import market size" is calculated as the ratio of imports of country *i* for product category *j* and the total world imports of product category *j* (Cuyvers *et al.*, 1995:178; Cuyvers, 2004:259-260).

Subsequently, a cut-off value for Filter 2 needs to be calculated. Cuyvers *et al.* (1995:179) argued that if the exporting country under consideration was already specialised in exporting a particular product category, the cut-off point for these markets had to be less stringent. Therefore, the Specialisation Index (SI) or Revealed Comparative Advantage (RCA) Index (Balassa, 1965) is used to define cut-off points for each of the above-mentioned sub-criteria.

$$ RCA = \left(\frac{X_{i,j}}{X_{w,j}} \right) / \left(\frac{X_{i,tot}}{X_{w,tot}} \right) $$

where:

$X_{i,j}$: exports of country *i* (which is the exporting country for which realistic export opportunities are identified) of product *j*;

$X_{w,j}$: worldwide exports of product *j*;

$X_{i,tot}$: total exports of country i; and

$X_{w,tot}$: worldwide exports of all product categories.

An RCA index of 0 means that country *i* either does not export, or exports very little of the product category. An RCA index larger than or equal to 1 means that country *i* is relatively specialised in exporting the product category under consideration (Cuyvers *et al.*, 1995:179).

Cut-off values for the variables of Filter 2 are defined as follows (Cuyvers, 1997:5; 2004:260):

For "short- and long-term import growth" a scaling factor, s_j, is firstly defined (Willemé & Van Steerteghem, 1993, as quoted by Cuyvers, 1997:5; 2004:260) in order to take the

should not lead to incorrect or unintentional analyses and interpretations. Due to the fact that the data used in the DSM is available in international data sources, the DSM can be applied to any exporting country for which international trade data is available.

exporting country's degree of specialisation in the exports of product category j into account when defining cut-off values:

$$S_j = 0.8 + \frac{1}{(RCA_j + 0.85) \exp^{(RCA_j - 0.01)}}$$

The cut-off values were then defined as (Willemé & Van Steerteghem, 1993:6-7, as quoted by Cuyvers, 1997:5; 2004:260):

$$g_{i,j} \geq G_j ;$$

with $g_{i,j}$ being the import growth rate of product category j by country i; and

$$G_j = g_{w,j} s_j, \text{ if } g_{w,j} \geq 0 ; \text{ or}$$

$$G_j = g_{w,j}/s_j, \text{ if } g_{w,j} < 0$$

with $g_{w,j}$ being the total world imports of product category j. Table 4.3 illustrates these cut-off points.

This procedure is carried out for both "short-term" and "long-term growth" rates (Cuyvers, 1997:6; 2004:260). If the above-mentioned criteria are met by a particular country for a specific product, a "1" is assigned in the "short-term" and/or "long-term import growth" columns in Table 4.5. A "0" is assigned in the case where the criteria are not met.

Furthermore, "the relative import market size" of country i for product category j was considered sufficiently large if (Cuyvers, 1997:6; 2004:260):

$$M_{i,j} \geq S_j$$

where $M_{i,j}$ is the import market size of country i for product category j; and

$$S_j = 0.02 M_{w,j}, \text{ if } RCA_j \geq 1 ; \text{ or}$$

$$S_j = [(3 - RCA_j) / 100] M_{w,j}, \text{ if } RCA_j < 1$$

Table 4.3. Illustration of cut-off points for short- and long-term growth.

	0 ≤ RCA < 1 (The exporting country for which the model is applied is not specialised in exporting product *j*.)	RCA ≥ 1 (The exporting country for which the model is applied is specialised in exporting product *j*.)
$g_{W,j} > 0$ (World short- or long-term growth rate in product *j* is positive.)	Country *i*'s short- or long-term import growth rate of product *j* (g_{ij}) must be between one and two times the world growth rate for product *j*. For example: If RCA = 0 and $g_{w,j}$ = 5%, then s_j = 1.988 and G_j (cut-off point) = 9.94% If RCA = 0.5 and $g_{w,j}$ = 5%, then s_j = 1.25 and G_j = 6.25%	Country *i*'s short- or long-term import growth rate of product *j* (g_{ij}) is allowed to be a bit lower than, or equal to, the world growth rate for product *j*. For example: If RCA = 1 and $g_{w,j}$ = 5%, then s_j = 1 and G_j = 5% If RCA = 1.5 and $g_{w,j}$ = 5%, then s_j = 0.895 and G_j = 4.475%
$g_{W,j} < 0$ (World short- or long-term growth rate in product *j* is negative.)	Country *i*'s short- or long-term import growth rate of product *j* (g_{ij}) must be higher than the world growth rate for product *j*. For example: If RCA = 0 and $g_{w,j}$ = -5%, then s_j = 1.988 and G_j = -2.5% If RCA = 0.5 and $g_{w,j}$ = -5%, then s_j = 1.25 and G_j = -4%	Country *i*'s short- or long term import growth rate of product *j* (g_{ij}) is allowed to be a bit lower than, or equal to, the world growth rate for product *j*. For example: If RCA = 1 and $g_{w,j}$ = -5%, then s_j = 1 and G_j = -5% If RCA = 1.5 and $g_{w,j}$ = -5%, then s_j = 0.895 and G_j = -5.59%

Source: Own table based on Cuyvers (1997:5; 2004:260).

Table 4.4 illustrates the implication of the above-mentioned cut-off points.

Table 4.4. Illustration of cut-off points for import market size.

$0 \leq RCA < 1$ (The exporting country for which the model is applied is not specialised in exporting product *j*.)	$RCA \geq 1$ (The exporting country for which the model is applied is specialised in exporting product *j*.)

Country *i*'s imports of product *j* (M_{ij}) must be between 2% and 3% of total world imports of product *j*.
 	
For example:
 	
If RCA = 0, then
 	
S_j (cut-off point) = 0.03 $M_{w,j}$ (3% of total world imports of product *j*)
 	
If RCA = 0.5, then
 	
S_j = 0.025 $M_{w,j}$ (2.5% of total world imports of product *j*)
	Country *i*'s imports of product *j* (M_{ij}) must be greater or equal to 2% of total world imports of product *j*.

Source: Own table based on Cuyvers (1997:6; 2004:260).

Again, each product-country combination is assigned a "0" or a "1" in the relative "import market size" column of Table 4.5, based on whether the above conditions as illustrated in Table 4.4 are fulfilled or not.

The selection of markets in Filter 2 is based on the categorisation illustrated in Table 4.5.

A product-country combination is selected to enter Filter 3 if it falls in category 3, 4, 5, 6 or 7 (Cuyvers, 1997:6; 2004:261). A market should therefore at least be growing adequately in the short or long term (see Table 4.3) and/or be of adequate size (see Table 4.4) to be considered for further analysis. The remaining product-country combinations subsequently enter Filter 3.

Table 4.5. Categorisation of product-country combinations in Filter 2.

Category	Short-term import market growth	Long-term import market growth	Relative import market size
0	0	0	0
1	1	0	0
2	0	1	0
3	0	0	1
4	1	1	0
5	1	0	1
6	0	1	1
7	1	1	1

Source: Cuyvers (1997:7; 2004:261).

4.3.3 Filter 3: Identifying probable and realistic export opportunities

According to Cuyvers et al. (1995:180), it holds true that being selected on the basis of size and growth does not necessarily mean that markets can be easily penetrated. In Filter 3 trade restrictions and other barriers to entry are considered to further screen the remaining possible export opportunities. Two categories of barriers are considered in this filter, namely the "degree of concentration" (Filter 3.1) and "trade restrictions" (Filter 3.2) (Cuyvers et al., 1995:180; Cuyvers, 1997:7; 2004:261).

4.3.3.1 Filter 3.1: Degree of import market concentration

According to Cuyvers et al. (1995:180), a market that is very "concentrated" is difficult to enter. A particular import market is considered to be concentrated if only a few exporting countries hold a relatively large market share and therefore have a lot of market knowledge and are well known by local customers. To confirm their argument, Cuyvers et al. (1995:180) carried out a partial analysis that revealed a negative correlation between export performance and market concentration. Cuyvers et al. (1995:180) concluded that it would be inefficient for export promotion organisations with limited resources to focus on heavily concentrated markets for which the chances of successful exporting are relatively small.

In the DSM the Herfindahl-Hirshmann-index (HHI) of Hirshmann (1964) is used to measure the degree of concentration in a market. The index is calculated as follows[6]:

6   The trade data needed to calculate this index were gathered from the World Trade Analyzer database of the International Trade division of Statistics Canada (SITC 4-digit) and the United Nations Comtrade Database (HS 6-digit) (UNCTAD, 2010).

$$HHI_{ij} = \sum \left(\frac{X_{k,ij}}{M_{tot,ij}}\right)^2$$

where:

$X_{k,ij}$: the exports of country k to country i for product category j; and

$M_{tot,ij}$: country i's total imports of product category j.

A HHI of 1 indicates that the importing market is only supplied by one exporting country and a HHI closer to 0 indicates a lower market concentration (importing market supplied by many exporting countries). It would, therefore, be more difficult for an exporting country to penetrate a particular market if the HHI for that market is relatively high (closer to 1) (Cuyvers *et al.* 1995:180; Cuyvers, 1997:7; 2004:261).

A cut-off point for market concentration had to be derived. Cuyvers *et al.* (1995:180) stated that it had to be kept in mind that concentration can be considered a bigger problem in a non-growing market (in which a market share will have to be won from often firmly established competitors) than in a large, growing market. Therefore, the cut-off point for market concentration was designed to be dependent on the category to which the various markets were assigned to in Filter 2 (see Table 4.5).

The cut-off points were defined as follows (Cuyvers, 1997:8; 2004:262):

$h_k \geq HHI_j$

with:

$h_k = \bar{x}_h - 0.05\alpha\sigma_h$, for category 3

$h_k = \bar{x}_h + 0.05\alpha\sigma_h$, for category 4, 5 and 6

$h_k = \bar{x}_h + 0.15\alpha\sigma_h$, for category 7

where:

$\bar{x}_h$: average of the HHI-values of all product-country combinations under investigation; and

σ_h: standard deviation of the HHI-values of all product-country combinations under investigation.

It is clear that a larger degree of concentration is tolerated for larger, growing markets. An α-value is selected where there is a "jump" in the number of product-country combinations selected (Cuyvers, 1997:8; 2004:262).

4.3.3.2 Filter 3.2: Trade barriers

The second set of accessibility criteria used in Filter 3 is "trade barriers". An index for "revealed absence of barriers to trade" was used in the Belgian and Thai studies as a proxy for trade barriers. The reason for this was that, at the time, for a large number of product-country combinations, no data were available on tariff and non-tariff barriers. Furthermore, the information that could be gathered was not available on the same product classification level (e.g. SITC 2-digit or SITC 4-digit level) as the trade data used in the rest of the DSM and it was very difficult to aggregate the information to the appropriate level (Cuyvers et al., 1995:180). There was, therefore, a need to follow a different approach, and the hypothesis was formulated that if the neighbours of Belgium or Thailand could establish a relatively strong market position in a particular market, it means that trade barriers in this market would not be too difficult for Belgium or Thailand to overcome (Cuyvers et al., 1995:181; Cuyvers, 1997:7; 2004:262). The revealed absence of barriers to trade ($M_{i,j}$) is calculated as follows[7]:

$$M_{i,j} = \cfrac{\cfrac{X_{Neighbour1,i,j}}{X_{Neighbour1,j}} + \cfrac{X_{Neighbour2,i,j}}{X_{Neighbour2,j}} + \cfrac{X_{Neighbour3,i,j}}{X_{Neighbour3,j}} + \dots}{\cfrac{X_{World,i,j}}{X_{World,j}}}$$

with:

$M_{i,j}$: the corrected market share of the neighbours of the country for which the model is applied in country i's imports of product category j;

$X_{Neighbour,i,j}$: the exports of each of the neighbouring countries of the country for which the model is applied, of product category j to country i;

$X_{World,i,j}$: total world exports of product category j to country i.

Again, a cut-off point for this criterion of Filter 3 had to be identified. The cut-off point was defined with the assumption in mind that a higher relative share $M_{i,j}$ reflects a relative lack or a revealed absence of barriers to trade (Cuyvers et al., 1995:181). Therefore, the higher

---

7   The trade data needed to calculate this index were gathered from the World Trade Analyzer database of the International Trade division of Statistics Canada (SITC 4-digit) and the United Nations Comtrade Database (HS 6-digit) (UNCTAD, 2010).

the $M_{i,j}$-value, the easier it would be for the country for which the model is applied to access the market in question (Cuyvers *et al.*, 1995:181). Cuyvers (1997:8; 2004:263) stated that no α could be determined unambiguously and that he was therefore compelled to apply the following rule of thumb to define a cut-off point for this criterion:

$M_{i,j} \geq 0.95$

This implies that, with a margin of error of 5%, if at least one of the neighbouring countries of the exporting country for which the model is applied, has a "revealed comparative advantage" (RCA) in exporting to a particular market, it is assumed that there are no "revealed barriers to trade" for the exporting country for which the model is applied in that market (Cuyvers, 1997:8; 2004:263).

To enter Filter 4, product-country combinations need to have adequately low market concentration and barriers to trade. Both the conditions in Filter 3 have to be met in order for a market to enter Filter 4.

4.3.4   Filter 4: Final analyses of opportunities

In the last stage of the analysis the realistic export opportunities identified in Filters 1 to 3 are categorised and prioritised and no markets are eliminated.

According to Cuyvers *et al.* (1995:181), the strength of an exporting country's position in a foreign market can be derived from criteria that determine its competitive advantage. For each of the markets that entered Filter 4, the relative market share of the exporting country (country *n*) of product category *j* in country *i* is calculated as follows:[8]

$$\mu_{n,ij} = \left(\frac{X_{n,ij}}{X_{w,ij}} \right) / \left(\frac{X_{n,j}}{X_{w,j}} \right)$$

where:

$X_{n,ij}$: country *n*'s exports of product category *j* to country *i*;

$X_{w,ij}$: world exports of product category *j* to country *i*;

$X_{n,j}$: country *n*'s total exports of product category *j*; and

$X_{w,j}$: world exports of product category *j*.

---

8   The trade data needed to calculate this index were gathered from the World Trade Analyzer database of the International Trade division of Statistics Canada (SITC 4-digit) and the United Nations Comtrade Database (HS 6-digit) (UNCTAD, 2010).

This is the same Specialisation Index (SI)/Revealed Comparative Advantage (RCA) that was used in Filter 2. It is now only calculated on a per market basis. The hypothesis of Cuyvers *et al.* (1995:182) was that a country has a comparative strength in doing business in a market if it has succeeded in obtaining a strong position in that market.

Subsequently, the relative market share of the exporting country ($\mu_{n,ij}$) is calculated for all markets that entered Filter 4. Also, the relative market share of the six countries with the largest exports in each product-country combination ($\mu_{SIX,ij}$) is calculated. A comparison can then be made between the relative market share of country *n* in each market that entered Filter 4 and the relative market share of the six largest exporting countries in these markets. By calculating the difference between country *n*'s relative market share and that of the six dominant exporting countries of product *j* to country *i*, it is possible to determine country *n*'s market importance in each market under consideration (Cuyvers, 1997:14; 2004:267).

The following categories of market importance are identified (Cuyvers, 1997:14; 2004:267):

$\mu_{six,ij} - \mu_{n,ij} > 3$: Country *n*'s relative market share is relatively small.

$1.5 < \mu_{six,ij} - \mu_{n,ij} \leq 3$: Country *n*'s relative market share is intermediately small.

$0 < \mu_{six,ij} - \mu_{n,ij} \leq 1.5$: Country *n*'s relative market share is intermediately large.

$\mu_{six,ij} - \mu_{n,ij} \leq 0$: Country *n*'s relative market share is relatively large.

The entire filtering process leads to the following matrix (Table 4.6) to categorise the realistic export opportunities that were identified in Filters 1 to 3 in terms of size and growth in demand and the exporting country's current market share in these markets.

It can be seen that the classification in the rows of Table 4.6 is obtained from Filter 2 (see Table 4.5), which indicates the size and growth of imports of the different markets, while the columns are based on the relative market share of the exporting country calculated in Filter 4.

From Table 4.6 it is evident that a total of 20 different kinds of markets are distinguished and the markets that entered Filter 4 are each assigned to one of these markets (Cuyvers *et al.*, 1995:182; Cuyvers, 1997:15; 2004:269). Each product-country combination that is identified by the DSM as an export opportunity is assigned a cell. The exporting country for which the model is applied will, therefore, know what the potential (demand) in the market is (import size and growth) and whether the exporting country has already utilised this opportunity or not (based on the relative market share already established). If a product-country combination is classified in Cell 5, for instance, it means that the demand in that market is large and growing in the short and long term, but the exporting country for which the model is applied has a relatively small market share in that market. This is, therefore, a market opportunity that is not exploited to its full potential by the exporting country.

Table **4.6.** Final categorisation of realistic export opportunities.

Size and growth of importing market	Market share of country *n* (Filter 4)			
	Relatively small	Intermediately small	Intermediately large	Relatively large
Large product market	Cell 1	Cell 6	Cell 11	Cell 16
Growing (short- and long-term) product market	Cell 2	Cell 7	Cell 12	Cell 17
Large product market with short-term growth	Cell 3	Cell 8	Cell 13	Cell 18
Large product market with long-term growth	Cell 4	Cell 9	Cell 14	Cell 19
Large product market with short- and long-term growth	Cell 5	Cell 10	Cell 15	Cell 20

Source: Cuyvers, 2004:269.

Export promotion organisations can also use these cells to formulate export promotion strategies for the markets (product-country combinations) identified in the DSM as realistic export opportunities. Cuyvers *et al.* (1995:183) suggest that an offensive market exploration export promotion strategy be used for export opportunities in Cells 1 to 10, based on the exporting countries' relatively small market share in these markets. An offensive market expansion strategy is suggested for export opportunities in Cells 11 to 15. Due to the fact that the exporting country already has an intermediately large market share in these markets and the demand in these markets is large and/or growing, market expansion is recommended. For export opportunities in Cells 16 to 20, a defensive export promotion strategy of market maintenance is recommended by Cuyvers *et al.* (1995:183).

It is, however, important to take the number of resources available by the export promotion organisation into consideration when choosing different export promotion strategies. As resources are limited, export promotion organisations are advised by Cuyvers (1997:14-15; 2004:270) not to actively promote export opportunities in Cells 1 to 10, but rather to gather market information on these opportunities and distribute this information to the relevant exporters. Such export promotion organisations can then rather focus on expanding markets in Cells 11 to 15 and maintaining markets in Cells 16 to 20.

In section 4.4 support from the international market selection literature for the variables used in the different filters of the DSM is summarised.

4.4 Support from the international market selection literature for the different filters of the DSM

Table 4.7 refers to other studies (firm-level and country-level, see also Chapter 3.2) from the international market selection literature that support the use of the different variables included in the DSM.

Table 4.7. Other literature supporting the use of the DSM variables.[9]

Filter/procedure used in the DSM:	Studies supporting:
Screening process (elimination of uninteresting opportunities)	Cavusgil (1985:29)
	Kumar *et al.* (1993:29)
	Jeanet & Hennessey (1998:138-142)
	Rahman (2003:120)
Filter 1: Country risk GDP / GNP / GDP per capita / GNP per capita / GDP / GNP growth	Verno (2008) (see section 3.3.8)
	Cavusgil (1985:29)
	Russow and Okoroafo (1996:50) (see section 3.3.3)
	Hoffman (1997:70)
	Arnold & Quelsh (1998:7-20) (see section 3.3.6)
	Papadopoulos *et al.* (2002:170-171) (see section 3.3.4)
	Rahman (2003:121-122)
	DTI (2004) (see section 3.3.7)
	Sakarya *et al.* (2007:209) (see section 3.3.6)
	Verno (2008) (see section 3.3.8)

---

9   An earlier version of this table was also published as conference proceedings of the International Academy of Business and Economics conference in Barcelona, Spain, June 2011 and published in the *Journal of International Business and Economics* (Cuyvers, L., Viviers, W. & Steenkamp, E.A (2011). The utilisation of export opportunities in the world market: a comparison of Belgium, South Africa and Thailand).

Filter/procedure used in the DSM:	Studies supporting:
Filter 2: Import market size and growth	Cavusgil (1985:29) Green and Allaway (1985:85-86) (see section 3.3.2) Kumar *et al.* (1993:33, 37) Russow and Okoroafo (1996:50) (see section 3.3.3) Rahman (2003:121-122) Williamson *et al.* (2006:74) (see section 3.3.2) Freudenberg *et al.* (2008:11-12) (see section 3.3.5) Verno (2008) (see section 3.3.8)
Filter 3 Market concentration (competitor analysis) Market accessibility/trade barriers	Cavusgil (1985:30) Kumar *et al.* (1993:33, 38) Jeanet and Hennessey (1998:144) Papadopoulos *et al.* (2002) (see section 3.3.4) Rahman (2003:121-122) Williamson *et al.* (2006:78-79) (see section 3.3.2) Sakarya *et al.* (2007:218-219) (see section 3.3.6) Verno (2008) (see section 3.3.8) Cavusgil (1985:30) Kumar *et al.* (1993:33,38) Papadopoulos *et al.* (2002:170-171) (see section 3.3.4) Rahman (2003:121-122) DTI (2004) (see section 3.3.7) Williamson *et al.* (2006:79) Freudenberg *et al.* (2008:11-12) (see section 3.3.5) Verno (2008) (see section 3.3.8)

In section 4.5 refinements to the original methodology of the DSM in several applications of the DSM approach that followed over time are discussed.

4.5   Refinements to the DSM methodology

As mentioned in Chapter 1, the DSM was originally developed by Cuyvers, De Pelsmacker, Rayp and Roozen and applied to Belgium in 1995. It was then applied to Thailand in 1997 and again in 2004. The model was refined and applied to South Africa in 2007 and 2009. In 2010 the DSM was run on a HS 6-digit level for the first time for South Africa and in order to do a comparative study (see Chapter 8), it was also applied on a HS 6-digit product level for Belgium and Thailand.

Throughout the years, five main refinements were made to the original methodology of the DSM as described. These include:

(i)   including GDP and GDP per capita growth values into the analysis in Filter 1.2;

(ii)   using the Harmonised System (HS) six-digit level trade data instead of the SITC 2- or 4-digit data;

(iii)   calculating a potential export value for each selected product-country combination in order to prioritise between export opportunities;

(iv)   taking the exporting country's production capacity into account; and

(v)   determining a new method of measuring the market accessibility of South Africa in the different product-country combinations (Filter 3.2).

In sections 4.5.1 to 4.5.5 a discussion of each of these refinements follows.

4.5.1   Including GDP growth and GDP per capita growth in Filter 1.2

In the applications of the DSM for South Africa in 2007, 2009 and 2010 as well as the 2010 applications for Belgium and Thailand, GDP and GDP per capita values were used instead of GNP and GNP per capita values. Also, GDP growth and GDP per capita growth rates were added as part of Filter 1.2. This was done to include countries that showed above average GDP and GDP per capita growth for three years in a row, even if the size of the market (GDP or GDP per capita) is not sufficient. Countries were, therefore, selected based on GDP growth and GDP per capita growth if the growth values were above the world average growth rates for the most recent three years for both growth measures. A country was selected to enter Filter 2 if it either qualified in terms of GDP *or* GDP per capita values *or* GDP growth *and* GDP growth values (Viviers & Pearson, 2007; Viviers *et al.*, 2009; 2010).

4.5.2 Using HS 6-digit product data

Harmonised System (HS) 6-digit level trade data were used in the 2010 applications of the DSM for Belgium, South Africa and Thailand instead of the SITC 2- and 4-digit data used in the previous applications of the model. This adjustment was made due to the fact that exporters mostly use the Harmonised System (HS) product classification to specify their goods in export ventures and documentation (Tempier, 2010). The HS 6-digit level product classification is also the most disaggregated level of product specifications that is standardised[10] throughout the world (Tempier, 2010). The introduction of HS 6-digit level trade data, therefore, contributes to the effective use and application of the results of the DSM by export promotion agencies and exporters.

4.5.3 Calculating a potential export value for each selected product-country combination

Although the previous applications of the model provided a list of realistic export opportunities; it did not give an indication of which opportunities are of a higher value than others. It was therefore difficult to prioritise between the identified export opportunities. For example, in the 2009 application of the DSM for South Africa, Turkey ranked in the seventh place with 261 products identified as export opportunities and the USA only ranked 14th with 230 products. It might, however, be that the potential export value of the 230 products in the USA exceeds the potential export value of the 261 products in Turkey. Therefore, the number of opportunities of a country is not necessarily an indication of the potential export value. Another example is small wares and toilet articles, which have export opportunities in 41 countries and rank second when compared with other products, while motor vehicles for the transportation of goods or materials ranked 20th with opportunities in 35 countries. Again, the size of the export opportunities was not considered and a ranking based on the number of opportunities is not accurate.

The potential export value for each product-country combination identified export opportunity was, therefore, calculated as follows in the 2010 applications of the DSM for Belgium, South Africa and Thailand (see Chapter 6):

$$\frac{\text{The total imports of country } i \text{ of product } j}{\text{number of countries that contributes 80\% of these imports } + 1.}$$

---

10 Standard product codes are used all over the world on a HS 6-digit level. For any higher level of product specification (8-, 10- or 12-digit level) the codes used are not standardised over the world and the code for a particular product, namely the national tariff line (NTL), in one country could differ from the NTL code used in another country.

This estimation of export potential gives an indication of the size of the import demand for each product-country combination and takes into consideration the possibility of South Africa being added (therefore, the plus one in the formula) to the group of countries which collectively represents 80% of the imports of product j to country i.

4.5.4 Taking the exporting country's production capability into consideration with RCA

So far, the DSM approach mostly focuses on the demand potential (size, growth, competitors, market access) for products in different countries and do not take into consideration the production capacity of the exporting country. It may therefore be that the DSM so far identifies export opportunities for a specific product in many countries, but the exporting country might not have the excess capacity to produce more of this product. However, by considering the exporting country's revealed comparative advantge (RCA) in producing and exporting the different products under consideration, it is ensured that only products in which the exporting country is relatively specialised are selected as export opportunities.

The revealed comparative advantage is an indication of the exporting country's relative specialisation in the production and exportation of a particular product (Balassa, 1965; Krugell & Matthee, 2009). The formula used to calculate exporting country n's revealed comparative advantage is:

$$RCA_j = \left(\frac{X_{n,j}}{X_{World,j}} \right) / \left(\frac{X_{n,tot}}{X_{World,tot}} \right)$$

where $X_{n,j}$ is the exporting country n's exports of product j, $X_{n,tot}$ is country n's total exports of all products, $X_{World,j}$ is the world's exports of product j and $X_{World,tot}$ is total world exports of all products (Balassa, 1965; Krugell & Matthee, 2009). In the 2010 applications of the DSM an additional criterion was introduced which involves that the exporting country should have a revealed comparative advantage of at least 0.7 (see Chapter 6) in a particular product in order for markets to be selected in the model.

4.5.5 Determining a new method of measuring the market accessibility of South Africa in the different product-country combinations (Filter 3.2)

An index for "revealed absence of barriers to trade" was used as a proxy for trade barriers in Filter 3.2 in the Belgian and Thai studies (see section 4.3.3.2). It was argued that if Belgium's (or Thailand's) neighbours could successfully export a particular product to a country, it would not be too difficult for Belgium (or Thailand) to also be able to overcome the trade barriers in that market (Cuyvers et al., 1995:181; Cuyvers, 1997:3-21; Cuyvers, 2004:262). In the application of the DSM to identify realistic export opportunities for South Africa specifically, this second part of Filter 3 could not be applied in the same way. Therefore, a different approach to the revealed absense of barriers proxy had to be followed in the South African study.

In the 2007 application of the DSM for South Africa, Viviers and Pearson (2007) used crow-fly distances between Pretoria, South Africa, and the capital cities of the countries that entered Filter 3 as a measure of trade barriers. After assessment of this proxy, it was found that this cannot be considered a very good estimation of market accessibility, and another proxy for market accessibility was developed (Viviers *et al.*, 2009:68). In the 2009 application of the model for South Africa, a new index for market accessibility was constructed by using distance, transport cost, the World Bank Logistics Performance Index (LPI), average applied tariffs per country and the frequency coverage ratio of non-tariff barriers per country (Steenkamp *et al.*, 2009; Viviers *et al.*, 2009).

Although this index overcame the limitations of using only distance as a measure of trade barriers, this index still had its own limitations. The main limitation of this measure of market accessibility (or barriers to trade) is that the index was only calculated on a country level and not a product-country level. A country can, therefore, perform well overall in terms of this measure/index, but specific products can still be highly protected or restricted in that country. With the purpose of the DSM to identify product-country combinations with the largest export potential, this country-level measure of market accessibility was not ideal.

Therefore in the 2010 application of the DSM for South Africa, a new way of measuring South Africa's market accessibility on a product-country level was, therefore, devised. The new index included the following variables:

(i)   "international shipment time" (ocean freight) from Durban harbour to the main port in the destination country (Linescape, 2010);

(ii)   "international shipment cost" (ocean freight) from Durban harbour to the main port in the destination country (quotes obtained from three main shipping lines per country);

(iii) "domestic time to import" including the time required for obtaining all necessary documents, inland transport and handling, customs clearance and inspections and port and terminal handling (Doing Business Report, The World Bank, 2009);

(iv)   "domestic cost to import" including the costs associated with all documentation, inland transport and handling, customs clearance and inspections, port and terminal handling and official costs (Doing Business Report, The World Bank, 2009);

(v)   "logistics performance index" measuring the efficiency of the customs clearance process; quality of trade and transport-related infrastructure; ease of arranging competitively priced shipments; competence and quality of logistics services; ability to track and trace consignments; and the frequency with which shipments reach the consignee within the scheduled or expected time (Arvis, Mustra, Ojala, Shepherd & Saslavsky, 2010);

(vi)   *ad valorem* equivalent tariffs per product-country combination (Market Access Map, ITC Comtrade database, 2010a);

(vii) *ad valorem* equivalent non-tariff barriers per product-country combination (Kee, Nicita & Olarreaga, 2008).

An index value for measuring market accessibility, incorporating all seven the above-mentioned variables, was calculated per product-country combination by means of a principle components analysis. Three factors that measure the market accessibility of a market were identified in the principle components analysis, namely a "domestic" factor that incorporates domestic time and cost and the LPI; an "international" factor that includes international shipping time and cost; and a "barrier" factor that includes tariff and non-tariff barriers. The three factor scores were then added[11] to arrive at a market accessibility index for each product-country combination that entered Filter 3. This market accessibility index provides a score for each product-country combination relative to all other product-country combinations included in the analysis. Each index value is, therefore, not very meaningful on its own. It places the position of each product-country combination relative to all other product-country combinations. For the purposes of this study, where the product-country combinations with the least accessibility for South Africa needed to be identified and eliminated, this index for market accessibility proved to be useful.

4.6   Conclusion

In this chapter, the development of the DSM methodology over time, and the adaptation and refinement thereof in various applications thereof, were discussed. Moreover, some new concepts, such as the average export value associated with each realistic export opportunity are unambiguously defined (see section 4.5.3).

In Part II the applications of the DSM approach, as applied to several countries between 1991 and 2010, will be discussed.

---

11 Since longer times to import, higher cost to import, higher tariffs and non-tariff barriers affect market accessibility negatively and a higher logistics performance index affects market accessibility positively, the signs of these variables were taken into consideration in the addition of the factor scores to calculate a market accessibility index value.

References

Arnold, D.J. & Quelsh, J.A. 1998. New strategies in emerging markets. *Sloan Management Review*, 40(1): 7-20.

Arvis, J.F., Mustra, M.A., Ojala, L., Shepherd, B. and Saslavsky, D. 2010. *Connecting to compete 2010: trade logistics in the global economy.* [Online.] Available from: http://siteresources. worldbank.org/INTTLF/Resources/LPI2010_for_web.pdf. Accessed 21 January 2010.

Balassa, B. 1965. *Trade liberalisation and revealed comparative advantage.* New Haven, CT: Yale University Economic Growth Centre.

Cavusgil, S.T. 1985. Guidelines for export market research. *Business Horizons*, 28(6): 27-33.

Cutts, S. & West, J. 1998. The arrangement on export credits. *OECD Observer*, 211: 12-14.

Cuyvers, L. 1997. Export opportunities of Thailand: a decision support model approach. *CAS discussion paper, no. 9.* [Online.] Available from: http://webhost.ua.ac.be/cas/PDF/CAS09.pdf. Accessed 17 January 2008.

Cuyvers, L. 2004. Identifying export opportunities: the case of Thailand. *International Marketing Review*, 21(3): 255-278.

Cuyvers, L., De Pelsmacker, P., Rayp, G. & Roozen, I.T.M. 1995. A decision support model for the planning and assessment of export promotion activities by government export promotion institutions: the Belgian case. *International Journal of Research in Marketing*, 12(2): 173-186.

DTI. *see* South Africa. Department of Trade and Industry.

Freudenberg, M., Paulmier, T., Ikezuki, T. & Conte, K. 2008. Export opportunity scan for Jordan: second draft. Unpubl. report of the International Trade Centre, Market Analysis Section.

Green, R.T. & Allaway, A.W. 1985. Identification of export opportunities: a shift-share approach. *Journal of Marketing*, 49(1): 83-88.

Hirshmann, A. 1964. The paternity of an index. *American Economic Review*, 54(5): 761-762.

Hoffman, J.J. 1997. A two-stage model for the introduction of products into international markets. *Journal of Global Marketing*, 11(1): 67-86.

IMF. 2010. World Economic Outlook. [Online.] Available from: http://www.imf.org/external/pubs/ ft/weo/2011/02/weodata/index.apsx. Accessed 27 November 2009.

ITC (International Trade Centre). 2010a. Market access map, detailed analysis, applied tariffs. [Online.] Available from: http://www.macmap.org/trademap/Applied.Tariffs.aspx. Accessed 18-29 January 2010.

Jeannet, J.P. & Hennessey, H.D. 1998. *International marketing management: strategies and cases.* Boston: Houghton Mifflin.

Kee, H.L., Nicita, A. & Olarreaga, M. 2008. Estimating trade restrictiveness indices. [Online.] Available from: http://siteresources.worldbank.org/INTRES/Resources/OTRIpaper.pdf. Accessed 4 November 2008.

Krugell, W. & Matthee, M. 2009. Measuring the export capability of South African regions. *Development Southern Africa*, 26(3): 459:476.

Kumar, V., Stam, A. & Joachimsthaler, E.A. 1993. An interactive multi-criteria approach to identifying potential foreign markets. *Journal of International Marketing*, 2(1): 29-52.

LINESCAPE. 2010. Independent search engine for ocean container schedules. [Online.] Available from: http://www.linescape.com. Accessed 1-12 February 2010.

Moravcsik, A.M. 1989. Disciplining trade finance: the OECD export credit arrangement. *International Organization*, 43(1): 173-205.

ONDD (Office National Du Ducroire). 2009. Country risks summary table. [Online.] Available from: http://www.ondd.be/webondd/Website.nsf/TRiskEn?OpenView&StartKey=A&Count=300&Expand=1. Accessed 27 October 2009.

ONDD (Office National Du Ducroire). 2011. Country risk explanation. [Online.] Available from: http://www.ondd.be/webondd/Website.nsf/weben/Country+risks_Explanations(Visitors)?OpenDocument. Accessed 15 March 2011.

Papadopoulos, N., Chen, H. & Thomans, D.R. 2002. Toward a trade-off model for international market selection. *International Business Review*, 11(2): 165-192.

Rahman, S.H. 2003. Modelling of international market selection process: a qualitative study of successful Australian international businesses. *Qualitative Market Research: An International Journal*, 6(2): 119-132.

Russow, L.C. & Okaroafo, S.C. 1996. On the way towards developing a global screening model. *International Marketing Review*, 13(1): 46-64.

Sakarya, S., Eckman, M. & Hyllegard, K.H. 2007. Market selection for international expansion: assessing opportunities in emerging markets. *International Marketing Review*, 24(2): 208-238.

South Africa. Department of Trade and Industry. 2004. A gravity model for the determination and analysis of trade potential for South Africa. [Online.] Available from: http://www.dti.gov.za/stats/gravity.pdf. Accessed 15 January 2011.

Steenkamp, E.A., Rossouw, R., Viviers, W. & Cuyvers, L. 2009. *Export market selection methods and the identification of realistic export opportunities for South Africa using a decision support model.* [Online.] Available from: http://www.sadctrade.org/node/281. Accessed 17 December 2009.

Tempier, L. 2010. *Harmonized system.* [Online.] Available from: http://www.gfptt.org/Entities/TopicProfile.aspx?tid=eba119e3-69fa-4e28-82fa-c2c788b51a02. Accessed 27 September 2010.

UNCTAD. 2010. *World Integrated Trade Solutions (WITS).* [Online.] Available from: http://wits.worldbank.org. Accessed January/February 2010.

Verno, C. 2008. *The trade opportunity matrix (TOM): an overview of Canadian export opportunities.* [Online.] Available from: http://www.edc.ca/english/docs/TOM_Final_Report_Dec2008_e.pdf. Accessed 24 January 2010.

Viviers, W. & Pearson, J.J.A.P. 2007. The construction of a decision support model for evaluating and identifying realistic export opportunities in South Africa. Unpubl. report prepared for the Department of Trade and Industry, South Africa, May. 92 p.

Viviers, W., Rossouw, R. & Steenkamp, E.A. 2009. The sustainability of the DSM for identifying realistic export opportunities for South Africa: 2007-2008. Unpubl. report prepared for the Department of Trade and Industry, South Africa, February. 105 p.

Viviers, W., Steenkamp, E.A. & Rossouw, R. & Cuyvers, L. 2010. Identification realistic export opportunities for South Africa: application of a decision support model (DSM) using HS 6-digit level product data. Unpubl. report prepared for the Department of Trade and Industry, South Africa, September. 57 p.

Williamson, N.C., Kshetri, N., Heijwegen, T. & Schiopu, A.F. 2006. An exploratory study of the functional forms of export market identification variables. *Journal of International Marketing*, 14(1): 71-97.

Willemé, P & Van Steerteghem, D. 1993. Een normatief model voor de planning van export-bevorderende activiteiten van de Vlaamse Dienst voor de Buitenlandse Handel. Brussels: Vlaamse Dienst voor de Buitenlandse Handel. (Unpubl.)

World Bank. 2009. Doing business 2010: reforming through difficult times. [Online.] Available from: http://web.worldbank.org/WBSITE/EXTERNAL/NEWS/0,,contentMDK:22301788~pagePK: 64257043~piPK:437376~theSitePK:4607,00.html. Accessed 21 January 2010.

World Bank. 2010. World Development Indicators. [Online.] Available from: http://data.worldbank. org/data-catalog/world-development-indicators. Accessed 27 November 2009.

Part II

Applications of the DSM in selected countries

Chapter 5

Belgium's export opportunities and export potentials in the world: A quantitative assessment using the DSM approach

Ludo Cuyvers, Ermie Steenkamp & Wilma Viviers

5.1 Introduction

In the early 1990s, the DSM was developed for use by the Flemish export promotion organisation (EPO) and applied first to identify export opportunities of Belgium (see Chapter 4). The original version used 2-digit SITC international trade data, after which subsequent runs of the DSM for Belgium, Thailand and the Philippines used SITC 4-digit data. The present version of the DSM as outlined in Chapter 4 follows the original filtering process and its four filters, but the international trade data used is HS-data at 6-digit level. This change in the international trade data source leads to a much more detailed product classification of the export opportunities identified. Moreover, the results of the DSM can be readily recognised and interpreted by the exporters, as they are familiar with their product's Harmonized System code which they have to fill in on their export declaration forms.

The aim of the present chapter is to discuss the results of the latest DSM run for Belgium, primarily as a detailed illustration of the DSM methodology as outlined in Chapter 4. We review in detail the results of the respective filters. Where possible, these results are also compared with the previous runs of the DSM using 1985-1989, 2000-2003 and 2004-2006 statistical data. This leads us to conclusions about which of Belgium's export opportunities can be found where, as well as about the impact of changes over time in the international environment and import demand conditions. Furthermore, it allows the comparison of the robustness of the DSM results over time.

5.2   Belgium's preliminary market opportunities

As indicated in Chapter 4, Filter 1 of the DSM consists of two sets of importing country criteria that are investigated. We first analyse importing country risks for 241 countries, after which macro-economic performance of importing countries are analysed.

Based on compound country risk scores, which were calculated using the ONDD political and commercial risk scores at individual country level and the threshold value of 9.286[1] (see Chapter 4 section 3.1.1), the importing countries showing the highest risk are deleted. This leaves us with 209 countries, i.e. 86.7% of the countries that entered Filter 1 are retained. This selection rate was only 62.6% in the first DSM run for Belgium (Cuyvers *et al.*, 1995:177), but 78.6% in the 2000-2003 run (as reported in Chapter 8) and even 91.2% in the 2006 run (Cuyvers & De Voet, 2008). Differences in the selection rate obviously reflect the general economic situation in the world as evidenced by the business cycle. The reason for the low selection rate in the first DSM run is, however, probably the finer scoring scale used by ONDD, which first used to be a 1-5 scale instead of the 1-7 scale in the more recent exercises.[2]

Among the countries that show too high political and/or commercial risk are Afghanistan, Cambodia, Congo, Cuba, Guinea, Haiti, Lao PDR, Lebanon, Pakistan, Rwanda, Sudan and Zimbabwe for example.

Macro-economic performance of the 209 importing countries that pass the risk score filter as potential export markets is assessed by using 2005-2007 indicators for current GDP and current GDP per capita, as well as GDP growth and GDP growth per capita. However, due to lacking macro-economic data, 13 countries had to be left out.

As described in Chapter 4 section 3.1.2, a critical value (CV) or cut-off point is used to identify the number of potential export markets that should be further investigated in terms of the two macro-economic variables, namely GDP and GDP per capita, as follows:

$$CV = \overline{X} - \alpha\, \sigma_x \dotfill (1)$$

where $\overline{X}$ is the average value and σ_x the standard deviation of the indicator under investigation. The value of α is chosen by means of a simulation process where its value is

---

1   This value corresponds to a short, medium and long-term political risk score of 6 and a commercial risk score of C.

2   The risk filtering of the DSM can for all practical purposes be regarded as identical whichever exporting country is considered. In the DSM runs for Thailand it was 65.8% in 1993 and 60.9% in 1997 (Cuyvers, 2004).

varied between 0 and 1 by increments of 0.001. Visual inspection then leads to the most appropriate alpha value (see Figure 5.1), which for GDP and GDP per capita is 0.07.

The number of countries selected in terms of GDP and GDP per capita amounts to 36 and 56 respectively.

Figure 5.1. Determining the Alpha Value for GDP and GDP per capita in Filter 1.

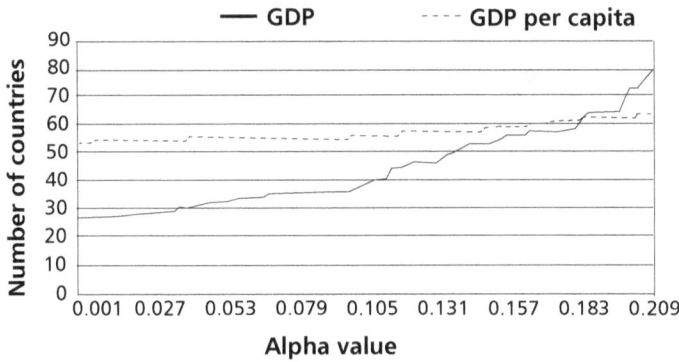

The average and the standard deviation of the distribution are calculated for all the 196 countries in the three years under consideration. The critical value is determined for each of the years. A country would be selected in terms of its GDP (GDP per capita) if the country's GDP (GDP per capita) were greater than the critical value for at least two of the three years under consideration. To be selected on the basis of both GDP and GDP per capita, the country should at least be selected in terms of one of these two indicators. In this way 67 countries are identified as preliminary market opportunities.

As pointed out in Chapter 4 section 3.1.2, weaker performing countries can have been eliminated in Filter 1 on the basis of their GDP and GDP per capita being too low. Yet, these countries can show export potential in certain product groups. Therefore, the countries not included during the first phase of Filter 1 can still be considered for further analysis if their average growth rate percentage for the two indicators (GDP growth and GDP per capita growth) are both higher than the average of all the countries for each of the individual years under consideration. Among the "growth economies" thus additionally selected, mention can be made of Armenia, Belarus, Bulgaria, Colombia, Jordan, Kazakhstan, Romania and Vietnam for example.

At the end of Filter 1, a total of 107 countries that passed the two sets of criteria are retained for analysis of detailed export potentials, which represents 54.6% of the countries with which this part of Filter 1 started. This percentage is considerably smaller than the 77.6% (59 countries) in the DSM run with 1985-1989 data, but in that run we had been confronted with more missing macro-economic data (Cuyvers, 1995:178). For comparison, this percentage amounted to 48.1% (90 countries) in the 2004-2006 run (Cuyvers & De Voet, 2008:9) and hardly 37.3% (69 countries) in the 2000-2003 run, a period of economic downturn.[3]

5.3 Belgium's possible export opportunities

In Filter 2, 2003-2007 import trade data from the United Nations Comtrade Database at HS 6-digit level are analysed for the countries that passed Filter 1. However, for some of these countries no import data were available, such as for Antigua and Barbuda, Puerto Rico, the Channel Islands, but also Taiwan. For some other countries, no 2007 international trade data were found, in which case the latest year was taken (e.g. 2006 for Vietnam and Macau, but e.g. even 2005 for the United Arab Emirates). In Filter 2, we finally are investigating 545,703 product-country combinations according to their size and their growth rates.

A given country's imports for a specific product will be considered as offering interesting export potential for Belgium if they show either sufficient volume and/or import growth in the short- and longer term. Critical values are calculated for each product group j at HS 6-digit level as explained in Chapter 4 section 3.2. To determine short-term growth of imports between 2006 and 2007, the simple percentage growth rate for each product group j in each country i is calculated. As for the long-term growth of imports, the compound percentage growth rate between 2003 and 2007 is calculated for each product group j in each country i.

The critical value, which determines whether a particular market shows potential in the growth of imports on the short and long term, is given as:

$$g_{ij} \geq G_j \quad \dotfill \quad (2)$$

where g_{ij} denotes the rate of growth of imports either in the short or long term of product group j by country i. If $g_{w,j}$ denotes the rate of growth of total world exports of product group j and s_j is the scaling factor which takes into account the degree of specialisation in the exports of Belgium of a product group j (Willemé & Van Steerteghem, 1993) as measured by the revealed comparative advantage index (Balassa, 1965) (see also Chapter 4 section 3.2), then

$$G_j = g_{w,j} \, s_j \quad \text{if} \quad g_{w,j} \geq 0 \text{ ; or}$$

$$G_j = g_{w,j} / s_j \quad \text{if} \quad g_{w,j} < 0$$

---

3   In the 1993 and 1997 DSM runs for Thailand this percentage was 58.8% (53 countries) and 63.9% (53 countries) respectively (Cuyvers, 2004:264-265).

Alternatively or additionally, to determine whether a particular market shows potential in terms of the relative import market size, another critical value can be calculated as follows:

$$M_{i,j} \geq S_j \quad\text{..} \quad (3)$$

where $M_{i,j}$ is the relative import market size of country i for product j and S_j denotes the cut-off point for relative import market size, taking into account the degree of specialisation of Belgium in product j such that:

$$S_j = 0.02\ M_{w,j} \quad \text{if} \quad RCA_j > 1$$

$$S_j = [(3 - RCA_j)/100]\ M_{w,j} \quad \text{if} \quad RCA_j \leq 1$$

where $M_{w,j}$ is the total import market of the world for product j and RCA_j denotes Balassa's revealed comparative advantage index of Belgium for product j. A market will be judged large enough if condition 3 is fulfilled. In line with our previous studies, we do not consider as having potential those product-country combinations that show neither sufficient size, nor sufficient growth in the short and long run. Nor are we further considering the product-country combinations that only show sufficient short-term growth (see Chapter 4, Table 4.5).

Using the above criteria we selected 150,528 product-country combinations, as possible realistic export opportunities for Belgium in the world market. These combinations represent 27.6% of the 545,703 possible product-country combinations at HS 6-digits. In 2003 and 2006, this percentage was 14.3% and 16.4% of the 59,780 and 82,320 product-country combinations at SITC 4-digits respectively (Cuyvers & De Voet, 2008:14; Chapter 8, Figure 8.1) which is the result of more detailed international trade data.[4]

5.4   Belgium's realistic export opportunities according to import market concentration

Filter 3 evaluates a country's ability to penetrate foreign markets. This ability depends on various trade barriers and restrictions. Although there are many tariff and non-tariff barriers, other trade barriers, such as transportation cost and lacking suitable infrastructure can severely hamper international trade between two countries. In this section it is assumed that also import market concentration is of sizeable influence on the potentials of an exporting country to tap possible export opportunities. Of course, concentration of supply of a given product j in a market relates to both domestic and foreign supply. As the combination

---

4   At 4 digits a product-country combination can fail the tests of the filter, although at 6-digit level a number of the product-country combinations, which are part of that at the 4-digit level, might pass.

of industrial production statistics and international trade statistics involves a complicated conversion procedure, we follow Cuyvers *et al.* (1995:180-181) and Cuyvers (2004:261-262), and restrict the analysis of concentration to imports of a product j and to the countries supplying these imports, using the Herfindahl-Hirschmann Index (HHI) (Hirschmann, 1964) as measure of the degree of market concentration, as follows:

$$HHI_{ij} = \sum \left(\frac{X_{k,ij}}{M_{tot,ij}} \right)^2 \quad \dots\dots\dots\dots\dots\dots\dots\dots\dots\dots\dots\dots\dots\dots\dots\dots\dots\dots\dots\dots \quad (4)$$

where $X_{k,ij}$ is country k's exports of product group j to country i and to country i's total import of product group j. If the **HHI** is low for a particular importing country, it can be safely assumed that Belgium will likely find it easier to penetrate that specific market, as it is less concentrated in terms of imports supply.

As in the previous filters a critical value will be determined for the degree of market concentration, as follows:

$h_k = \overline{x}_h - 0.1 \, \alpha \, \sigma_h$, for large volume product-country combinations;

$h_k = \overline{x}_h + 0.1 \, \alpha \, \sigma_h$, for other (not-large) product-country combinations showing growth in the long and short term, or large product-country combinations which combine either short- or long-term growth;

$h_k = \overline{x}_h + 0.3 \, \alpha \, \sigma_h$, for large product-country combinations, which also show, short- and long-term growth.

As explained in Chapter 4 section 3.3.1, the formulas for the critical values are different for the various categories, with the first mentioned (product-country combination showing only a large size of imports) being allowed less market concentration, than the second group of categories. These, in turn, are considered as less interesting than the last mentioned category (product-country combinations showing large size of imports, together with sufficiently high growth rates in the short and the long term) and for which the formula for h_k allows the highest concentration ratio of all. In other words, our filtering process is least restrictive for that category and most restrictive for the first mentioned above.

To determine whether or not a particular product-country combination will be included for further analysis, the following condition has to be fulfilled:

$$h_k \geq HHI_{ij} \quad \dots\dots\dots\dots\dots\dots\dots\dots\dots\dots\dots\dots\dots\dots\dots\dots\dots\dots\dots\dots\dots\dots\dots\dots \quad (5)$$

with h_k the cut-off point for market concentration.

If condition (5) is fulfilled, those product-country combinations will be included for further analysis. The cut-off point h_k is determined by first selecting α, which was done heuristically by looking for breaks in the number of "eliminated" product-country combinations when α increases (see Chapter 4 section 3.3.1).

As Figure 5.2 shows, this number of "eliminated" product-country combinations mostly decreases monotonously for increasing α, apart from two small downwards jumps when α is increased from 0.75 to 0.77, leading to 50,819 eliminations at $\alpha = 0.76$ (coming from 50,840) and another one when α is increased with 0.01 from 11.57. It was decided to choose $\alpha = 0.76$, leading to the h_k cut-off values as defined above, of:

h_k = 0.4767, for large volume product/country combinations

h_k = 0.4990, for other (not-large) product/country combinations showing growth in the long and short term, or large product/country combinations which combine either short- or long-term growth

h_k = 0.5212, for large product/country combinations which also show short- and long-term growth.

Thus, if an import market for a large volume product-country combination shows a HHI > 0.48, it is not selected due to being too concentrated. The same applies to large product-country combinations which also show short- and long-term growth with HHI > 0.52.

Figure 5.2. Determining the Alpha value for HH concentration index in Filter 3.

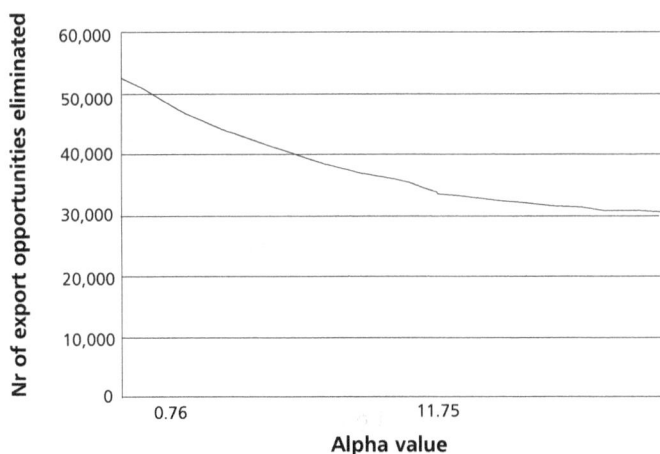

Using these cut-off values, leads us to select 99,709 product-country combinations as showing import market concentration ratios, which are smaller than the respective h_k's, or 66.2% of the product-country combinations coming out of Filter 2. In the 2003 and 2006 run of the DSM for Belgium this percentage was 79.9% and 78% respectively (see Chapter 8, Figure 8.1; Cuyvers & De Voet, 2008:15-19), which is likely due to the use of international trade data at 6-digit level in the present run of the DSM. A comparison with the h_k's in e.g. the 2006 run reveals that these were much less restrictive for "other (not-large) product-country combinations showing growth in the long and short term, or large product-country combinations which combine either short- or long-term growth" and "large product-country combinations which also show short- and long-term growth" which make up the vast majority of the product-country combinations (De Voet, 2008:56-57). This lower restrictiveness in 2006, as compared to the results in the present run, is probably due to the more buoyant state of international trade at that time.

5.5 Belgium's realistic export opportunities based on import market restrictions

As in previous research on realistic export opportunities of Belgium and Thailand (Cuyvers *et al.*, 1995, Cuyvers, 1996, Cuyvers, 2004), no attempt is made here to quantify the various market access barriers, but instead an index $M_{i,j}$ of "revealed absence of barriers to trade" is used as proxy:

$$M_{i,j} = \frac{\dfrac{X_{nij}}{X_{nj}} + \dfrac{X_{gij}}{X_{gj}} + \dfrac{X_{fij}}{X_{fj}}}{\dfrac{X_{wij}}{X_j}}$$

With X_{nij} = the exports of the Netherlands (Germany or France, respectively) of product group *j* to country *I*,

X_{nj} = the total exports of the Netherlands (Germany or France, respectively) of product group *j*,

X_{wij} = the total exports of the world of product group *j* to country *i*,

X_{wj} = the total world exports of product group *j*.

This index shows the share of Belgium's continental neighbouring countries' exports to country *i* of product group *j* in their respective exports of product group *j*, corrected for the share of that country *i* in world trade of product group *j*. As like in the previous runs of the

DSM, no α could be determined unambiguously here, we were compelled to use the rule of thumb:

$$M_{ij} \geq 0.95$$

which implies that, apart from a margin of error of 5%, Belgium is assumed to have no "revealed barriers to trade" in a market if at least one of its three continental neighbouring countries has a "revealed comparative advantage" in exporting to that market.

Applying this criterion, leads to the selection of 98,792 product-country combinations with an apparent market accessibility which is similar to that which at least one of Belgium's neighbouring countries is experiencing for the same product group in the same importing country. This number represents 65.6% of these that entered Filter 3, as compared to 57.4% and 62% in 2003 and 2006 (Chapter 8, Figure 8.1; Cuyvers & De Voet, 2008:22). The increasing percentage of product-country combinations passing this filter of market restrictiveness probably reflects the general increase in trade liberalisation, as well as the growing integration of new emerging markets in the world economy.

5.6 The categorisation of Belgium's realistic export opportunities according to import market characteristics and import market share

As for realistic export opportunities (REOs), it is assumed that the respective import markets are sufficiently accessible and reasonably competitive (less concentrated), the union of the product-country combinations selected on the basis of import market concentration and market accessibility leads to the list of such REOs. The union thus constructed contains 61,051 REOs, which is 40.6% of the product-country combinations, which entered Filter 3 (as compared to 45.6% and 53.6% in 2003 and 2006)(Chapter 8, Figure 8.1; Cuyvers & De Voet, 2008:22). The complete filtering process is summarised in Figure 5.3.

Based on this output as well as on output from the individual filters, the REOs identified can now be further categorised according to the import market characteristics and the import market share for each REO taken separately. This categorisation is done by constructing Tables 5.1a, 5.1b and 5.1c.

Whereas the import characteristics are those defined in Filter 2, the categorisation according to import market share, as explained in Chapter 4 section 3.4, is linked to $\mu_{n,ij}$, the degree of market importance of country n's exports of product group j to country:

$$\mu_{n,ij} = \left(\frac{X_{n,ij}}{X_{w,ij}}\right) / \left(\frac{X_{n,j}}{X_{w,j}}\right),$$

where $X_{n,ij}$ is country n's exports of product group j to country i, $X_{World,ij}$ is the world's exports of product group j to country i, $X_{n,j}$ is country n's total exports of product group j, and $X_{World,j}$ is the world's total exports of product group j.

Figure 5.3. The filtering process of Belgium's realistic export opportunities.

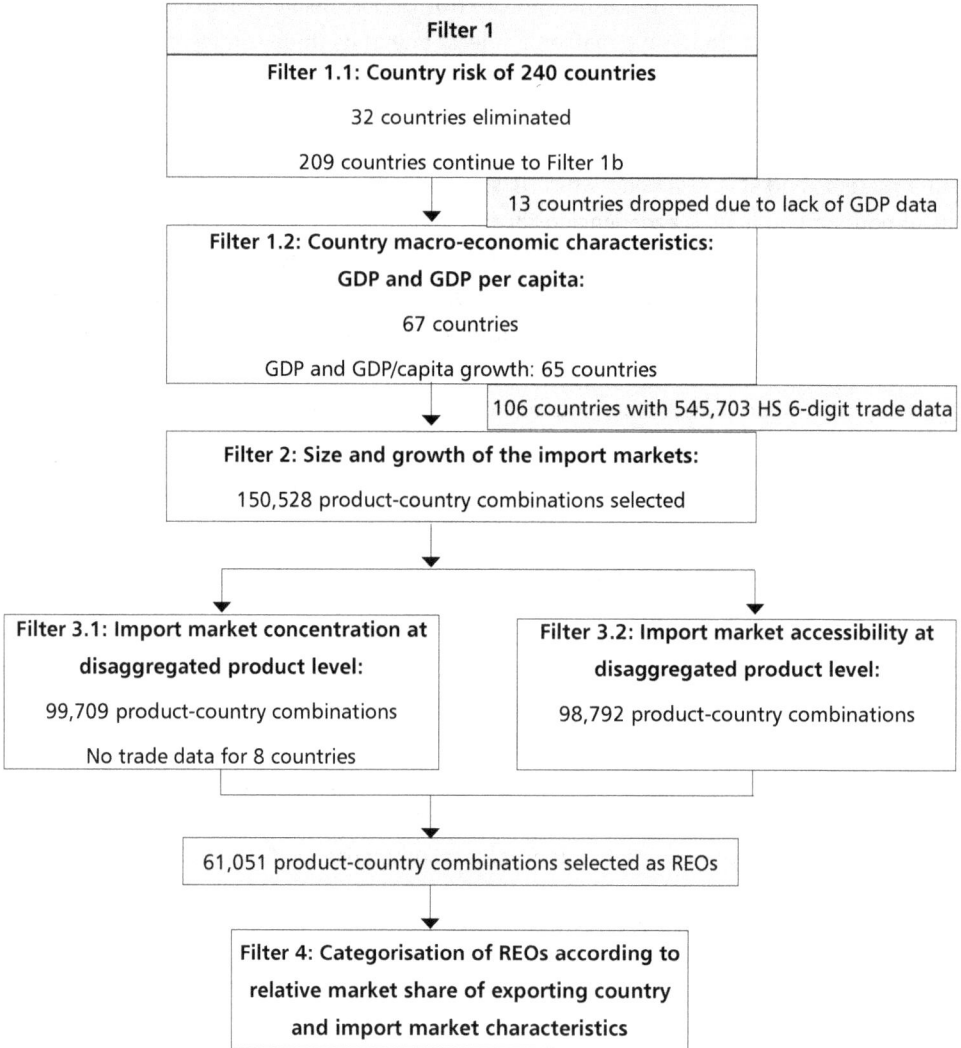

Filter 1
Filter 1.1: Country risk of 240 countries
32 countries eliminated
209 countries continue to Filter 1b

13 countries dropped due to lack of GDP data

Filter 1.2: Country macro-economic characteristics:
GDP and GDP per capita:
67 countries
GDP and GDP/capita growth: 65 countries

106 countries with 545,703 HS 6-digit trade data

Filter 2: Size and growth of the import markets:
150,528 product-country combinations selected

Filter 3.1: Import market concentration at disaggregated product level:	**Filter 3.2: Import market accessibility at disaggregated product level:**
99,709 product-country combinations	98,792 product-country combinations
No trade data for 8 countries	

61,051 product-country combinations selected as REOs

Filter 4: Categorisation of REOs according to relative market share of exporting country and import market characteristics

In order to indicate whether Belgium's market share is small or large, or intermediately small or large, for any particular product-country combination selected as REO, $\mu_{Belgium,ij}$ is compared with $\mu_{six,ij}$, the combined degree of market importance of the six exporting countries with the largest exports of the product category to the country in question. Following Cuyvers *et al.* (1995) and Cuyvers (2004), the following rules of thumb are used:

$\mu_{six,ij} - \mu_{Belgium,ij} > 3$: the relative market share of Belgium is relatively small;

$1.5 \leq \mu_{six,ij} - \mu_{Belgium,ij\,j} \leq 3$: the relative market share of Belgium is intermediately small;

$0 < \mu_{six,ij} - \mu_{Belgium,ij} \leq 1.5$: the relative market share of Belgium is intermediately high; and

$\mu_{six,ij} - \mu_{Belgium,ij} \leq 0$: the relative market share of Belgium is relatively high.

Table 5.1a shows the distribution of the 61,051 REOs, whereas Table 5.1b depicts the distribution of the REOs for which Belgium has a reasonably high comparative advantage, say, RCA ≥ 0.7.

Table 5.1a. Distribution of Belgium's potential realistic export opportunities according to relative market position and market characteristics.

	Market share of Belgium relatively small	Market share of Belgium intermediately small	Market share of Belgium intermediately large	Market share of Belgium relatively large	Total
Large product market	(Cell 1) 2,295 (3.76%)	(Cell 6) 1,377 (2.26%)	(Cell 11) 1,744 (2.86%)	(Cell 16) 1,716 (2.81%)	7,132 (11.68%)
Growing (long- and short-term) product market	(Cell 2) 27,226 (44.60%)	(Cell 7) 3,222 (5.28%)	(Cell 12) 3,114 (5.10%)	(Cell 17) 4,542 (7.44%)	38,104 (62.41%)
Large product market, short-term growth	(Cell 3) 1,266 (2.07%)	(Cell 8) 774 (1.27%)	(Cell 13) 1,053 (1.72%)	(Cell 18) 1,182 (1.94%)	4,275 (7.00%)
Large product market, long-term growth	(Cell 4) 1,062 (1.74%)	(Cell 9) 587 (0.96%)	(Cell 14) 759 (1.24%)	(Cell 19) 678 (1.11%)	3,086 (5.05%)
Large product market, short- and long-term growth	(Cell 5) 3,000 (4.91%)	(Cell 10) 1,604 (2.63%)	(Cell 15) 2,073 (3.40%)	(Cell 20) 1,777 (2.91%)	8,454 (13.85%)
Total	34,849 (57.08%)	7,564 (12.39%)	8,743 (14.32%)	9,895 (16.21%)	61,051 (100%)

A comparison with the percentage distribution of the REOs based on the 2003 and 2006 DSM results, for which much less detailed international trade data were used, reveals both striking similarities as well as differences. The distribution of the 2003 REOs according to import market characteristics and Belgium's relative market position (based on the information in Chapter 8, Table 8.1), is by and large similar to the REO distribution according to Table 5.1a (in spite of no 2003 REOs in the "large product market" row), but differs significantly from that of the 2006 REOs. The difference of the 2003 and present REOs distribution, and that of 2006, is apparently the result of the large share in 2006 of the REOs for which Belgium's relative market position is very small (93.8%, as compared to 44.6% in 2003 and 57.1% according to the above Table 5.1a). In particular, the share of the 2006 REOs in Cell 2 (long- and short-term growing product-country combinations) seems to be large (70%, as compared to 37.6% in 2003 and 44.6% according to Table 5.1a). It is challenging to attribute the difference with 2006 to the booming world economy at that time.

Table 5.1a can also be compared with the 2003 and 2006 DSM results as reported by Cuyvers and De Voet (2008), De Voet (2008) and Van Mol (2003), by ranking the cells of the respective Filter 4 output matrices. The Spearman rank correlation coefficient between the ranking of the 2006 and present 2008 cells is 0.632 and that between the 2003 and present ranking 0.520, which is moderate, thus being evidence for apparent shifts in the importance of the respective cells. To illustrate these shifts we can e.g., mention that the 2008 cell showing the largest number of REOs is Cell 2, followed by Cell 17, which in 2006 ranked fifth and sixth respectively. Some extreme examples of shift in importance show Cell 19 which in 2008 is ranked 19th, but 8th in 2006, or Cell 11 which in 2008 is ranked 9th, but 17th in 2006. One might be inclined, at first sight, to attribute these shifts to the different product classification and its level of aggregation. However, a similar Spearman rank correlation coefficient is found between the ranking of the cells in 2003 and 2006 (0.617) going together with similarly dramatic shifts in importance of the cells, in spite of the DSM results being based on SITC 4-digit international trade data. Therefore, the shifts over time within the categorisation of the REOs according to relative market position and market characteristics must be due to shifts in the country composition, which in turn depends on changes in country risks, and changing import demand conditions.

A comparison of Table 5.1a and 5.1b reveals that by imposing the condition RCA ≥ 0.7, the number of REOs decreased from 61,061 to 29,968. However, in spite of the halving of the number of REOs, their percentage distribution according to import market characteristics and Belgium's market position remains remarkably similar. The imposition of the RCA ≥ 0.7 condition dramatically negatively affects the large (not growing) product-country combinations, but positively the large product-country combinations among the REOs that also show both short- and long-term growth. We have no explanation for this, although it seems to indicate that Belgium's future export performance can benefit from it, if the country and its exporters would decide as a priority to tap into these large and growing product-country combinations. Yet, it should not be forgotten that for approximately half (52.3%) of all REOs of Belgium (see Table 5.1b) that can be considered as actual and present opportunities, Belgium has acquired only negligible, if any, market share, thus tentatively indicating a potential source of rapid success for Belgium's export promotion. Although providing evidence for the power of the DSM as a tool for designing and prioritising export promotion activities, a further analysis of the implications is, unfortunately, beyond the scope of this chapter.

Table 5.1b. Distribution of Belgium's realistic export opportunities with RCA ≥ 0.7, according to relative market position and market characteristics.

	Market share of Belgium relatively small	Market share of Belgium intermediately small	Market share of Belgium intermediately large	Market share of Belgium relatively large	Total
Large product market	(Cell 1) 601 (2.01%)	(Cell 6) 469 (1.57%)	(Cell 11) 644 (2.15%)	(Cell 16) 718 (2.40%)	2,432 (8.12%)
Growing (long- and short-term) product market	(Cell 2) 12,758 (42.57%)	(Cell 7) 1,881 (6.28%)	(Cell 12) 1,829 (6.10%)	(Cell 17) 2,221 (7.41%)	18,689 (62.36%)
Large product market, short-term growth	(Cell 3) 413 (1.38%)	(Cell 8) 357 (1.19%)	(Cell 13) 542 (1.81%)	(Cell 18) 631 (2.11%)	1,943 (6.48%)
Large product market, long-term growth	(Cell 4) 446 (1.49%)	(Cell 9) 353 (1.18%)	(Cell 14) 482 (1.61%)	(Cell 19) 472 (1.58%)	1,753 (5.85%)
Large product market, short- and long-term growth	(Cell 5) 1,467 (4.90%)	(Cell 10) 1,027 (3.43%)	(Cell 15) 1,438 (4.80%)	(Cell 20) 1,219 (4.07%)	5,151 (17.19%)
Total	15,685 (52.34%)	4,087 (13.64%)	4,935 (16.47%)	5,261 (17.56%)	29,968 (100%)

Whereas Table 5.1a and 5.1b relate to numbers of REOs, Table 5.1c shows the distribution of the REOs according to potential export values. In an attempt to make a rough estimate of the potential export values behind the REOs, we calculated following Viviers *et al.* (2010) per REO the average value of imports from the exporting countries which represent 80% of these imports, and assume that this average approximates sufficiently Belgium's export potential, measured in US$. Instead of adding up numbers of REOs, we then proceed by adding up the potential export values of the REOs thus estimated.

Table 5.1c. Distribution of the estimated US$ values (x1,000) of Belgium's potential realistic export opportunities according to relative market position and market characteristics.

	Market share of Belgium relatively small	Market share of Belgium inter- mediately small	Market share of Belgium inter- mediately large	Market share of Belgium relatively large	Total
Large product market	(Cell 1) 39,869,550 (3.92%)	(Cell 6) 64,054,192 (6.30%)	(Cell 11) 129,323,263 (12.71%)	(Cell 16) 72,392,980 (7.12%)	305,639,985 (30.04%)
Growing (long- and short-term) product market	(Cell 2) 68,237,276 (6.71%)	(Cell 7) 18,252,229 (1.79%)	(Cell 12) 24,859,216 (2.44%)	(Cell 17) 36,133,474 (3.55%)	147,482,195 (14.50%)
Large product market, short- term growth	(Cell 3) 33,704,814 (3.31%)	(Cell 8) 57,186,221 (5.62%)	(Cell 13) 47,236,954 (4.64%)	(Cell 18) 36,572,291 (3.59%)	174,700,280 (17.17%)
Large product market, long- term growth	(Cell 4) 11,373,054 (1.12%)	(Cell 9) 16,288,254 (1.60%)	(Cell 14) 27,931,761 (2.75%)	(Cell 19) 41,778,883 (4.11%)	97,371,952 (9.57%)
Large product market, short- and long-term growth	(Cell 5) 52,896,602 (5.20%)	(Cell 10) 42,489,891 (4.18%)	(Cell 15) 102,999,705 (10.12%)	(Cell 20) 93,733,246 (9.21%)	292,119,444 (28.71%)
Total	206,081,296 (20.26%)	198,270,787 (19.49%)	332,350,899 (32.67%)	280,610,874 (27.58%)	1,017,313,856 (100%)

From Table 5.1c it can be concluded that Belgium's potential REOs represent some 1,017 billion US$, However, the potential US$ value of each REO should not be considered as a true estimate of the export value that can be attained, but rather as a means to weigh each REO against all others.

Comparing Table 5.1a with 5.1c, we can clearly see how weighing the REOs by the assumed US$ value of their respective export potential, makes quite a difference in the distribution of the REOs. Particularly, it appears that the importance of the REOs with a small or negligible market share of Belgium is much lower, although still representing 20.3%, which means that in this column we find many REOs with small potential export value. The reduction of the share of Cells 1-5 is largely due to the impact of weighing on Cell 2, which now represents only 6.7%, as compared to 44.6% if unweighted.

5.7   Top 30 of Belgium's realistic export opportunities

Before investigating Belgium's export potential per broad product category and per import region in the world, it is interesting to briefly look into the highest ranked HS 6-digits products according to number of REOs that can be associated with these, as well as in terms of potential export value, which is determined as just explained.

Table 5.2 below shows the Top 30 list of products according to potential export value. It can be clearly seen that merely counting the number of REOs here, can easily lead to wrong conclusions, from the point of view of public export promotion. Having to promote exports of e.g. HS 901839 – Needles, catheters, cannulae, etc. (medical), the product that ranks highest on the Top 30 list according to number of REOs (which is identical to number of countries where the REO at issue is found), in 59 countries and hoping to reach potential exports of that product of merely $2,070,058, would waste scarce public resources for a meagre export return.

The product that ranks highest in Table 5.2 is an "umbrella" product category, which consists of products, that are difficult to categorise. We, therefore, should rather devote attention to the second product, HS 300490 – Medicaments n.e.s., in dosage, which is found in 52 different countries and promises a potential export value of $35,878,950. From the point of view of export promotion, this product still needs promotion in too many countries. The same argument holds for HS 870324 – Automobiles, spark ignition engine of >3000 cc or HS 870323 – Automobiles, spark ignition engine of 1500-3000 cc. Moreover, these products are produced by large multinational companies (MNCs) which, following their own global strategies, can hardly be influenced by the export promotion activities in the countries where they produce.

This aspect illustrates the limitations of export promotion in a world dominated by MNCs. It is these conglomerates which evidently benefit most from the existing export opportunities. Attracting these MNCs to Belgium or keeping their investment in the country, by well-designed investment promotion "sticks and carrots" allows Belgium to benefit in terms of export potential and employment, be it that any attempt to link these foreign affiliates to Belgium's export promotion targets must largely remain futile.

We clearly have to descend a rather long way down in the Top 30 to find products the exports of which can to some extent be incited by the export promotion organisations (EPOs) in Belgium, which evidently implies that in designing product targeted export promotion activities, the Belgian EPOs have to consult and cooperate closely with the sectoral organisations and the exporters. The output of the DSM can help to prioritise efforts towards the most promising import markets for the products offering the highest potential export value.

Table 5.2. Top 30 Belgian products according to potential export value.

Ranking	HS 6-digit product category	Product ranking based on number of REOs	Potential export value (US$ thousands)	Number of countries for which the product is selected
1	300490 – Medicaments n.e.s., in dosage	3	35,878,950	52
2	870324 – Automobiles, spark ignition engine of >3000 cc	53	28,645,480	39
3	870323 – Automobiles, spark ignition engine of 1500-3000 cc	12	26,752,468	44
4	270900 – Petroleum oils, oils from bituminous minerals, crude	3,601	25,160,977	5
5	870332 – Automobiles, diesel engine of 1500-2500 cc	54	15,043,985	39
6	271019 – Light petroleum distillates n.e.s.	678	14,783,495	23
7	854221 – Monolithic integrated circuits, digital	2,282	11,738,462	12
8	847330 – Parts and accessories of data processing equipment ne	191	11,213,026	32
9	710239 – Diamonds (jewellery) worked but not mounted or set	1,145	10,110,193	19
10	271011 – Aviation spirit	1,951	10,048,119	13
11	852520 – Transmit-receive apparatus for radio, TV, etc.	832	9,190,521	22

Ranking	HS 6-digit product category	Product ranking based on number of REOs	Potential export value (US$ thousands)	Number of countries for which the product is selected
12	841191 – Parts of turbo-jet or turbo-propeller engines	2,245	8,201,127	12
13	880240 – Fixed wing aircraft, unladen weight > 15,000 kg	3,324	8,027,382	7
14	300210 – Antisera and other blood fractions	683	7,616,974	23
15	293399 – Heterocyclic comps. with nitrogen hetero-atom(s) only	2,734	6,703,764	9
16	847130 – Portable digital computers < 10kg	1,046	6,352,009	20
17	852990 – Parts for radio/TV transmit/receive equipment, n.e.s	743	6,177,845	23
18	880330 – Aircraft parts nes	838	5,748,841	22
19	847989 – Machines and mechanical appliances n.e.s	3,307	4,843,573	7
20	950390 – Toys n.e.s	569	4,601,720	25
21	870899 – Motor vehicle parts n.e.s	26	4,447,469	42
22	841112 – Turbo-jet engines of a thrust > 25 KN	2,626	4,418,697	10
23	293499 – Nucleic acids & their salts, whether or not chemically defined, n.e.s.	681	4,179,096	23
24	851790 – Parts of line telephone/telegraph equipment, n.e.s	2,650	3,928,245	10
25	870840 – Transmissions for motor vehicles	370	3,773,607	28
26	740311 – Copper cathodes and sections of cathodes unwrought	3,068	3,730,956	8
27	901890 – Instruments, appliances for medical, etc science, n.e.s.	13	3,583,597	44

Ranking	HS 6-digit product category	Product ranking based on number of REOs	Potential export value (US$ thousands)	Number of countries for which the product is selected
28	852540 – Still image video camera	230	3,557,355	31
29	870322 – Automobiles, spark ignition engine of 1000-1500 cc	653	3,425,992	24
30	8443990 – Parts of printing machinery and ancillary equipment	3,302	3,264,837	7

5.8   An analysis of Belgium's export potential per broad product category and import region

In this section, we limit ourselves to a brief overview of the characteristics of the list of REOs identified, based on the product composition and export destination. Of course, a much deeper overview and analysis is possible, but is beyond the scope of this chapter. We then proceed to analyse Belgium's REOs according to the geographical region in the world. Table 5.3a shows Belgium's REOs per broad product category.

Table 5.3a. Belgium's REOs per broad product category.

	Potential export value (US$ thousands)	Percentage of total potential export value	Number of REOs	Percentage of number of REOs
01 – 05 Animal and animal products	13,813,352	1.36%	1,567	2.57%
06 – 15 Vegetable products	22,738,321	2.24%	2,984	4.89%
16 – 24 Foodstuffs	30,718,776	3.02%	2,542	4.16%
25 – 27 Mineral products	70,137,009	6.89%	831	1.36%
28 – 38 Chemicals and allied industries	132,492,719	13.02%	8,281	13.56%
39 – 40 Plastic/Rubbers	43,311,319	4.26%	3,574	5.85%
41 – 43 Raw hides, skins, leather, and furs	8,974,827	0.88%	790	1.29%
44 – 49 Wood and wood products	26,844,884	2.64%	2,840	4.65%

	Potential export value (US$ thousands)	Percentage of total potential export value	Number of REOs	Percentage of number of REOs
50 – 63 Textiles	41,015,960	4.03%	9,119	14.94%
64 – 71 Stone / Glass	45,494,660	4.47%	2,965	4.86%
72 – 83 Metals	90,366,607	8.88%	6,851	11.22%
84 – 85 Machinery / Electrical	241,971,577	23.79%	11,382	18.64%
86 – 89 Transportation	131,948,034	12.97%	1,663	2.72%
90 – 97 Miscellaneous	117,485,811	11.55%	5,662	9.27%
Grand Total	1,017,313,856	100.00%	61,051	100.00%

Machinery and electrical equipment represents the largest share of the REOs, both weighted (23.8%) or unweighted (18.6%), followed by chemicals (13% when weighted by average export values) and transportation equipment (13% when weighted by average export values). It is difficult to compare with earlier DSM results due to a different product classification, but tentatively HS 01-24 which, according to the present results, contribute 11.6% of the total number of REOs, largely corresponds with SITC 0 (food and live animals) which in 2003 and 2006 represented 15.6% and 16.7% of the REOs, and HS 84-89 with 21.4% of the total number of REOs in the present results corresponds with SITC 7 (machines and transport equipment) making up 18.9% and 16.9% of the total number of 2003 and 2006 REOs, respectively (based on data in Van Mol, 2005 and De Voet, 2008). This seems to imply that more recently the REOs identified have shifted to machinery and transport equipment, which is probably related to the quick rise of the Central and Eastern European Countries (CEEC).

The distribution of Belgium's REOs according to geographical region in the world can be consulted in Table 5.3b, from which it can be seen that the EU-15[5] alone, with 36.4% of all REOs, accounts for more than half of their total potential export value (56.3%). The Central and East European Countries (CEEC)[6] in turn, a number of which became EU member

---

5   EU-15 consists of Austria, Belgium, Denmark, Finland, France, Germany, Greece, Ireland, Italy, Luxemburg, Netherlands, Portugal, Spain, Sweden and United Kingdom.

6   The group of Central and Eastern European Countries (CEEC) consists of the former Soviet Union and the "East Bloc" countries, plus former Yugoslavia: Albania, Armenia, Belarus, Bosnia and

countries more recently, contribute 28.2% of the REOs, which, however, only contribute 7.6% of the potential export value of all REOs. Surprisingly, the number of REOs of Belgium in ASEAN[7] and Central Asia[8] together represents only 6.1% of all REOs and 10.2% of the potential export value of Belgium's REOs. Adding South Asia[9] doesn't change much.

Table 5.3b. Belgium's REOs per region in the world.

Region	Potential export value (US$ thousand)	Percentage of total pot. export value	No. of REOs	Percentage of number of REOs
Africa	14,298,790	1.41%	3,000	4.91%
ASEAN	23,155,072	2.28%	1,545	2.53%
CEEC	77,168,688	7.59%	17,190	28.16%
Central America and Caribbean	8,353,030	0.82%	842	1.38%
Central Asia	80,718,518	7.93%	2,160	3.54%
EU 15	573,125,025	56.34%	22,204	36.37%
Middle East	25,178,862	2.48%	3,531	5.78%
North America	159,253,602	15.65%	2,018	3.31%
North Europe (non-EU)	5,884,249	0.58%	1,750	2.87%
Oceania	9,299,150	0.91%	1,028	1.68%
South America	11,802,938	1.16%	2,707	4.43%
South Asia	6,611,225	0.65%	983	1.61%
South Europe (non-EU)	22,464,707	2.21%	2,093	3.43%
Grand Total	1,017,313,856	100.00%	61,051	100.00%

It is interesting to compare the ranking of the countries according to number of REOs with the ranking in the past, say according to the 2003 results. Concentrating on the 55 countries that the present ranking and that of 2003 have in common, the Spearman ranking correlation coefficient is -0.3703, showing weak negative correlation between the two series, basically for reasons listed above. The comparative ranking is depicted in Table 5.4.

Herzegovina, Bulgaria, Croatia, Czech Republic, Estonia, Georgia, Hungary, Kazakhstan, Latvia, Lithuania, Poland, Romania, Russia, Serbia, Slovakia, Slovenia, Turkmenistan and Uzbekistan.

7   ASEAN, the Association of South East Asian Nations, consists of Brunei Darussalam, Cambodia, Indonesia, Lao PDR, Malaysia, Myanmar (Burma), Philippines, Singapore, Thailand and Vietnam.

8   Central Asia consists of China, Hong Kong, Japan, Macau, Mongolia and South Korea.

9   South Asia consists of Bangladesh, Bhutan, India and Sri Lanka.

Table 5.4. Comparative country ranking of 2008 and 2003 according to number of REOs.

Country	No. of 2008 REOs	2008 Ranking	2003 Ranking
Germany	3,180	1	8
France	2,829	2	4
United Kingdom	2,700	3	1
Italy	2,503	4	3
Spain	2,244	5	2
Russia	1,865	6	16
Poland	1,818	7	10
Netherlands	1,808	8	5
United States	1,710	9	9
Switzerland	1,296	12	29
Austria	1,234	13	19
Denmark	1,110	15	11
China	1,105	16	23
Sweden	1,066	18	14
Norway	1,018	19	26
Portugal	823	24	7
India	818	25	21
Finland	800	26	15
Saudi Arabia	762	27	28
Brazil	758	28	48
Iceland	732	31	20
Greece	641	38	12
Egypt	620	39	13
Ireland	617	40	6
Israel	609	41	18
Japan	601	42	24
Turkey	599	43	17

Country	No. of 2008 REOs	2008 Ranking	2003 Ranking
Cyprus	531	44	30
Singapore	468	46	43
Australia	451	47	33

Source: 2008 ranking based on own calculations, 2003 ranking from Van Mol (2003)

The country ranked 10th and 11th in the 2008 list is Romania and the Czech Republic, two countries which are not in the 2003 ranking. The same holds for country ranked 14th, 17th and 20th, which is Bulgaria, Lithuania and Slovakia, etc. showing how the emergence and rapid rise of the Central and Eastern European Countries (CEEC) affects the 2008 ranking dramatically.

Evidently, the quickness to make use of the 2008 REOs depends on Belgium already having gained sufficient comparative advantage. For this analysis we could take, as before in this chapter, a revealed comparative index (RCA) of 0.7 as cut-off value and consider only the REOs relating to products for which the RCA is at least equal to 0.7. We have to refrain from conducting this analysis, as it would unnecessarily repeat the Belgian part of the comparison of "actual REOs" and "potential REOs" between Belgium, South Africa and Thailand in Chapter 6, to which the reader is referred.

5.9 Conclusions

It is only by applying the DSM that its usefulness can be judged. The present chapter illustrates the DSM methodology, outlined in Chapter 4, as applied to Belgium, using statistical data up to 2008. Two types of conclusions can be drawn. The first type of conclusions relate to the results, the second to the stability of the results over time and its implications.

As to the results of the present "run" of the DSM for Belgium, the following can be concluded. Starting with 240 countries, these showing the highest country risks were eliminated, after which the remaining countries are evaluated based on their GDP and/or GDP per capita record, which identifies 67 countries as providing preliminary market opportunities. A further criterion related to the economic growth performance of the countries is used, such that 107 countries pass Filter 1 of the DSM.

Based on HS international trade data at 6-digit level, all product/country combinations for the 107 countries are assessed in the next filter based on market size and import market growth, after which, in Filter 3, the output of Filter 2 is evaluated based on import market concentration and "revealed absence" of barriers to trade. This leads to the identification of 61,051 realistic export opportunities, which in total represent a potential export value of

1,017 billion US$. How many of these realistic export opportunities, or to what extent they are already tapped is not analysed, as it is beyond the scope of the present chapter (see Chapter 6).

Further data on relative market position of Belgium for each realistic export opportunity, as well as on basic import market characteristics, allows putting the potentials for immediate use into perspective. Also looking into Belgium's degree of specialisation at product level, based on the revealed comparative advantage index, allows some further assessment of these potentials.

In the Top 30 of these realistic export opportunities based on potential export values, automobiles, oil products, pharmaceuticals and integrated circuits figure prominently. Production of these products is dominated by multinational companies, and therefore promoting such exports looks rather nonsensical. One has to descend a rather long way down in the Top 30 to find products the exports of which can to some extent be incited by the trade promotion organisations (TPOs) in Belgium.

It is clear that the output of the DSM can offer a lot of input for identifying, prioritising, designing, planning and executing concrete export promotion activities by the Belgian export promotion organisations. However, as the results of the DSM are inescapably based on statistical data which are at least two years old, there is a need to have the realistic export opportunities assessed by experts "in the field" such as panels of exporters, representatives of sector organisations, commercial attachés at diplomatic missions abroad, etc.

Relating to the second type of conclusions, it should be stressed that we were unable to perform an inter-temporal robustness check of the results, but that the differences with previous DSM runs can be explained. However, even a superficial comparison of the present results with these for 2003 and 2006 should lead to some further caution. A thorough comparison is hampered by the different and more detailed product classification underlying the present DSM run. In addition, a somewhat lower selection rate of the countries based on country risk is achieved in Filter 1, probably due to the finer scoring scale used by ONDD on which the selection was performed for 2003 and 2006. In Filter 2 this seems to be compensated by a higher percentage of the product/country combinations identified as possible realistic export opportunities, as compared to the previous runs, probably due to the more detailed international trade data used presently. In turn, the selection rate in Filter 3 seems to be somewhat lower than for 2003 and 2006.

In sheer number, machines and transport equipment represent the bulk of the opportunities and their share seems to have increased somewhat, as compared to the results for 2003 and 2006. This is likely related to the importance of the EU-15 market and to the quick rise in prominence of the Central and Eastern European Countries (CEEC) among the countries offering potential, which is in contrast with the results for 2003 and 2006. It presents a deep challenge for government export promotion, as the result illustrates that the economic environment can change so rapidly, that an export promotion strategy at product and country level, which by definition should aim at a sustained longer-term focus, runs the risk of being surpassed by events.

The same can be said when we look at the changes over time in the categorisation of the export opportunities. Comparing the present Belgian DSM results with these for 2003 and 2006 it was found that the rankings of the Filter 4 categories of realistic export opportunities for 2008, 2006 and 2003, although showing some reasonable correlation, sometimes changed dramatically. We did not confirm whether this also applies to the individual opportunities, as such an analysis is beyond the scope of this chapter. There is, however, no reason why this should not be the case, although the phenomenon is probably not widespread. Again, for those opportunities of which the categorisation changes, the export promotion strategies also have to be adapted (see Chapter 9).

Is government export promotion, therefore, another exercise in shooting from the hip at a moving target? Are a continuously changing international environment, country performances and risks, and import demand conditions, not making any attempt by the public sector to direct exporters to selected markets a predictable failure? We are convinced this is not the case. Rather, a repeated use of the DSM to identify realistic export opportunities will allow the export promotion organisation to better prioritise its activities, concentrating on the most promising and stable opportunities, be it that additional expert opinion on recent and expected future changes by privileged experts – both at country and product level – is required to optimise the use of the DSM results. The DSM seems to be a necessary, but not a sufficient condition for an efficient public export promotion programme.

References

Balassa, B. 1965. Trade Liberalisation and Revealed Comparative Advantage, Centre Paper 63, Yale University Economic Growth Centre, New Haven.

Cuyvers, L. 1996. Export opportunities of Thailand: a decision support model approach. *Journal of Euro-Asian Management*, I2(2): 71-96.

Cuyvers, L. 2004. Identifying export opportunities: the case of Thailand. *International Marketing Review*, 21(3): 255-278.

Cuyvers, L., De Pelsmacker, P., Rayp, G. & Roozen, I.T.M. 1995. A decision support model for the planning and assessment of export promotion activities by government export promotion institutions: the Belgian case. *International Journal of Research in Marketing*, 12: 173-186.

Cuyvers, L. & De Voet, A. 2008. Application of the decision support model to Belgium: last update and results, Powerpoint presented at the workshop *Export Opportunities and Public Export Promotion*, University of Antwerp, 11-12 September 2008.

De Voet, A. 2008. Exportmogelijkheden van België: Resultaten van het normatief model. Unpublished master's thesis. Antwerp: University of Antwerp, Faculty of Applied Economics.

Hirschmann, A.O. 1964. The Paternity of an Index. *American Economic Review*, 54(5): 761-762.

Viviers, W., Steenkamp, E., Rossouw, R. & Cuyvers, L. 2010. Identifying realistic export opportunities for South Africa: application of a decision support model (DSM) using HS 6-digit level product data. Report prepared for the Department of Trade and Industry, South Africa, September 2010, 56 pp.

Van Mol, L. 2003. Exportmogelijkheden van België: Resultaten van het normatief model. Unpublished master's thesis. Antwerp: University of Antwerp, Faculty of Applied Economics.

Willemé, P. & Van Steerteghem, D. 1993. Een normatief model voor de planning van exportbevorderende activiteiten van de Vlaamse Dienst voor de Buitenlandse Handel, Brussels: Vlaamse Dienst voor de Buitenlandse Handel, Brussels. (Unpublished report).

Chapter 6

Realistic export opportunities and export potentials: a comparison using DSM results for Belgium, South Africa and Thailand

Ludo Cuyvers, Ermie Steenkamp, Wilma Viviers & Riaan Rossouw

6.1   Introduction

This chapter reports on the 2007 realistic export opportunities (REOs) of Belgium, South Africa and Thailand, according to the latest run of the DSM, and compares the results. As the same macro-economic and international trade data are used, a comparison can be made between these results. More specifically, this chapter will concentrate on a comparison of the REOs of Belgium, South Africa and Thailand according to the import market characteristics and the mentioned three countries' market position in the respective import markets. In addition, the broad product composition of the list of REOs at HS 2-digit level[1] will be compared and contrasted with the REOs for which the three countries' comparative advantage (measured using Balassa's revealed comparative advantage index RCA, see Balassa, 1965) is sufficiently large to warrant relatively rapid export success (see Chapter 4 section 3.4). The REOs without taking the exporting country's comparative advantage into account can be considered as potential REOs. We call the REOs for which the exporting country has acquired relatively large RCA (say, of at least 0.7) actual REOs. A comparison of the actual and potential REOs according to various criteria, will in turn allow some conclusions on the immediate use the three countries investigated can possibly make of their potential REOs, thus providing evidence on whether a country is sufficiently tapping its existing export potentials in the world. The analysis will end with a comparison of the REOs of the three countries, according to the geographical position and the level of economic development of the import markets.

---

1   The detailed analysis is carried out at HS 6 digits, after which we have grouped categories at 2-digit level.

Belgium is a high income OECD country that, as a small but rich economy, is very open to the international trade and investment flows of the rest of the world. It is at the crossroads of the major physical distribution channels (roads, railways, ports) in Western Europe. As founding member of the European Union and as host of the European Union institutions, Belgium is at the centre of the European single market. Thailand, on the other hand, is an Asian lower middle-income economy, whereas South Africa is an African upper middle-income country. However, Thailand is a fast-growing economy and often considered as a "next tier Newly Industrialising Economy" which is part of an economically dynamic region in the world – the backyard of Japan, South Korea and China – which has evolved following the so-called "flying geese" pattern of industrialisation. South Africa, on the other hand, is mostly described as a "dual society" with a rich upper class of people, which compare to the rich population strata in the high-income countries and also share important cultural characteristics with the "West", and a vast number of poor and very poor with low-quality education levels and often divided along tribal lines. The poverty headcount ratio at the national poverty line (% of the population) in South Africa amounts at 22% (2008, but 38% in 2000), against 13.6% (1998, in the middle of the "Asian crisis") in Thailand. Moreover, South Africa is located in a much less economically dynamic region of the world.

As we lack a standard or reference for the comparison of the product and country structure of the realistic export opportunities of exporting countries, or the use that is made of the opportunities, we are compelled to limit ourselves to the comparison of the DSM results for Belgium, South Africa and Thailand. In contrast to Chapter 7, where only South Africa's export opportunities in the rest of the African continent are investigated, the comparison in the present chapter relates to the export opportunities of Belgium, Thailand and South Africa respectively, in the rest of the world.

As the selection of the REOs for Belgium, South Africa and Thailand proceeds in the same way, using the same macro-economic and international trade data, one would expect the REOs of the countries to be very similar. Yet, a comparison of the distribution of the REOs according to the relative market share of the exporting country and the import market characteristics will show remarkable differences. The reasons for these differences must evidently be found in the differences in the export market shares of the selected countries in the import markets.

However, as will be pointed out below, the product composition of the set of potential realistic export opportunities of the three exporting countries researched does not seem to show much difference. We, therefore, also look at the actual REOs. Moreover, a comparison of actual and potential REOs allows providing evidence on whether a country is sufficiently tapping its existing export potentials in the world.

6.2 Comparison of the REOs identified for Belgium, South Africa and Thailand

In this section we analyse the distribution of the potential REOs according to relative market share of Belgium, South Africa and Thailand respectively and market characteristics of the import markets involved in the REOs. We first consider the number of potential REOs detected, counting the product-country combinations involved, after which we analyse the distribution using the US$ values involved.[2]

6.2.1 Comparison based on the distribution of the number of potential REOs according to relative export market position and import market characteristics

In Table 6.1a, 6.1b and 6.1c, the number of the potential REOs of Belgium, South Africa and Thailand, and their percentage distribution are depicted according to the relative market share of these countries[3] in the respective import markets, as well as the import market characteristics of the individual REO.

Table 6.1a. Distribution of Belgium's potential realistic export opportunities according to relative market position and market characteristics.

	Market share of Belgium relatively small	Market share of Belgium inter- mediately small	Market share of Belgium inter- mediately large	Market share of Belgium relatively large	Total
Large product market	2,295	1,377	1,744	1,716	7,132
	(3.756%)	(2.26%)	(2.86%)	(2.81%)	(11.68%)
Growing (long- and short-term) product market	27,226	3,222	3,114	4,542	38,104
	(44.60%)	(5.28%)	(5.10%)	(7.44%)	(62.41%)
Large product market, short- term growth	1,266	774	1,053	1,182	4,275
	(2.07%)	(1.27%)	(1.72%)	(1.94%)	(7.00%)
Large product market, long-term growth	1,062	587	759	678	3,086
	(1.74%)	(0.96%)	(1.24%)	(1.11%)	(5.05%)

2   These values were calculated following the methodology outlined in Viviers *et al.* (2010) and Chapter 4 section 5.3. It consists at calculating per product group at HS 6-digit level the average value of imports of the exporting countries, which represent 80% of these imports.

3   For the cut-off values of the relative market share used to distinguish between market shares that are relatively small, intermediately small, intermediately high and relatively high, we refer to Cuyvers *et al.* (1995) and Cuyvers (1996, 2004), as outlined in Chapter 4, Table 4.6.

	Market share of Belgium relatively small	Market share of Belgium inter-mediately small	Market share of Belgium inter-mediately large	Market share of Belgium relatively large	Total
Large product market, short- and long-term growth	3,000 (4.91%)	1,604 (2.63%)	2,073 (3.40%)	1,777 (2.91%)	8,454 (13.85%)
Total	34,849 (57.08%)	7,564 (12.39%)	8,743 (14.32%)	9,895 (16.21%)	61,051 (100%)

Source: Authors' own calculations based on DSM results

Table 6.1b. Distribution of South Africa's potential realistic export opportunities according to relative market position and market characteristics.

	Market share of South Africa relatively small	Market share of South Africa inter-mediately small	Market share of South Africa inter-mediately large	Market share of South Africa relatively large	Total
Large product market	9,279 (11.88%)	1,272 (1.63%)	1,104 (1.41%)	569 (0.73%)	12,224 (15.65%)
Growing (long- and short-term) product market	44,037 (56.39%)	531 (0.68%)	442 (0.57%)	1,771 (2.27%)	46,781 (59.90%)
Large product market, short-term growth	4,558 (5.84%)	516 (0.66%)	455 (0.58%)	241 (0.31%)	5,770 (7.39%)
Large product market, long-term growth	3,066 (3.93%)	275 (0.35%)	262 (0.34%)	177 (0.23%)	3,780 (4.84%)
Large product/market short- and long-term growth	7,717 (9.88%)	723 (0.93%)	707 (0.91%)	396 (0.51%)	9,543 (12.22%)
Total	68,657 (87.91%)	3,317 (4.245%)	2,970 (3.80%)	3,154 (4.04%)	78,098 (100%)

Source: Authors' own calculations based on DSM results

Table 6.1c. Distribution of Thailand's potential realistic export opportunities according to relative market position and market characteristics.

	Market share of Thailand relatively small	Market share of Thailand inter-mediately small	Market share of Thailand inter-mediately large	Market share of Thailand relatively large	Total
Large product market	852 (3.94%)	361 (1.67%)	288 (1.33%)	121 (0.56%)	1,622 (7.51%)
Growing (long- and short-term) product market	12,094 (55.96%)	755 (3.49%)	584 (2.70%)	465 (2.15%)	13,898 (64.31%)
Large product market, short-term growth	705 (3.26%)	288 (1.33%)	199 (0.92%)	72 (0.33%)	1,264 (5.85%)
Large product market, long-term growth	645 (2.98%)	245 (1.13%)	169 (0.78%)	58 (0.27%)	1,117 (5.17%)
Large product market, short- and long-term growth	2,164 (10.01%)	760 (3.52%)	615 (2.85%)	172 (0.80%)	3,711 (17.17%)
Total	16,460 (76.16%)	2,409 (11.15%)	1,855 (8.58%)	888 (4.11%)	21,612 (100%)

Source: Authors' own calculations based on DSM results

From the tables above it appears that among the potential REOs of South Africa and Thailand, 88% and 76% respectively are product-country combinations with a relatively small market share. For Belgium this group of potential REOs represents 57% of all REOs. This percentage is around 90% for Thailand (93%) and Belgium (88%) when growing product-country combinations are considered, and for South Africa 84%. As such, according to the theoretical insights on the role of comparative advantage of nations which determines the specialisation of countries in the world market, such large shares would not come too much as a surprise.

The number of potential REOs with an intermediately large or even large market share for Belgium, South Africa and Thailand accounts for 30%, 8% and 12% of the total number of potential REOs of these countries respectively.

6.2.2 Comparison based on the distribution of the estimated values of the potential REOs according to relative export market position and import market characteristics

Tables 6.2a, 6.2b and 6.2c show the distribution of the estimated US$ values of the potential REOs according to the relative market share of the three exporting countries considered and the import market characteristics.

Table 6.2a. Distribution of the estimated US$ values of Belgium's potential realistic export opportunities according to relative market position and market characteristics.

	Market share of Belgium relatively small	Market share of Belgium inter-mediately small	Market share of Belgium inter-mediately large	Market share of Belgium relatively large	Total
Large product market	3.92%	6.30%	12.71%	7.12%	30.04%
Growing (long- and short-term) product market	6.71%	1.79%)	2.44%	3.55%)	14.50%
Large product market, short-term growth	3.31%	5.62%	4.64%	3.59%	17.17%
Large product market, long-term growth	1.12%	1.60%	2.75%	4.11%	9.57%
Large product market, short- and long-term growth	5.20%	4.18%	10.12%	9.21%	28.71%
Total	20.26%	19.49%	32.67%	27.58%	100%

Source: Authors' own calculations based on DSM results

Table 6.2b. Distribution of the estimated US$ values of South Africa's potential realistic export opportunities according to relative market position and market characteristics.

	Market share of South Africa relatively small	Market share of South Africa inter-mediately small	Market share of South Africa inter-mediately large	Market share of South Africa relatively large	Total
Large product market	16.40%	7.13%	14.14%	3.08%	40.74%
Growing (long- and short-term) product market	7.95%	0.52%	0.49%	0.33%	9.29%
Large product market, short-term growth	6.78%	4.55%	3.27%	0.63%	15.23%

	Market share of South Africa relatively small	Market share of South Africa inter-mediately small	Market share of South Africa inter-mediately large	Market share of South Africa relatively large	Total
Large product market, long-term growth	3.98%	0.95%	2.86%	0.64%	8.44%
Large product market, short- and long-term growth	13.94%	4.80%	4.85%	2.71%	26.30%
Total	49.04%	17.95%	25.61%	7.40%	100%

Source: Authors' own calculations based on DSM results

Table 6.2c. Distribution of the estimated US$ values of Thailand's potential realistic export opportunities according to relative market position and market characteristics.

	Market share of Thailand relatively small	Market share of Thailand inter-mediately small	Market share of Thailand inter-mediately large	Market share of Thailand relatively large	Total
Large product market	5.16%	10.70%	8.15%	2.91%	26.92%
Growing (long- and short-term) product market	10.03%	2.51%	2.25%	1.28%	16.07%
Large product market, short-term growth	4.63%	3.09%	1.53%	0.80%	10.05%
Large product market, long-term growth	2.78%	2.71%	2.70%	1.24%	9.43%
Large product market, short- and long-term growth	10.02%	8.13%	16.75%	2.63%	37.54%
Total	32.62%	27.14%	31.37%	8.87%	100%

Source: Authors' own calculations based on DSM results

From Tables 6.2a – c it can be concluded that many potential REOs have relatively low export values. South Africa's REOs with a relatively low South African market share, which represented 88% of all REOs, accounts for 49% of the total potential export value. In the

Thai case the 76% of all potential REOs represent 33% of the total potential export value. These percentages for Belgium are 57% and 20% respectively. In terms of values concerned the potential REOs with an intermediately large or even large market share for Belgium, South Africa and Thailand account for 60%, 33% and 40% of the total potential export value of these countries respectively.

6.2.3 Comparison based on the product distribution of the potential and actual REOs

The Tables 6.3a and 6.3b below allow some comparison between the DSM results based on the product distribution of the REOs. One should keep in mind, however, that the comparison with the South African results is somewhat hampered due to a different way of proxying the impact of trade barriers in Filter 3, which seems to have increased both the number of the South African REOs and their value. In spite of this, we assume that percentage distribution of the number of REOs and their value allows comparison of the Belgian and Thai REOs with the South African REOs.

Table 6.3a. Distribution of the potential realistic export opportunities of Belgium, South Africa and Thailand based on product (HS 2 digit).

HS 2 digit	Number of REOs			Value of REOs		
	Belgium	South Africa	Thailand	Belgium	South Africa	Thailand
01 – 05 Animal and animal products	2.57%	2.58%	2.52%	1.36%	1.13%	0.99%
06 – 15 Vegetable products	4.89%	4.90%	4.78%	2.24%	2.17%	2.12%
16 – 24 Foodstuffs	4.16%	3.82%	4.15%	3.02%	1.84%	2.33%
25 – 27 Mineral products	1.36%	2.08%	1.30%	6.89%	15.48%	6.92%
28 – 38 Chemicals and allied industries	13.56%	13.30%	11.56%	13.02%	8.77%	10.40%
39 – 40 Plastic/Rubbers	5.85%	4.83%	5.77%	4.26%	2.90%	2.82%
41 – 43 Raw hides, skins, leather, and furs	1.29%	1.40%	1.42%	0.88%	0.77%	1.04%
44 – 49 Wood and wood products	4.65%	5.06%	4.57%	2.64%	2.43%	2.26%
50 – 63 Textiles	14.94%	15.38%	16.06%	4.03%	3.76%	4.12%
64 – 71 Stone/Glass	4.86%	5.19%	5.19%	4.47%	5.25%	4.77%
72 – 83 Metals	11.22%	12.45%	11.00%	8.88%	8.52%	7.82%

HS 2 digit	Number of REOs			Value of REOs		
	Belgium	South Africa	Thailand	Belgium	South Africa	Thailand
86 – 89 Transportation	2.72%	2.59%	2.68%	12.97%	8.55%	13.37%
90 – 97 Miscellaneous	9.27%	8.27%	9.31%	11.55%	10.54%	13.39%
Grand total	100%	100%	100%	100%	100%	100%

The percentage distributions of the potential REOs of the three countries, according to the HS 2-digit product categories, are very similar. However, the South African share of mineral products in the total value of the REOs is much higher than in Belgium and Thailand, and the corresponding South African share of chemicals and allied industries and transportation are somewhat lower. This similarity should not come as a surprise, as in the filtering process that leads to the REOs, no account is taken of the comparative advantages of the respective countries.

Table 6.3b below shows the distribution of the REOs of the three countries when considering only these for which the respective countries have a RCA ≥ 0.7, which we call "actual realistic export opportunities".

Table 6.3b. Distribution of the actual realistic export opportunities of Belgium, South Africa and Thailand based on product (HS 2 digit).

HS 2 digit	Number of REOs			Value of REOs		
	Belgium	South Africa	Thailand	Belgium	South Africa	Thailand
01 – 05 Animal and animal products	2.53%	3.00%	2.36%	1.64%	1.52%	0.95%
06 – 15 Vegetable products	4.42%	7.05%	3.51%	2.19%	2.57%	1.07%
16 – 24 Foodstuffs	5.41%	6.13%	5.37%	3.99%	3.91%	2.41%
25 – 27 Mineral products	1.70%	3.90%	0.91%	6.17%	17.42%	7.46%
28 – 38 Chemicals and allied industries	19.69%	16.95%	6.56%	22.25%	6.71%	2.58%
39 – 40 Plastic/Rubbers	8.68%	4.26%	9.12%	7.47%	2.46%	5.33%
41 – 43 Raw hides, skins, leather, and furs	0.66%	1.59%	1.45%	0.78%	0.61%	0.85%
44 – 49 Wood and wood products	5.34%	4.41%	3.82%	3.56%	2.65%	1.69%

HS 2 digit	Number of REOs			Value of REOs		
	Belgium	South Africa	Thailand	Belgium	South Africa	Thailand
64 – 71 Stone/Glass	4.79%	5.43%	6.24%	6.05%	12.57%	8.67%
72 – 83 Metals	11.72%	19.21%	11.17%	10.63%	20.97%	7.20%
84 – 85 Machinery/ Electrical	12.55%	14.04%	19.78%	10.64%	11.77%	34.85%
86 – 89 Transportation	2.89%	2.91%	2.72%	14.37%	12.85%	16.61%
90 – 97 Miscellaneous	6.82%	4.34%	7.44%	5.47%	2.88%	5.35%
Grand total	100%	100%	100%	100%	100%	100%

When only considering the REOs for which the respective countries show a sufficient comparative advantage (RCA ≥ 0.7), the distributions are much different. Belgium's percentage share of actual REOs in product category chemicals and allied industries (22.25%) is higher as compared to that of South Africa (6.71%) and Thailand (2.58%). South Africa is leading in metals (20.97% of its actual REOs) and minerals (17.42%). Thailand's share of machinery and transportation in its actual REOs are highest, representing 34.85% and 16.61%.

Also the countries' distributions of the values associated with the actual REOs show marked differences, actually making the differences in the distribution of the actual REOs more outspoken for a number of product categories, with textile products and transport equipment being extreme cases. It is also found, for instance that product category machinery and electrical equipment now represents 34.85% of the total value of Thailand's actual REOs. It would be interesting to investigate whether these REOs are more in import markets where Thailand's market share is small or rather large, but such a more detailed analysis is beyond the scope of the present study.

In terms of the values associated with the actual REOs, mineral products and metals represent for South Africa 17.42% and 20.97% respectively, against only 3.90% and 19.21% in numbers.

6.2.4 Comparison of actual and potential REOs

A comparison of the actual and potential REOs provides some interesting insights in the degree a country is adapted to the export opportunities in the world, taking into account its present comparative advantage.

Table 6.4. Actual as compared to potential realistic export opportunities of Belgium, South Africa and Thailand based on product (HS 2 digit).

HS 2 digit	Number of REOs			Value of REOs		
	Belgium	South Africa	Thailand	Belgium	South Africa	Thailand
01 – 05 Animal and animal products	48.37%	29.67%	36.61%	61.56%	24.93%	32.84%
06 – 15 Vegetable products	44.37%	36.63%	28.69%	49.89%	22.04%	17.29%
16 – 24 Foodstuffs	63.81%	40.93%	50.54%	67.20%	39.36%	35.19%
28 – 38 Chemicals and allied industries	71.26%	32.46%	22.20%	86.98%	14.22%	8.46%
39 – 40 Plastic/Rubbers	72.80%	22.47%	61.74%	89.36%	15.77%	64.54%
41 – 43 Raw hides, skins, leather, and furs	25.19%	28.92%	39.97%	45.09%	14.70%	27.94%
44 – 49 Wood and wood products	56.37%	22.19%	32.71%	68.70%	20.23%	25.48%
64 – 71 Stone/Glass	48.40%	26.67%	47.03%	68.85%	44.50%	62.05%
72 – 83 Metals	51.26%	39.32%	39.73%	60.92%	45.75%	31.41%
84 – 85 Machinery/ Electrical	33.05%	19.70%	39.28%	22.78%	7.85%	42.96%
86 – 89 Transportation	52.13%	28.61%	39.61%	56.39%	27.95%	42.37%
90 – 97 Miscellaneous	36.08%	13.37%	31.27%	24.10%	5.07%	13.62%
Grand total	49.09%	25.48%	39.11%	50.91%	18.59%	34.10%

From Table 6.4 it appears that on average Belgium is best adapted to its potential export opportunities in the world market, with half of these showing comparative advantages. Belgium is followed by Thailand with a ratio of actual to potential REOs of 39.11% and 34.10% respectively according to number and values of REOs. South Africa's potential REOs are only covered for 25.48% and 18.95%, which seems dismally low.

There are, however, striking differences according to the product categories at HS 2-digit level. In terms of values behind the potential REOs, Belgium's potentials in plastics/rubbers (HS 39-40) and chemical products (HS 28-38) can be almost completely materialised (89.36% and 86.98% respectively), followed by stone/glass (68.85%), wood and wood products (68.70%) and foodstuffs (67.20%). Considering South Africa's potentials, it has the highest ratio in metals (45.75%) and stone/glass (44.50%), but it can be assumed that it will face tough competition from many other countries, as also Belgium and Thailand have a relatively high ratio for this category (60.92% and 31.41% respectively in metals and 68.85% and 62.05% respectively in stone/glass). Thailand's potentials, in terms of export values considered, can mostly be materialised in plastic/rubber (64.54%) and stone/glass (62.05%), where it seems that Belgium's possibilities to do likewise are highest of the three countries (89.36% and 68.85% respectively).

It is also interesting to look at textile products, for which Belgium seems to be adapted most of the three countries to cater to the export opportunities in the world with a ratio of actual to potential REOs in value terms of 60.57%. It is followed by Thailand in this product group with a ratio of 41.11%. South Africa's textile products for which there is comparative advantage hardly correspond to the REOs in the world (5.59%).

6.2.5   Comparison based on the level of development of the importing countries and on the geographical distribution of the REOs

It is also possible to compare the DSM results according to their geographical distribution. Based on international trade theory it can be expected that the REOs are differently distributed as a result of distance between exporting and importing country and as a result of their level of economic development.

6.2.5.1 Comparison based on the level of development of the importing countries for potential and actual REOs of Belgium, South Africa and Thailand

Table 6.5a and 6.5b below provide the distribution of actual and potential REOs of the three exporting countries according to the level of development of the importing countries. Following the World Bank Atlas definition four groups of importing countries are distinguished according to level of development, using their 2009 GNI per capita, as follows:

(i)   High-income economies with a GNI per capita of $12,196 or more,

(ii)   Upper middle-income economies with a GNI per capita of $3,946 – $12,195

(iii)   Lower middle-income economies with a GNI per capita of $996 – $3,945

(iv)   Low-income economies with a GNI per capita of $995 or less.

Table 6.5a. Potential REOs of Belgium, South Africa and Thailand according to the level of development of the importing countries.

	Number of REOs			Value of REOs		
	Belgium	South Africa	Thailand	Belgium	South Africa	Thailand
High-income economies	67.87%	64.22%	70.26%	85.05%	76.99%	85.02%
Upper middle-income economies	21.34%	18.43%	19.47%	7.58%	5.18%	7.19%
Lower middle-income economies	9.85%	14.41%	9.34%	7.05%	17.62%	7.67%
Low-income economies	0.94%	2.93%	0.93%	0.33%	0.21%	0.12%
Total	100%	100%	100%	100%	100%	100%

Again, as far as the distribution of potential REOs of Belgium, South Africa and Thailand is concerned, these are very similar, with the exception of the high share of the lower middle-income economies for South Africa, and its corresponding lower share of the high-income and upper middle-income economies.

Table 6.5b. Actual REOs of Belgium, South Africa and Thailand according to the level of development of the importing countries.

	Number of REOs			Value of REOs		
	Belgium	South Africa	Thailand	Belgium	South Africa	Thailand
High-income economies	69.12%	66.71%	71.75%	86.65%	77.93%	84.43%
Upper middle-income economies	20.79%	16.72%	8.19%	8.46%	5.93%	5.65%
Lower middle-income economies	9.22%	13.60%	1.05%	4.35%	15.63%	0.23%
Low-income economies	0.88%	2.98%	19.02%	0.54%	0.51%	9.69%
Total	100%	100%	100%	100%	100%	100%

Also the actual REOs of Belgium and Thailand are mostly distributed similarly according to the level of development of the importing economies, with an exception for the higher share of the low-income economies for Thailand (particularly in number terms), and a corresponding lower share of the middle-income economies. The actual REOs of South Africa show relatively higher concentration in the lower middle-income economies, than these of Belgium and Thailand, but South Africa's share of the low-income economies, in terms of potential exporting value, is almost the same as that of Belgium. Taking into account that in the near future the most dynamic markets can be assumed to be in the high income and upper middle income economies, and probably not the low income economies, this implies that, taking into account the comparative advantage of the three exporting countries, Belgium is best positioned, followed by Thailand, with South Africa coming third.

6.2.5.2 Comparison based on the geographical distribution of potential and actual REOs of Belgium, South Africa and Thailand separately

Tables 6.6a, 6.6b and 6.6c show the potential and actual REOs of Belgium, South Africa and Thailand, grouped according to the region of the world where these REOs can be found.

Table 6.6a. Belgium's potential and actual REOs according to region.

	Potential REOs				Actual REOs			
	Sum of potential export value		Sum of number of products selected in this country		Sum of potential export value		Sum of number of products selected in this country	
	(US$ thousands)	%	Nrs	%	(US$ thousands)	%	Nrs	%
Africa	14,298,790	1.41%	3000	4.91%	7,490,151	1.45%	1455	4.86%
ASEAN	23,155,072	2.28%	1545	2.53%	5,531,737	1.07%	723	2.41%
CEEC*	77,168,688	7.59%	17190	28.16%	41,275,755	7.97%	8609	28.73%
Central America and Caribbean	8,353,030	0.82%	842	1.38%	5,562,244	1.07%	425	1.42%
Central and East Asia	80,718,518	7.93%	2160	3.54%	26,246,841	5.07%	908	3.03%
EU 15	573,125,025	56.34%	22204	36.37%	319,431,869	61.68%	11053	36.88%
Middle East	25,178,862	2.48%	3531	5.78%	12,786,885	2.47%	1699	5.67%
North America	159,253,602	15.65%	2018	3.31%	65,596,644	12.67%	763	2.55%
North Europe (non-EU)	5,884,249	0.58%	1750	2.87%	3,607,742	0.70%	907	3.03%
Oceania	9,299,150	0.91%	1028	1.68%	5,321,317	1.03%	544	1.82%
South America	11,802,938	1.16%	2707	4.43%	7,379,979	1.42%	1338	4.46%
South Asia	6,611,225	0.65%	983	1.61%	2,735,152	0.53%	412	1.37%
South Europe (non-EU)	22,464,707	2.21%	2093	3.43%	14,951,743	2.89%	1132	3.78%
Grand total	1,017,313,856	100%	61051	100%	517,918,059	100%	29968	100%

* Central and East European countries

From Table 6.6a it appears that the distribution of the actual and potential REOs of Belgium in terms of values and numbers involved respectively is very similar, although the distribution according to values as compared to that based on numbers is different (e.g. North America accounts for 12 to 16% of the total potential when values are considered, but only 2 to 3% based on numbers). As we will see immediately, the same observation holds for South Africa and Thailand, but the percentages evidently differ.

It is interesting to look into the shares of Asia and Latin America in South Africa's REOs according to Table 6.6b. In a previous study (Pearson et al., 2010), it was found that the number of potential REOs in Brazil was 51, in China 259 and in India 198. Although the level of detail of the product-country combinations is far from the same, it is the proportions that interest us here, which are: for each REO in Brazil, 5 were detected in China and 4 in India. On the basis of the present calculations for South Africa, 1,153 potential REOs were detected in Brazil, against 2,321 in China and 1,475 in India. The reason for the divergence with the previous results is due to the different levels of aggregation and product classification (SITC at 4 digits in Pearson et al., 2010, against HS 6-digit level in this study) and the impact of trade barriers and market concentration in the import markets, which were not sufficiently taken into account in Pearson et al. (2010).

Table 6.6b. South Africa's potential and actual REOs according to region.

	Potential REOs				Actual REOs			
	Sum of potential export value		Sum of number of products selected in this country		Sum of potential export value		Sum of number of products selected in this country	
	(US$ thousands)	%	Nrs	%	(US$ thousands)	%	Nrs	%
Africa	7,438,520	0.49%	3,553	4.55%	2,578,317	0.92%	948	4.76%
ASEAN	87,440,482	5.80%	5,621	7.20%	14,023,239	5.00%	1,501	7.54%
CEEC *	59,925,151	3.97%	18,676	23.91%	13,463,243	4.80%	4,561	22.92%
Central America and Caribbean	1,436,631	0.10%	814	1.04%	619,304	0.22%	234	1.18%
Central and East Asia	348,629,836	23.12%	5,335	6.83%	54,868,642	19.58%	1,216	6.11%
EU 15	505,836,786	33.55%	23,884	30.58%	89,846,273	32.06%	6,232	31.32%
Middle East	37,689,661	2.50%	5,485	7.02%	11,947,288	4.26%	1,404	7.06%
North America	366,710,535	24.32%	4,039	5.17%	67,378,925	24.04%	919	4.62%
South America	17,892,536	1.19%	2,825	3.62%	4,069,061	1.45%	657	3.30%

	Potential REOs				Actual REOs			
	Sum of potential export value		Sum of number of products selected in this country		Sum of potential export value		Sum of number of products selected in this country	
	(US$ thousands)	%	Nrs	%	(US$ thousands)	%	Nrs	%
South Asia	36,063,108	2.39%	2,093	2.68%	10,104,680	3.61%	507	2.55%
South Europe (non-EU)	17,580,111	1.17%	2,078	2.66%	4,594,902	1.64%	593	2.98%
Grand total	1,507,828,144	100%	78,098	100%	280,283,304	100%	19,897	100%

* Central and East European countries

Table 6.6c. Thailand's potential and actual REOs according to region.

	Potential REOs				Actual REOs			
	Sum of potential export value		Sum of number of products selected in this country		Sum of potential export value		Sum of number of products selected in this country	
	(US$ thousands)	%	Nrs	%	(US$ thousands)	%	Nrs	%
Africa	6,738,238	0.79%	2,384	4.31%	3,200,778	1.11%	976	4.52%
ASEAN	18,902,762	2.23%	1,029	1.86%	10,992,617	3.80%	305	1.41%
CEEC *	61,837,697	7.28%	14,765	26.72%	29,092,766	10.05%	6,178	28.59%
Central America and Caribbean	8,139,306	0.96%	741	1.34%	5,388,721	1.86%	291	1.35%
Central and East Asia	77,666,045	9.15%	2,008	3.63%	21,619,978	7.47%	624	2.89%
EU 15	451,728,306	53.21%	21,586	39.06%	144,969,830	50.07%	8,262	38.23%
Middle East	20,196,643	2.38%	3,216	5.82%	8,975,706	3.10%	1,279	5.92%
North America	156,857,500	18.48%	1,976	3.58%	46,862,008	16.19%	527	2.44%
South America	9,079,254	1.07%	2,370	4.29%	4,304,301	1.49%	892	4.13%
South Asia	6,274,544	0.74%	900	1.63%	2,268,155	0.78%	278	1.29%
South Europe (non-EU)	18,575,561	2.19%	1,820	3.29%	5,900,696	2.04%	836	3.87%
Grand total	848,937,247	100%	55,259	100%	289,518,044	100%	21,612	100%

* Central and East European countries

In the Thailand case we want to draw attention to the small share of ASEAN in the potential REOs (see Table 6.6c). In 1997, ASEAN accounted for 343 of Thailand's REOs (15%), as compared to 199 REOs in the USA (9%), 179 in Japan (8%), 144 in China (6%) and 114 in India (5%) (Cuyvers, 2004). Using 2007 data and a more disaggregated HS product classification, the share of ASEAN in Thailand's REOs is merely 1.86% (in potential value terms only 2.23%). The share of the USA is 3% (17% in value terms), Japan's share 1% (2.26% in terms of value), China's 1.85% (6.02% in terms of value), India's 1.37% (0.73% in terms of value). This draws a rather gloomy picture of ASEAN as an export driven growth engine for the member countries, in particular for Thailand. In contrast, the EU-15 represents 39.06% of all Thailand's REOs (even 53.21% in terms of value), against some 22% in 1997. These differences with previous results have to be analysed further in detail in order to find out whether they are robust over time and when using, as previously, SITC international trade data.[4]

Two more comparisons are appropriate. In section 6.2.6, we first compare the distributions between Belgium, South Africa and Thailand, after which, in section 6.2.7, the respective ratios of actual to potential REOs for the three countries in the respective regions are looked at in some detail.

6.2.6 Comparison based on the geographical distribution of potential and actual REOs between Belgium, South Africa and Thailand

Referring to the percentages in Table 6.6a – 6.6c, it can be concluded that the broad geographical distribution of the potential REOs of Belgium, South Africa and Thailand is very similar. When looking at the number of REOs, the EU-15 and the Central and Eastern European Countries have the largest share (although somewhat smaller for South Africa's REOs). At first sight this should not be too surprising as the same product providing a REO in e.g. France, the United Kingdom and Spain is counted three times, i.e. not as one single REO in the EU-15. However, when we look at the geographical distribution of the REOs based on potential export value, the share of EU-15 is even larger (but almost the same as far as South Africa is concerned), while North America and Central and East Asia are now ranking second and third. When considering the potential export value of South Africa's REOs the EU-15 represents 33.55% of South Africa's REOs, against 24.32% in North America and 23.12% in Central and East Asia. That EU-15 makes up 56.34% of the potential value of Belgium's REOs, against 15.65% in North America and 7.93% in Central and East Asia, is not surprising at all, considering EU-15 as Belgium's "hinterland" and taking into account that Belgium is a member country of the European single market. As mentioned above, it is more surprising

---

4   The geographical distributions might have been biased due to the importance of intra-EU trade. Therefore, the calculations were done by only focusing on the potential export values in EU-15 as a whole, instead of adding up the potential export values of the EU-15, which evidently include these of the other EU-15 countries into each other's market.

to see that EU-15 represents 53.21% of the potential export value of Thailand's REOs, and Central and East Asia only 9.15%.

When considering the sheer numbers of actual REOs (potential REOs for which the respective exporting countries have a RCA ≥ 0.7), the geographical distributions of Belgium, South Africa and Thailand are remarkably similar, with the EU-15 providing the highest number of potential REOs (36-39% for Belgium and Thailand, but only 33.55% for South Africa), followed second by the Central and Eastern European countries (about 26 – 28% for Belgium and Thailand, and 23% for South Africa).

However, when the potential export values are considered, the distributions are much less similar. The share of EU-15 is still highest, but differs significantly between Belgium (61.68% of the potential export value of Belgium's actual REOs), South Africa (32.06%) and Thailand (50.07%). The region of North America comes second, Central and East Asia comes third, but surprisingly for Thailand the share of the actual REOs in Central and East Asia in value terms only represents 7.5%.

6.2.7 Comparison of actual and potential REOs according to geographical region

A comparison of the ratios of actual and potential REOs for an exporting country according to the region of the world where these REOs occur, also allows some tentative conclusions about the possibilities to cater to the world taking into account the present degree of specialisation (RCA ≥ 0.7). Table 6.7 below shows the ratios of actual to potential REOs according to the region. The ratios can be interpreted as showing the overall potential degree of utilisation of the REOs in a region by the exporting country, or the degree of immediate utilisation of the export potentials in a region of the world. However, as we are not investigating the one-by-one correspondence at product level between actual and potential REOs, the comparison should not be used to draw other conclusions than as to the degree a potential existing in a region can possibly be tapped. A comparison with e.g. the real export values at product level from the exporting country into the various regions would shed more light on the use that is made of the almost immediately existing export potentials. Such a comparison is, however, a topic for a separate study and, therefore, beyond the scope of the present study.

In terms of potential export values, Belgium has the highest potential degrees of utilisation (except for, based on number of REOs, Thailand in ASEAN, which is understandable given the geographical and cultural proximity), followed by Thailand, with South Africa coming last in the ranking. This seems to reflect the degree of adaptation of the exporting countries to their potential export opportunities in the world market. The picture that emerges is a reflection of the basic reality, which we already came across while analysing similar ratios according to product composition of the REOs. When looking at the potential degrees of utilisation-based on the number of actual and potential REOs, the same can be concluded.

The degree of immediate utilisation of the export potentials of Belgium is highest based on number of REOs in Central America and the Caribbean, where it reaches 66.59%. This ratio is 66.56% in South Europe and around 53-56% in the Central and Eastern European countries and in the EU-15. The lowest ratio for Belgium is found in ASEAN. Thailand's degree of immediate utilisation of its export potentials is also highest in Central America and the Caribbean. Not surprisingly, the same ratio amounts at some 58.15% in ASEAN, but it appears that the potentials in Europe can only to a limited extend be tapped, which is even more the case for Central and East Asia. South Africa shows little capacity to immediately use the export potentials.

Table 6.7. Potential degree of utilisation of REOs according to region.

	Based on potential export value of REOs			Based on number of REOs		
	Belgium	South Africa	Thailand	Belgium	South Africa	Thailand
Africa	48.50%	26.68%	40.94%	52.38%	34.66%	47.50%
ASEAN	46.80%	26.70%	29.64%	23.89%	16.04%	58.15%
CEEC *	50.08%	24.42%	41.84%	53.49%	22.47%	47.05%
Central and East Asia	42.04%	22.79%	31.08%	32.52%	15.74%	27.84%
EU 15	49.78%	26.09%	38.27%	55.74%	17.76%	32.09%
Middle East	48.12%	25.60%	39.77%	50.78%	31.70%	44.44%
North America	37.81%	22.75%	26.67%	41.19%	18.37%	29.88%
North Europe (non-EU)	51.83%	29.26%	47.12%	61.31%	29.51%	43.89%
Oceania	52.92%	31.61%	47.45%	57.22%	33.06%	47.10%
South America	49.43%	23.26%	37.64%	62.53%	22.74%	47.41%
South Asia	41.91%	24.22%	30.89%	41.37%	28.02%	36.15%
South Europe (non-EU)	54.09%	28.54%	45.93%	66.56%	26.14%	31.77%
Grand total	49.09%	25.48%	39.11%	50.91%	18.59%	34.10%

* Central and East European countries

In value terms, a similar picture emerges for Belgium, with Central America and the Caribbean, the CEEC and EU-15 showing an immediate utilisation ratio of around 50%. For Thailand this ratio amounts at about 39 to 41% for the REOs potential export value in the CEEC, Africa and Central America and the Caribbean, but highest in Oceania and the North-European market. As for South Africa, the ratios are remarkably low, even in the African market.

6.3   Conclusions

The present chapter compares the realistic export opportunities (REOs) of Belgium, South Africa and Thailand in the world market at large. These REOs were identified using a decision support model for export promotion purposes. We analyse the distribution of potential REOs with actual REOs. Potential REOs are REOs, which disregard the comparative advantage in exporting the goods at issue by the exporting country. Actual REOs are the REOs for which the revealed comparative advantage index of the exporting country is at least 0.7.

We have shown that these concepts and a comparison of the distributions of the actual and potential REOs between the three exporting countries according to numbers involved or underlying export values provide a powerful tool to assess the capacity of an exporting country to tap into the export opportunities in the world. A comparison of the ratios of actual and potential REOs for an exporting country according to the region of the world where these REOs occur, also allows some tentative conclusions about the possibilities to cater to the world market's needs, taking into account the exporting country's present degree of specialisation. In fact, such ratios can be interpreted as giving the overall potential degree of utilisation of the REOs in a region by the exporting country.

We have illustrated the use that can be made by such comparisons for Belgium, South Africa and Thailand. No doubt, the concepts used and the comparison made allows a more detailed analysis about which product groups and which countries and regions in the world need improvement in the exports of a country. This in turn is an important input in discussions about a country's export strategy.

Our comparison revealed that in terms of export values concerned, the potential REOs with an intermediately large or even large market share for Belgium, South Africa and Thailand account for 60%, 33% and 40% of their total potential export value. We also found that, on average, Belgium is most adapted to its potential export opportunities in the world market, with half of these showing comparative advantages. Belgium is followed by Thailand with a ratio of actual to potential REOs of 39.11% and 34.10% respectively according to number and values of REOs. South Africa's potential REOs are only covered for 25.48% and 18.95%, which seems dismally low.

We also considered the level of economic development of the import markets in the world. When it is assumed that in the near future the most dynamic markets are most likely to be found in the high-income and upper middle-income economies, and probably not the low-income economies, our results imply that, taking into account the comparative advantage of the three exporting countries, Belgium is best positioned in these countries, followed by Thailand, with South Africa coming third.

On the other hand, some results were obtained that beg for further research and analysis. In the Thailand case, for instance we found that ASEAN only has a small share in Thailand's potential REOs, thus, unexpectedly, downgrading ASEAN as an export driven growth engine for the member countries, in particular for Thailand. In contrast, for the three exporting countries considered, the EU-15 seems to show high export potential. The region of North America comes second: 12.67% of the potential value of Belgium's, 24.04% of South Africa's, and 16.19% of Thailand's actual REOs. Central and East Asia comes third: 5.07% of the potential value of Belgium's actual REOs is located in that region, and even 19.58% of South Africa's, but surprisingly hardly 8% of these of Thailand.

Belgium has the highest potential degrees of utilisation of potential export values (except for Thailand in ASEAN, which is understandable given the geographical and cultural proximity), followed by Thailand, with South Africa coming last in the ranking. This result seems to reflect the degree of adaptation of the three exporting countries to their potential export opportunities in the world market.

It would be interesting to extend the analysis to actual and potential production networks by linking e.g., Belgium's REOs in Thailand or South Africa, which can be considered as relating to intermediate products, to Thailand's or South Africa's REOs of final products that are produced using the said intermediate products. In this way, interdependencies between exporting/importing countries could be assessed as factors, which reinforce the potentials of the REOs and could become important input in the discussions on the relationship between the characteristics of the REOs and appropriate public export promotion strategies at product level. Moreover, such analysis could be linked to foreign direct investment potentials in exporting/importing countries and thus become an element of public investment promotion as well. This is evidently beyond the scope of the present chapter. The issue of how to derive appropriate export promotion strategies for the REOs identified is covered by Chapter 9.

References

Balassa, B. 1965. Trade liberalisation and revealed comparative advantage. *Centre Paper 63*. New Haven: Yale University Economic Growth Centre.

Cuyvers, L. 1996. Export opportunities of Thailand: a decision support model approach. *Journal of Euro-Asian Management*, 2(2): 71-97.

Cuyvers, L. 2004. Identifying export opportunities: the case of Thailand. *International Marketing Review* 21(3): 255-278.

Cuyvers, L., De Pelsmacker, P., Rayp, G. & Roozen, I.T.M. 1995. A decision support model for the planning and assessment of export promotion activities by government export promotion institutions: the Belgian case. *International Journal of Research in Marketing*, 12: 173-186.

Pearson, J.J.A., Viviers, W., Cuyvers, L. & Naudé, W. 2010. Identifying export opportunities for South Africa in the southern engines: a DSM approach. *International Business Review*, 19(4): 345-359.

Viviers, W., Steenkamp, E.A., Rossouw, R. & Cuyvers, L. 2010. *Identifying realistic export opportunities for South Africa: application of a decision support model (DSM) using HS 6-digit level product data*. Report prepared for the Department of Trade and Industry, South Africa, September 2010, 56 p.

Chapter 7

The identification of export opportunities for South Africa in the rest of the African content

Ermie Steenkamp & Wilma Viviers

7.1   Introduction

Export development can be regarded an economic tool that enables a nation to employ citizens, build overseas exchange reserves and ultimately create a higher standard of living (Shankarmahesh, Olsen & Honeycutt, 2005:203; Edwards & Stern, 2007:1-22). However, governments and individual firms that want to stimulate growth through export development must distinguish between a vast number of export combinations due to the fact that in most circumstances a large number of export opportunities exists, and only a limited number of these can be explored because of scarce resources (Papadopoulos & Denis, 1988:38).

Therefore, the challenge that governments and individual firms face was in choosing specific markets for export promotion (Shankarmahesh *et al.*, 2005:204). In order to yield a higher return on investment and to make sure that resources are not wasted on less attractive export markets, they should focus their efforts and resources on a limited set of export markets that holds the highest export potential (Shankarmahesh *et al.*, 2005:204). Furthermore, selecting the "right" market is important as a first step to ensure export success (Papadopoulos & Denis, 1988:38).

The DSM was specifically designed to select the most promising markets for a given exporting country in order to assist export promotion organisations in planning and assessing their export promotion activities (see Chapter 2). In this chapter the DSM methodology (as discussed in Chapter 4) is applied to identify realistic export opportunities for South African products in the rest of the African continent.

The strengthening of trade and economic links with countries in Africa is regarded a priority in the trade policies of the South African government (DTI, 2006). The South African government's strategic objectives include support to economic development in Africa through regional integration, increased intra-African trade and capacity building and strengthening SADC, SACU, NEPAD and the AU institutions (DTI, 2006). The reasons for prioritising the strengthening of trade and economic links with countries in Africa include the following (DTI, 2006):

(i)   South Africa's economic development is linked to the economic development of the rest of the African continent.

(ii)   South Africa is the leading economy in Africa. This presents unique trade and investment opportunities for South Africa, but also presents a responsibility to contribute to the continent's economic development.

(iii)   Other countries around the world are seeking increased presence in the African continent through various trade initiatives. South Africa needs to compete with this growing competition for markets in Africa.

Furthermore, according to the DTI (2010), the African continent is amongst the most important and fastest growing destinations for South African exports. South Africa's exports to the rest of the African continent also include more higher value-added products compared to other continents. To increase South Africa's exports to other African countries is also part of South Africa's industrial and employment objectives (DTI, 2010).

In section 7.2 the methodology of the DSM specifically applied to identify export opportunities for South Africa in the rest of the African continent, will be discussed. The results of this unique application of the DSM will be discussed in section 7.3.

7.2   Method

The methodology of the DSM was discussed in detail in Chapter 4. For identifying export opportunities for South Africa specifically in the rest of the African continent, it was decided to change the sequence of the filters.

The reason for this is that in a study to determine South Africa's export opportunities to the rest of the world, 42 African countries were already eliminated in Filter 1 (Steenkamp & Viviers, 2011). Sixteen (16) African countries were eliminated based on too high commercial and political risk ratings and another 27 countries eliminated based on too low GDP/GDP per capita levels as well as GDP/GDP per capita growth values in Filter 1. Therefore, in total, 42 of the 52 African countries were eliminated in Filter 1, leaving only 10 African countries to be analysed in Filters 2 to 4 (for more detail, see Steenkamp & Viviers, 2011).

Based on the strategic importance of increasing and diversifying South Africa's exports to other African countries (as indicated in section 7.1) and, therefore, the importance of identifying export opportunities for South Africa in the rest of the African continent, it was decided to start the DSM approach with Filter 2. Therefore, all 52 African countries entered the analysis.

7.3   Results

The filtering process of the DSM applied to identify export opportunities for South Africa in the rest of the African continent is illustrated in Figure 7.1. For a detailed description of the filters applied, see Chapter 4.3: the sequential filtering process of the DSM.

Figure 7.1. Selection of realistic export opportunities for South Africa in Africa.

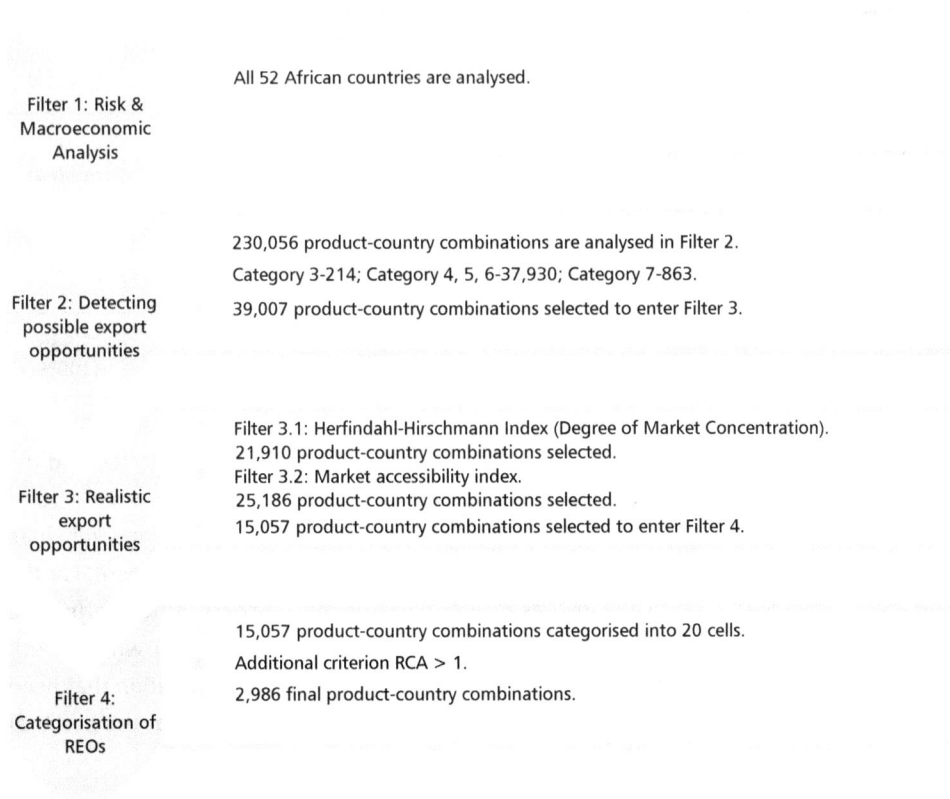

Filter 1: Risk & Macroeconomic Analysis

All 52 African countries are analysed.

Filter 2: Detecting possible export opportunities

230,056 product-country combinations are analysed in Filter 2.
Category 3-214; Category 4, 5, 6-37,930; Category 7-863.
39,007 product-country combinations selected to enter Filter 3.

Filter 3: Realistic export opportunities

Filter 3.1: Herfindahl-Hirschmann Index (Degree of Market Concentration).
21,910 product-country combinations selected.
Filter 3.2: Market accessibility index.
25,186 product-country combinations selected.
15,057 product-country combinations selected to enter Filter 4.

Filter 4: Categorisation of REOs

15,057 product-country combinations categorised into 20 cells.
Additional criterion RCA > 1.
2,986 final product-country combinations.

From a possible 280,956[1] product-country combinations in Africa 2,986 were identified as having export opportunities for South Africa in the rest of the African continent. These product-country combinations are categorised according to South Africa's relative market share and the importers' market characteristics in Table 7.1 and 7.2 (see Chapter 4 section 3.4).

Table 7.1. Number of realistic export opportunities in Africa according to South Africa's relative market share and the importers' market characteristics.

	Market share of South Africa relatively small	Market share of South Africa inter-mediately small	Market share of South Africa inter-mediately large	Market share of South Africa relatively large	Total
Large product market	(Cell 1) 5 (0.17%)	(Cell 6) 0 (0.00%)	(Cell 11) 1 (0.03%)	(Cell 16) 7 (0.23%)	13 (0.44%)
Growing (long- and short-term) product market	(Cell 2) 1248 (41.80%)	(Cell 7) 58 (1.94%)	(Cell 12) 63 (2.11%)	(Cell 17) 1,499 (50.20%)	2,868 (96.05%)
Large product market, short-term growth	(Cell 3) 6 (0.20%)	(Cell 8) 0 (0.00%)	(Cell 13) 0 (0.00%)	(Cell 18) 3 (0.10%)	9 (0.30%)
Large product market, long-term growth	(Cell 4) 6 (0.20%)	(Cell 9) 1 (0.03%)	(Cell 14) 0 (0.00%)	(Cell 19) 8 (0.27%)	15 (0.50%)
Large product market, short- and long-term growth	(Cell 5) 37 (1.24%)	(Cell 10) 3 (0.10%)	(Cell 15) 7 (0.23%)	(Cell 20) 34 (1.14%)	81 (2.71%)
Total	1,302 (43.60%)	62 (2.08%)	71 (2.38%)	1,551 (51.94)	2,986 (100%)

It is interesting to note that both in terms of the number of opportunities selected and the potential export value, most export opportunities fall into either Cells 1 to 5 or Cells 16 to 20. South Africa, therefore, mostly has either a very small or a relatively large market share in the markets identified as export opportunities in the rest of the African continent. For the markets in which South Africa already has a relatively large market share, little interference from export promotion organisations are probably needed. For markets in which South Africa has a very low market share there is still much exploration and preparation that need to take place. For a further analysis of these results, see section 7.3.5 and for the practical

1   Fifty-two (52) African countries (excluding South Africa) x 5,403 HS 6-digit product classifications.

implications of the cells for government export promotion, see the case studies discussed in Chapter 9.

Table 7.2. Potential export values of therealistic export opportunities in Africa according to South Africa's relative market and the importers' market characteristics (thousands of US$).

	Market share of South Africa relatively small	Market share of South Africa inter- mediately small	Market share of South Africa inter- mediately large	Market share of South Africa relatively large	Total
Large product market	(Cell 1) 44,852 (0.63%)	(Cell 6) 0 (0%)	(Cell 11) 15,061 (0.21%)	(Cell 16) 71,506 (1.01%)	131,419 (1.85%)
Growing (long- and short-term) product market	(Cell 2) 2,352,359 (33.06%)	(Cell 7) 560,910 (7.88%)	(Cell 12) 123,776 (1.74%)	(Cell 17) 2,803,259 (39.40%)	5,840,304 (82.09%)
Large product market, short-term growth	(Cell 3) 35,888 (0.50%)	(Cell 8) 0 (0.00%)	(Cell 13) 0 (0.00%)	(Cell 18) 50,845 (0.71%)	86,733 (1.22%)
Large product market, long-term growth	(Cell 4) 195,906 (2.75%)	(Cell 9) 377 (0.01%)	(Cell 14) 0 (0.00%)	(Cell 19) 23,374 (0.33%)	219,657 (3.09%)
Large product market, short- and long-term growth	(Cell 5) 396,232 (5.57%)	(Cell 10) 307,66 (0.43%)	(Cell 15) 54,671 (0.77%)	(Cell 20) 354,579 (4.98%)	836,248 (11.75%)
Total	3,025,237 (42.52%)	592,053 (8.32%)	193,508 (2.72%)	3,303,563 (46.44%)	7,114,361 (100%)

It is also interesting to note from Tables 7.1 and 7.2 that in total, 96.05% (in terms of the number of opportunities selected) or 82.09% (in terms of the potential export value) of the total export opportunities selected in Africa is in growing in the short and long term, but not large markets (Cells 2, 7, 12 and 17).

In the following sections the results will be presented according to regions, countries, sectors (HS 2-digit), and products (HS 6-digit).

7.3.1 Regional results of the Africa DSM

In this section the results of the DSM applied to identify export opportunities for South Africa in the rest of the African continent will be reported per region, namely Northern Africa, Eastern Africa, Southern Africa, Middle Africa and Western Africa[2]. Figures 7.2 and

2   Regions as defined by the United Nations (2010).

7.3 provide graphical illustrations of the DSM results per region based on the number of opportunities identified and the potential export values of these opportunities respectively.

Figure 7.2. Regional distribution of export opportunities in Africa: share in total number of opportunities.

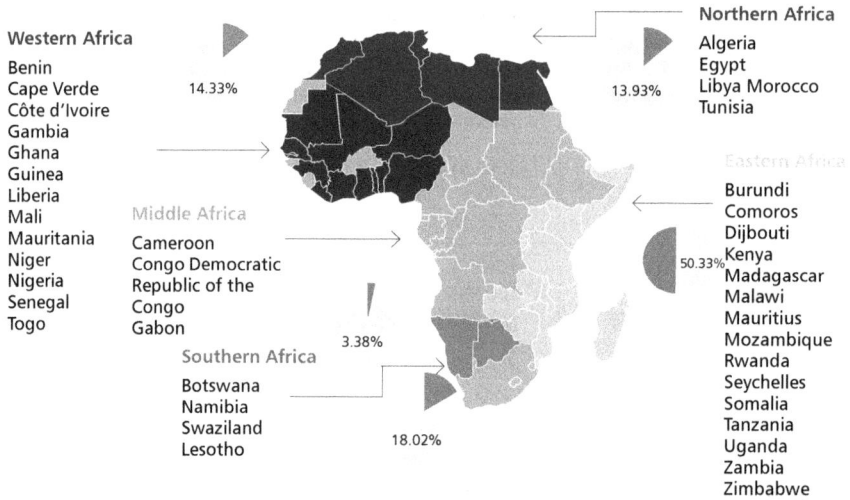

From Figure 7.2 it is clear that in terms of number of opportunities, Eastern Africa holds the highest export potential for South Africa with 50.33% of the opportunities in this region. Southern Africa follows with 18.92%. Western Africa (14.33%) and Northern Africa (13.95%) are in the third and fourth places, followed by Middle Africa with only 3.38% of the total number of opportunities identified in this region. This picture changes when the potential export values of the different export opportunities are considered (see Figure 7.3).

From Figure 7.3 it is clear that while Eastern Africa holds 50.33% of the number of export opportunities in Africa (see Figure 7.2), these change when the potential export values of the export opportunities identified are considered. Eastern Africa still holds the largest percentage of the export opportunities (29.22%), followed by Western and Northern Africa with 28.89% (as opposed to 14.33% in terms of number of opportunities) and 21.85% (as opposed to 13.93% in terms of number of opportunities) of the export opportunities in each of these regions.

Figure 7.3. Regional distribution of export opportunities in Africa: share in total potential export value.

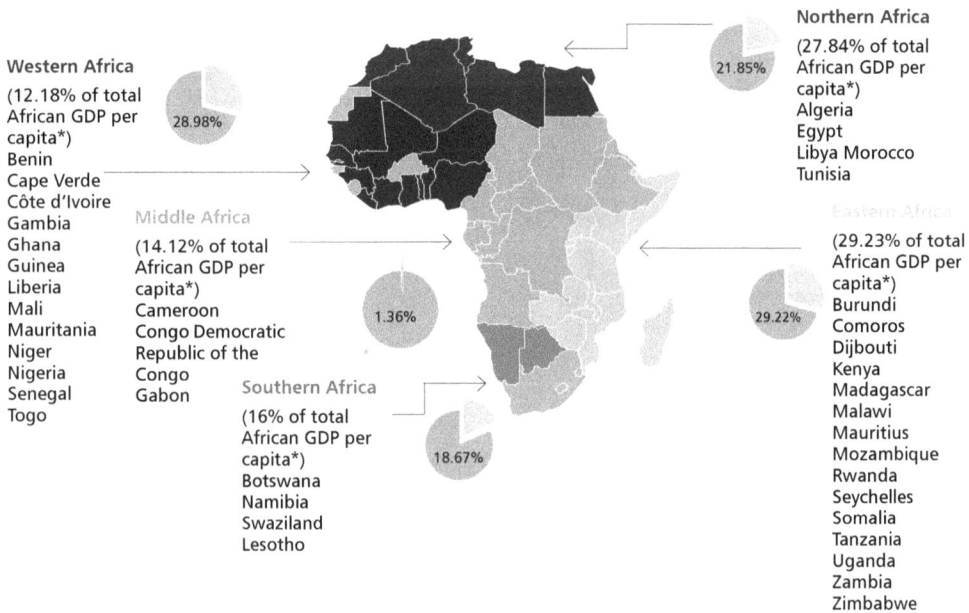

Western Africa
(12.18% of total African GDP per capita*)
Benin
Cape Verde
Côte d'Ivoire
Gambia
Ghana
Guinea
Liberia
Mali
Mauritania
Niger
Nigeria
Senegal
Togo

28.98%

Middle Africa
(14.12% of total African GDP per capita*)
Cameroon
Congo Democratic Republic of the Congo
Gabon

1.36%

Northern Africa
(27.84% of total African GDP per capita*)
Algeria
Egypt
Libya Morocco
Tunisia

21.85%

Eastern Africa
(29.23% of total African GDP per capita*)
Burundi
Comoros
Djibouti
Kenya
Madagascar
Malawi
Mauritius
Mozambique
Rwanda
Seychelles
Somalia
Tanzania
Uganda
Zambia
Zimbabwe

29.22%

Southern Africa
(16% of total African GDP per capita*)
Botswana
Namibia
Swaziland
Lesotho

18.67%

Source: GDP per capita data from World Bank (2011).

Southern Africa still holds around 18% of the export opportunities, while Middle Africa is still in the last place with only 1.36% of the total potential export value of the export opportunities identified for South Africa that fall in this region.

When one compares each region's share in the total African[3] GDP per capita to it's share in the total potential value of the export opportunities identified, as indicated in Figure 7.3, these percentages correlate well in Northern Africa, Eastern Africa and Southern Africa. Although Western Africa's 12,81% share in total African GDP per capita is considerably less than it's share in total African potential export value (28.89%), it holds 28.55% of total African GDP, which correlates well with the share in total potential export value. The same applies for Middle Africa that holds a 5.74% share of the total African GDP, and correlating better to its share in the total potential export value (1.36%).

Figure 7.4 provides an illustration of South Africa's actual exports to the product-country combinations identified as export opportunities in each region. This analysis will shed some light on the degree to which South Africa is utilising its export potential in each region.

3   This excludes South Africa and the countries in which no export opportunities were identified.

Figure 7.4. Regional distribution of South Africa's actual exports to Africa.

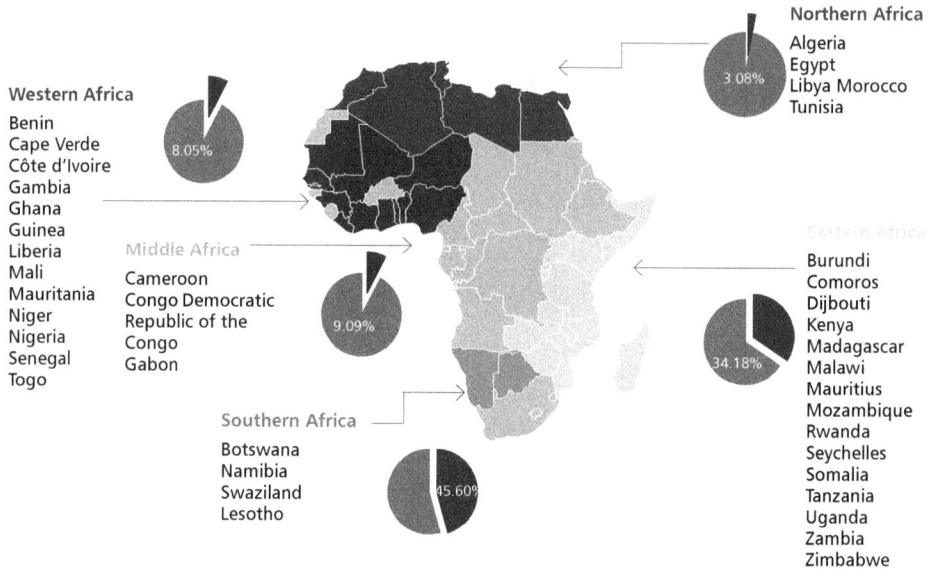

Northern Africa

Algeria
Egypt
Libya Morocco
Tunisia

3.08%

Western Africa

Benin
Cape Verde
Côte d'Ivoire
Gambia
Ghana
Guinea
Liberia
Mali
Mauritania
Niger
Nigeria
Senegal
Togo

8.05%

Middle Africa

Cameroon
Congo Democratic
Republic of the
Congo
Gabon

9.09%

Eastern Africa

Burundi
Comoros
Djibouti
Kenya
Madagascar
Malawi
Mauritius
Mozambique
Rwanda
Seychelles
Somalia
Tanzania
Uganda
Zambia
Zimbabwe

34.18%

Southern Africa

Botswana
Namibia
Swaziland
Lesotho

45.60%

From Figure 7.3 and 7.4 it can be noted that South Africa is on the right track in exporting to Eastern, Southern and Middle Africa, but might be missing many export opportunities in Western and Northern Africa. To elucidate this situation, Figure 7.5 illustrates the differences between the potential and actual exports of the export opportunities identified in each of the African regions.

Figure 7.5. Potential export value realised in actual export values per African region (US$ thousand).

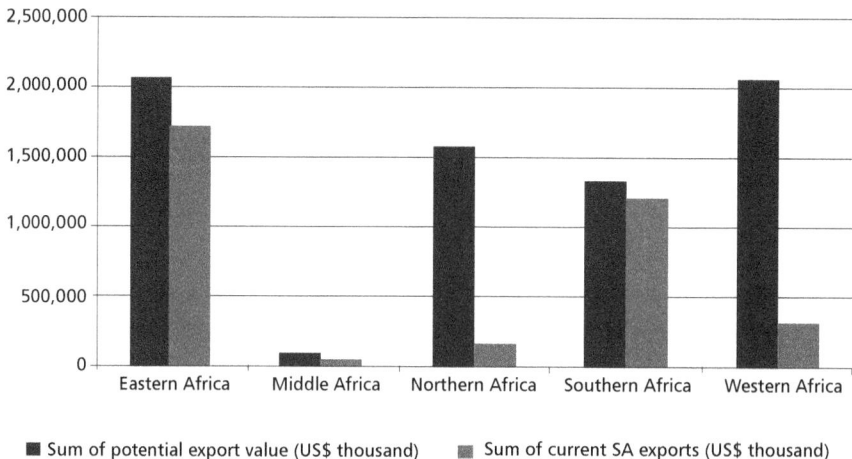

■ Sum of potential export value (US$ thousand)   ■ Sum of current SA exports (US$ thousand)

Figure 7.5 confirms that South Africa is utilising its export potential to a large extent in Eastern, Southern and Middle Africa, but falls short in Northern and Western Africa.

In order to be more specific, the specific countries with the highest export potential for South Africa in the rest of the African continent will be determined in section 7.3.2.

7.3.2 Country-level results of the Africa DSM

The top 20 African countries in terms of total potential export value are provided in Table 7.3. The African countries with the highest potential export values for South Africa are situated in Western Africa, Eastern Africa and Northern Africa. Nigeria presents the highest potential export value for South Africa, but South Africa only tapped into 13.35% of this country's potential.

Table 7.3. Top 20 African countries based on total export potential values.

Ranking	Country	Potential export value (2007)[4] (US$ thousand)	Current export value (2007) (US$ thousand)	% of the total potential export value realised in actual exports[5]
1	Nigeria	1,213,631	162,028	13.35%
2	Namibia	1,019,333	924,307	90.68%
3	Ghana	631,990	127,986	20.25%
4	Egypt	573,624	19,200	3.35%
5	Morocco	544,189	134,985	24.80%
6	Zambia	523,376	504,549	96.40%
7	Kenya	342,553	241,339	70.45%
8	Tunisia	333,054	7,790	2.34%
9	Zimbabwe[6]	253,928	232,902	91.72%
10	Mauritius	230,736	165,817	71.86%
11	Botswana	230,272	198,877	86.37%
12	Mozambique	195,143	171,385	87.83%
13	Uganda	158,208	86,775	54.85%
14	Tanzania	114,348	94,153	82.34%
15	Malawi	105,616	98,218	93.00%
16	Madagascar	99,606	73,906	74.20%
17	Côte d'Ivoire	86,544	9,009	10.41%

Ranking	Country	Potential export value (2007)[4] (US$ thousand)	Current export value (2007) (US$ thousand)	% of the total potential export value realised in actual exports[5]
18	Swaziland	78,868	77,064	97.71%
19	Senegal	70,341	8,269	11.76%
20	Algeria	67,017	233	0.35%

Countries in which South Africa has, to a relatively large degree, tapped into the export potential include Namibia, Zambia, Zimbabwe, Botswana, Mozambique, Tanzania, Malawi and Swaziland which are all SADC countries. Countries that hold high potential for exporters, that are not adequately utilised by South Africa, are Tunisia (2.45%), Egypt (3.35%), Côte d'Ivoire (10.41%), Senegal (11.76%), Nigeria (13.35%), Ghana (20.25%) and Morocco (24.80%).

In section 7.3.3 a sector-level analysis (HS 2 digit) of the results follows.

7.3.3 Sector-level (HS 2-digit level) results of the Africa DSM

This section will report in more detail on the sector-level (HS 2-digit level) results of the DSM applied to identify export opportunities for South Africa in the rest of the African continent. Firstly, to gain an overview of the different types of product groups identified as export opportunities in Africa, a comparison of the potential export values for each product category is provided in Figure 7.6.

The product groups with the highest export potential for South Africa in the rest of the African continent include mineral products, metals and transportation. Chemicals and allied industries also hold high export potential for South Africa in Africa.

Table 7.4 presents the percentages of the potential export values for the different product categories realised in actual exports. These percentages should be interpreted together with the relative size of the export potential in each product category as illustrated in Figure 7.7.

---

4   The most recent trade data in the database obtained from the International Trade Centre are for 2007.

5   This ratio is the sum of the actual exports of only the products for which realistic export opportunities was identified divided by the potential export value thereof per country.

6   The export opportunities identified in Zimbabwe should be interpreted bearing the current political and economic instability in Zimbabwe in mind.

Figure 7.6. Comparison of potential export values per product group in Africa (HS 2-digit level) (US$ thousand).

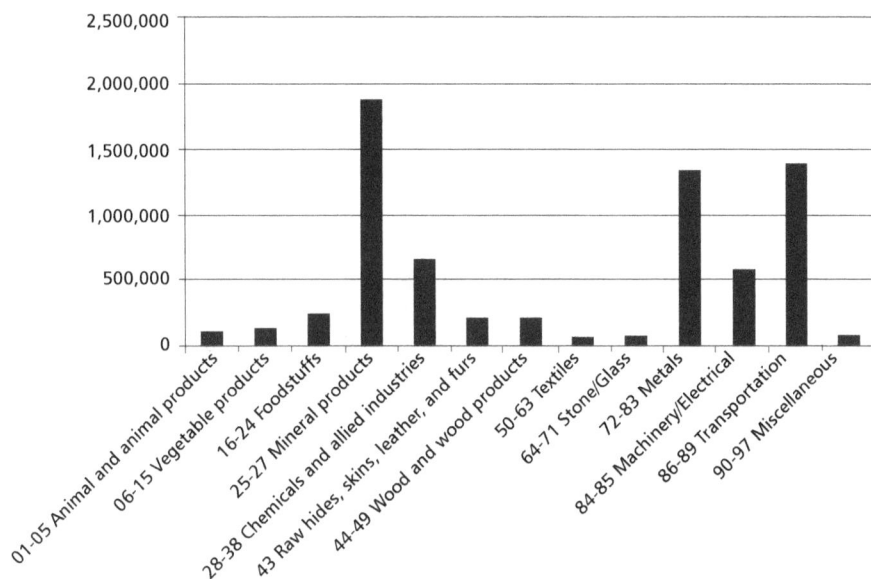

Table 7.4. Potential export value realised in actual export values for export opportunities identified per HS 2-digit product group in Africa.

	Potential export value (US$ thousand)	Actual SA export value (US$ thousand)	% of the total potential export value realised in actual exports
01 – 05 Animal and animal products	127,657	33,191	26.00%
06 – 15 Vegetable products	134,132	96,612	72.03%
16 – 24 Foodstuffs	247,491	174,843	70.65%
25 – 27 Mineral products	1,908,724	719,517	37.70%
28 – 38 Chemicals and allied industries	665,812	428,658	64.38%
41 – 43 Raw hides, skins, leather and furs	213,906	112,598	52.64%
44 – 49 Wood and wood products	236,105	113,377	48.02%
50 – 63 Textiles	57,499	26,441	45.99%
64 – 71 Stone/Glass	81,280	27,571	33.92%
72 – 83 Metals	1,344,067	722,214	53.73%
84 – 85 Machinery/Electrical	585,196	300,264	51.31%
86 – 89 Transportation	1,397,269	591,355	42.32%
90 – 97 Miscellaneous	115,223	69,253	60.10%
Total	**7,114,361**	**3,415,894**	**48.01%**

Figure 7.7. Potential export value realised in actual export values per product group in Africa (US$ thousand).

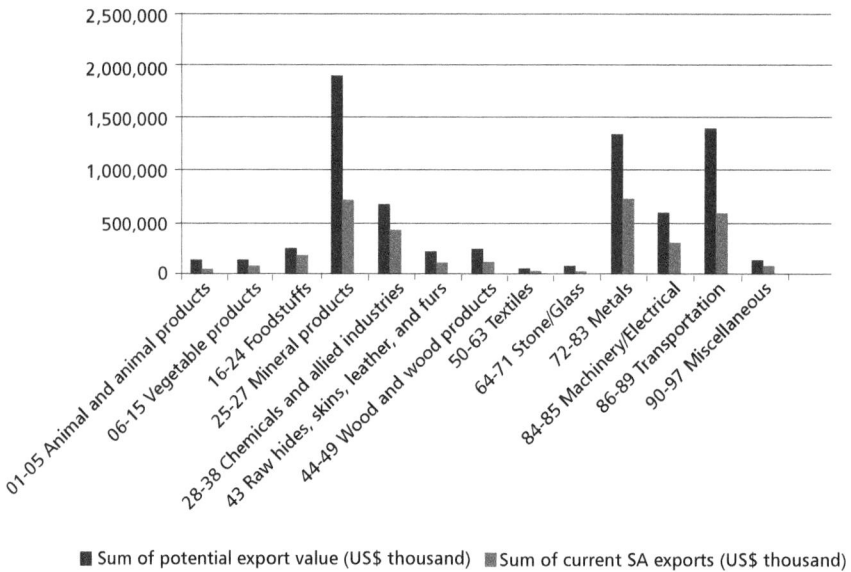

■ Sum of potential export value (US$ thousand) ■ Sum of current SA exports (US$ thousand)

From Table 7.4 and Figure 7.7 it is clear that the sectors with the highest export potential and the biggest shortfalls in actual exports versus potential export values are mineral products, transportation products and metals. The export promotion of these product groups in African countries can therefore be regarded as first priorities on which the South African export promotion organisations should focus their export promotion activities.

In order to combine the regional (section 7.3.1) and sector-level results (section 7.3.3), the product groups with the most potential in each African region have been identified in Figure 7.8.

Mineral products to Western Africa far outweigh the other export opportunities for South Africa in the rest of the African continent. Metals to Eastern Africa, transportation products to Western Africa, mineral products and metals to Northern Africa, mineral and transportation products to southern Africa as well as chemicals and allied industries to Eastern Africa also hold relatively large export potential for South Africa.

Following on the sector-level analysis of the results of the African DSM, the specific HS 6-digit level products with the highest export potential for South Africa in the rest of the African continent will be discussed in section 7.3.4.

Figure 7.8. Potential export values of the different product groups per African region (US$ thousand).

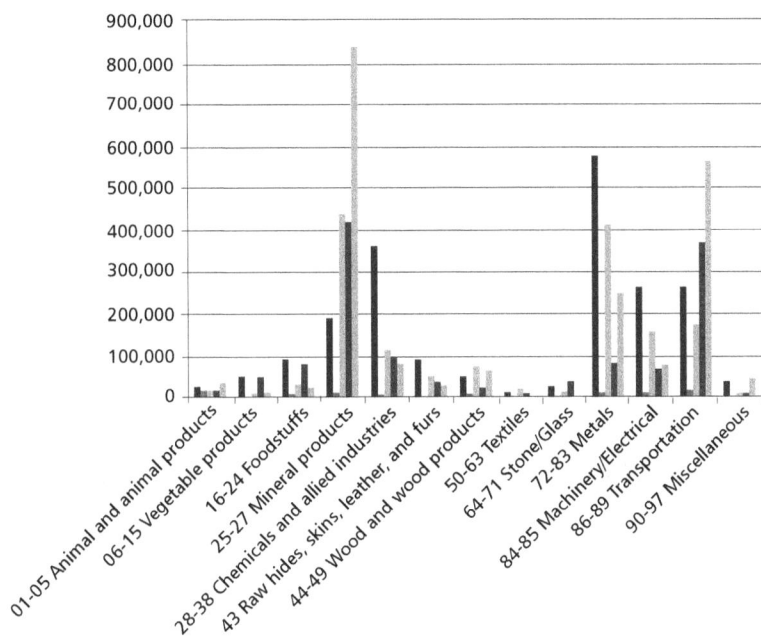

7.3.4   Product and product-country level results of the Africa DSM

The top 50 HS 6-digit products in Africa that hold the highest export potential values for South Africa are provided in Table 7.5.

Table 7.5. Top 50 products with the highest export potential for South Africa in Africa.

Rank	Product category	Potential export value (US$ thousand)	Actual SA export value (US$ thousand)	% of potential value realised
1	271011 – Aviation spirit	1,249,734	426,635	34.14%
2	870323 – Automobiles, spark ignition engines of 1500-3000 cc	827,972	248,884	30.06%
3	870421 – Diesel powered trucks weighing less than 5 tons	237,282	183,876	77.49%
4	270119 – Coal except anthracite or bituminous, not agglomerate	223,845	197,650	88.30%

Rank	Product category	Potential export value (US$ thousand)	Actual SA export value (US$ thousand)	% of potential value realised
5	720839 – Flat-rolled products/coils of iron/non-alloy steel of a thickness less than 3 mm	220,096	141,362	64.23%
6	260112 – Iron ores and concentrates, excluding iron pyrites, agglomerated	177,938	0	0.00%
7	720719 – Semi-finished products of iron/non-alloy steel, containing by weight less than 0.25% of carbon, n.e.s.	113,974	7,162	6.28%
8	250300 – Sulphur of all kinds	109,700	21,810	19.88%
9	870322 – Automobiles, spark ignition engines of 1000-1500 cc	105,051	2,546	2.42%
10	870410 – Dump trucks designed for off-highway use	100,867	82,396	81.69%
11	730890 – Structures and parts of structures of iron or steel, n.e.s.	95,682	84,078	87.87%
12	730410 – Line pipe of iron or steel used for oil or gas pipelines	93,479	276	0.30%
13	310520 – Nitrogen-phosphorus-potassium fertilizers, pack >10 kg	73,761	50,894	69.00%
14	847490 – Parts of machinery for mineral sorting, screening, mixing, etc.	72,679	54,444	74.91%
15	390210 – Polypropylene in primary forms	72,642	41,858	57.62%
16	401120 – Pneumatic tyres new of rubber for buses or lorries	66,375	32,223	48.55%
17	030374 – Mackerel, frozen, whole	61,039	945	1.55%
18	721391 – Bars and rods of circular cross-section, less than 14 mm in diameter	60,623	21,286	35.11%
19	760110 – Aluminium unwrought, not alloyed	54,312	51,371	94.58%
20	720918 – Flat-rolled products of iron /non-alloy steel, in coils, less than 0.5 mm thick	53,742	15,093	28.08%
21	841381 – Pumps n.e.s.	53,301	27,069	50.79%
22	730690 – Tube/pipe/hollow profile of iron/steel, n.e.s.	47,373	35,687	75.33%
23	721049 – Flat-rolled products of iron or non-alloy steel, coated with zinc, of a width of 600 mm or more, other than corrugated	45,696	27,197	59.52%
24	710231 – Diamonds (jewellery) unworked or simply sawn, cleaved	43,386	6,714	15.48%
25	360200 – Prepared explosives, except propellant powders	42,115	37,091	88.07%
26	847420 – Machines to crush or grind stone, ores and minerals	41,813	20,022	47.88%

Rank	Product category	Potential export value (US$ thousand)	Actual SA export value (US$ thousand)	% of potential value realised
27	721633 – Angles, shapes and sections of iron/ non-alloy steel, H-sections, hot-rolled/ hot-drawn/ extruded of a height of 80 mm or more	39,979	12,281	30.72%
28	852510 – Transmission apparatus for radio, telephone and TV	39,570	2,295	5.80%
29	280700 – Sulphuric acid, oleum	38,356	27,133	70.74%
30	902830 – Electricity supply, production and calibrating meters	37,466	24,462	65.29%
31	380830 – Herbicides, sprouting and growth regulators	37,187	16,041	43.14%
32	730820 – Towers and lattice masts of iron or steel	35,478	32,961	92.91%
33	721310 – Bars and rods of iron or non-alloy steel, hot-rolled in irregular wound coils	35,403	31,779	89.76%
34	030379 – Fish n.e.s., frozen, whole	32,842	12,329	37.54%
35	310590 – Fertilizers, mixes, n.e.s.	32,291	29,248	90.58%
36	940600 – Prefabricated buildings	32,120	21,010	65.41%
37	310230 – Ammonium nitrate, including solution, in pack >10 kg	30,249	9,031	29.86%
38	491199 – Printed matter, n.e.s.	29,810	16,662	55.89%
39	480256 – Paper and paperboard, not cont, fibres obt by a mech/chemi-mech process	29,369	26,779	91.18%
40	854460 – Electric conductors for over 1,000 volts, n.e.s.	29,122	13,641	46.84%
41	760511 – Wire, aluminium, not alloyed, of which the cross-sectional dimension > 7 mm	28,922	1,236	4.27%
42	170199 – Refined sugar, in solid form, n.e.s., pure sucrose	28,771	27,665	96.16%
43	260700 – Lead ores and concentrates	28,765	0	0.00%
44	310240 – Ammonium nitrate limestone, etc mixes, pack >10 kg	27,780	27,780	100.00%
45	480421 – Sack kraft paper, unbleached, uncoated	26,476	1,738	6.56%
46	300680 – Waste pharmaceuticals	24,025	20,110	83.70%
47	220421 – Grape wines n.e.s., fortified wine or must, pack < 2l	23,943	21,413	89.43%
48	720852 – Flat-rolled products of iron/on-alloy steel, in coils, less than 4.75 mm thick	22,971	19,138	83.31%
49	721190 – Flat-rolled iron or non-alloy steel of a width less than 600 mm, not clad/ plated/coated, n.e.s.	22,945	22,688	98.88%
50	240120 – Tobacco, unmanufactured, stemmed or stripped	22,717	5,174	22.78%

These products are diverse, but those with the highest potential export values include mineral products (e.g. aviation spirit, coal, iron ores, sulphur), transportation products (e.g. 1000-3000 cc automobiles, diesel trucks weighing less than five tons and dump trucks for off-highway use) and metals (e.g. flat-rolled products of iron/non-alloy steel of different thicknesses, semi-finished products of iron/non-alloy steel, iron or steel structures and parts of structures, line pipe used for oil/gas pipelines of iron or steel).

South Africa has tapped into the potential to a relatively large extent in the following products: ammonium nitrate limestone mixes, flat-rolled iron/non-alloy steel, refined sugar, aluminium, iron or steel towers and lattice masts, paper and paperboard, fertilizers, hot rolled bars, grape fines, coal, prepared explosives, structures and pars of structures of iron or steel, waste pharmaceuticals, dump trucks for off-highway use, diesel powered trucks weighing less than 5 tons and tube, pipe and hollow profile of iron or steel.

However, for the following products South Africa has not adequately tapped into the export potential in the identified markets[7]: lead ores, iron ore, line pipe used for oil/gas pipelines of iron or steel, frozen mackerel, 1000-1500 cc automobiles, aluminium wire, transmission apparatus for radio, telephone and television, semi-finished products of iron or non-alloy steel, sack kraft paper, unworked diamonds, sulphur and tobacco.

The 50 product-country combinations with the highest export potential for South Africa in the rest of the African continent are provided in Table 7.6.

Table 7.6. Top 50 product-country combinations in Africa.

Country	HS 6-digit product code and description	Filter 4 Cell classifi-cation[8]	Potential export value (US$ thousand)	Actual SA Exports (US$ thousand)
Nigeria	271011 – Aviation spirit	2	781,698	63,025
Namibia	271011 – Aviation spirit	17	391,642	350,000
Ghana	870323 – Automobiles, spark ignition engine of 1500-3000 cc	7	317,623	486
Namibia	870323 – Automobiles, spark ignition engine of 1500-3000 cc	17	249,881	223,563
Egypt	260112 – Iron ores and concentrates, excluding iron pyrites, agglomerated	4	164,777	0
Nigeria	870323 – Automobiles, spark ignition engine of 1500-3000 cc	17	153,468	13,589
Morocco	270119 – Coal except anthracite or bituminous, not agglomerate	20	128,331	102,147

Country	HS 6-digit product code and description	Filter 4 Cell classifi-cation[8]	Potential export value (US$ thousand)	Actual SA Exports (US$ thousand)
Tunisia	720719 – Semi-finished products of iron/non-alloy steel, containing by weight less than 0.25% of carbon, n.e.s.	5	106,802	0
Kenya	720839 – Flat-rolled products/coils of iron/non-alloy steel of a thickness< 3 mm	17	79,686	79,686
Egypt	870322 – Automobiles, spark ignition engine of 1000-1500 cc	2	66,427	1,925
Morocco	720839 – Flat-rolled products/coils of iron/non-alloy steel of a thickness < 3 mm	2	59,468	0
Zimbabwe	870421 – Diesel powered trucks weighing less than 5 tons	2	56,106	47,102
Morocco	250300 – Sulphur of all kinds	5	56,052	0
Mauritius	270119 – Coal except anthracite or bituminous, not agglomerate	17	51,473	51,473
Nigeria	720918 – Flat-rolled products of iron /non-alloy steel, in coils, < 0.5 mm thick	18	48,086	10,486
Zambia	730890 – Structures and parts of structures of iron or steel, n.e.s.	17	44,599	44,599
Nigeria	730410 – Line pipe of iron or steel used for oil or gas pipelines	5	41,057	0
Zambia	870410 – Dump trucks designed for off-highway use	17	39,458	39,458
Tanzania	720839 – Flat-rolled products/coils of iron/non-alloy steel of a thickness < 3 mm	17	38,548	31,755
Ghana	870421 – Diesel powered trucks weighing less than 5 tons	17	36,876	36,876
Zambia	847490 – Parts of machinery for mineral sorting, screening, mixing, etc	17	35,205	35,205
Kenya	870421 – Diesel powered trucks weighing less than 5 tons	7	35,054	18,093
Uganda	271011 – Aviation spirit	2	35,032	3,243
Botswana	870410 – Dump trucks designed for off-highway use	17	33,373	33,373
Botswana	710231 – Diamonds (jewellery) unworked or simply sawn, cleaved	7	32,572	5,513

7   These products are successfully exported by South Africa (RCA >1), but are not exported to the markets in Africa with high export potential for South Africa.

8   See Table 4.6 for the meaning of the different cell classifications.

Country	HS 6-digit product code and description	Filter 4 Cell classifi-cation[8]	Potential export value (US$ thousand)	Actual SA Exports (US$ thousand)
Ghana	760110 – Aluminium unwrought, not alloyed	17	31,374	31,374
Tunisia	250300 – Sulphur of all kinds	1	30,166	0
Namibia	870421 – Diesel powered trucks weighing less than 5 tons	7	29,203	25,562
Tunisia	870323 – Automobiles, spark ignition engine of 1500-3000 cc	2	29,111	0
Uganda	870421 – Diesel powered trucks weighing less than 5 tons	2	28,994	15,507
Uganda	720839 – Flat-rolled products/coils of iron/non-alloy steel of a thickness < 3 mm	17	28,974	28,648
Morocco	260700 – Lead ores and concentrates	2	28,765	0
Zambia	280700 – Sulphuric acid, oleum	16	27,771	25,638
Senegal	721391 – Bars and rods of circular cross-section, less than 14 mm in diameter	12	27,132	858
Zimbabwe	310520 – Nitrogen-phosphorus-potassium fertilizers, pack >10 kg	17	27,008	23,814
Morocco	870322 – Automobiles, spark ignition engine of 1000-1500 cc	12	26,716	621
Mozambique	270119 – Coal except anthracite or bituminous, not agglomerate	17	26,031	26,031
Zambia	310590 – Fertilizers, mixes, n.e.s.	20	26,027	23,606
Algeria	730410 – Line pipe of iron or steel used for oil or gas pipelines	5	24,976	58
Ghana	852510 – Transmission apparatus for radio, telephone and TV	10	24,870	228
Zambia	300680 – Waste pharmaceuticals	16	24,025	20,110
Nigeria	401120 – Pneumatic tyres new of rubber for buses or lorries	7	22,861	294
Egypt	721633 – Angles, shapes and sections of iron/non-alloy steel, H-sections, hot-rolled/hot-drawn/extruded of a height of 80 mm or more	2	22,804	0
Malawi	310520 – Nitrogen-phosphorus-potassium fertilizers, pack >10 kg	7	22,722	22,722
Morocco	721190 – Flat-rolled iron or non-alloy steel of a width less than 600 mm, not clad/plated/coated, n.e.s.	17	22,253	22,253
Kenya	760110 – Aluminium unwrought, not alloyed	2	22,093	19,152
Zambia	250300 – Sulphur of all kinds	20	21,810	21,810

Country	HS 6-digit product code and description	Filter 4 Cell classification[8]	Potential export value (US$ thousand)	Actual SA Exports (US$ thousand)
Kenya	721310 – Bars and rods of iron or non-alloy steel, hot-rolled in irregular coils	17	21,351	21,351
Egypt	390210 – Polypropylene in primary forms	2	20,767	0
Côte d'Ivoire	870323 – Automobiles, spark ignition engine of 1500-3000 cc	7	20,619	2

The countries in which the top 50 export opportunities for South Africa are located include, in order of highest to lowest total export potential value, Nigeria, Namibia, Ghana, Morocco, Egypt, Zambia, Tunisia, Kenya, Uganda, Zimbabwe, Botswana, Mauritius, Tanzania, Senegal, Mozambique, Algeria, Malawi and Côte d'Ivoire.

The products with the highest potential export values in the top 50 product-country combinations for South Africa in Africa are mineral products (aviation spirit, iron ore, sulphur and coal) and transportation products (1500-3000 cc automobile engines and diesel powered trucks weighing less than 5 tons).

Amongst the product-country combinations with the highest potential for South Africa in the rest of the African continent, there are product-country combinations to which South Africa has not exported at all. It means that South Africa is not tapping the export potential of these markets even though the demand is sizable and/or growing, the competition is not too fierce, barriers to trade are not too high, South Africa is specialised in producing and exporting the product and the potential export value is high. Examples of such product-country combinations include iron ore to Egypt, semi-finished iron or non-alloy steel products to Tunisia, flat-rolled products of iron/non-alloy steel in coils less than 3 mm thick to Morocco, sulphur to Morocco and Tunisia, pipe line of iron or steel for oil or gas pipelines to Nigeria, 1500-3000 cc automobiles to Tunisia, lead ores to Morocco, polypropylene to Egypt and H sections angles, shapes and sections of iron/non-alloy steel of a height of 80 mm or more to Egypt. It is interesting to note that most of these opportunities are in Northern Africa.

On the other hand, there are product-country combinations to which South Africa has utilised the export potential to a relatively large degree. These product-country combinations include flat-rolled products of iron/non-alloy steel in coils less than 3 mm thick and hot-rolled bars and rods of iron/non-alloy steel to Kenya, coal to Mauritius and Mozambique, structures and parts of structures of iron and steel, parts for mineral sorting, screening and mixing machinery, sulphur, sulphuric acid and fertilizers to Zambia, dump trucks for off-highway use to Botswana and Zambia and diesel powered trucks weighing less than 5 tons and aluminium to Ghana. It is interesting to note that most of these opportunities are situated in Eastern Africa.

If the export promotion organisations (EPOs) want to focus their export promotion efforts and their resources, they can do so by focusing on prioritised product-country combinations. In order to determine on which product-country combinations the focus should be, it is necessary to determine the so-called "low hanging fruits" for export promotion organisations. In section 7.3.5 recommendations for focused export promotion into Africa is discussed.

7.3.5 Focused export promotion by export promotion organisations into Africa

Cuyvers *et al.* (1995:183) and Cuyvers (1997:14-15; 2004:270) recommend that when resources are limited, export promotion agencies should not actively promote export opportunities in Cells 1 to 10, where South Africa's market share is small, but rather focus on expanding markets in Cells 11 to 15. Furthermore, resources should not be used to actively promote exports to markets in Cells 16 to 20, where South Africa already has a large market share and exporters are familiar with their markets. These markets should rather be maintained by the exporters themselves.

In total, there are 71 export opportunities identified in Cells 11 to 15 for South Africa in the rest of the African continent. In Table 7.7 the top 50 product-country combinations selected in Africa, which are categorised in Cells 11 to 15, are provided.

The top 50 export opportunities in Cells 11 to 15 with the highest export potential values are situated in Northern Africa (Egypt and Morocco), Eastern Africa (Kenya, Zambia and Tanzania) and Western Africa (Senegal and Ghana).

Table 7.7. Top 50 African product-country combinations in Cells 11 to 15.

Country	HS 6-digit product code and description	Filter 4 Cell classifi-cation	Potential export value (US$ thousand) (2007)	Actual SA export value (US$ thousand) (2007)
Senegal	721391 – Bars and rods of circular cross-section, less than 14 mm in diameter	12	27,132	858
Morocco	870322 – Automobiles, spark ignition engine of 1000-1500 cc	12	26,716	621
Ghana	283711 – Cyanides and cyanide oxides of sodium	15	15,324	107
Egypt	480421 – Sack kraft paper, unbleached, uncoated	11	15,061	248

Country	HS 6-digit product code and description	Filter 4 Cell classification	Potential export value (US$ thousand) (2007)	Actual SA export value (US$ thousand) (2007)
Zambia	360200 – Prepared explosives, except propellant powders	15	14,463	13,977
Tanzania	730820 – Towers and lattice masts of iron or steel	12	12,959	12,959
Egypt	320710 – Pigment, opacifier, colours, etc for ceramics or glass	15	10,005	18
Kenya	440310 – Poles, treated or painted with preservatives	15	9,490	5,208
Egypt	480255 – Paper and paperboard	12	9,197	544
Nigeria	480419 – Paper, kraft liner, other than unbleached, uncoated	12	5,492	96
Kenya	842919 – Bulldozers and angledozers, wheeled	15	3,178	290
Madagascar	310520 – Nitrogen-phosphorus-potassium fertilizers, pack >10 kg	12	3,068	1,385
Uganda	852510 – Transmission apparatus for radio, telephone and TV	12	2,955	492
Ghana	940180 – Seats n.e.s	12	2,506	92
Egypt	843629 – Poultry-keeping machinery, other than poultry incubators and brooders	12	2,476	13
Morocco	300230 – Vaccines, veterinary use	12	2,235	75
Tunisia	842123 – Oil/petrol filters for internal combustion engines	12	2,150	59
Morocco	580890 – Ornamental trimmings in the piece	15	2,033	266
Tunisia	380830 – Herbicides, sprouting and growth regulators	12	1,930	257
Uganda	850433 – Electrical transformers having a power capacity of 16-500 kVA	12	1,679	251
Ghana	842123 – Oil/petrol filters for internal combustion engines	12	1,531	82
Botswana	630629 – Tents, of textile material n.e.s	12	1,529	1,529
Tanzania	730690 – Tube/pipe/hollow profile of iron/steel, n.e.s	12	1,186	618
Ghana	842131 – Intake air filters for internal combustion engines	12	1,123	91
Egypt	380400 – Residual lyes from the manufacture of wood pulp	12	1,083	314
Tunisia	291612 – Acrylic acid esters	12	1,058	217

Country	HS 6-digit product code and description	Filter 4 Cell classifi- cation	Potential export value (US$ thousand) (2007)	Actual SA export value (US$ thousand) (2007)
Egypt	843050 – Construction equipment, self-propelled n.e.s	12	1,052	20
Kenya	847490 – Parts of machinery for mineral sorting, screening, mixing, etc	12	913	508
Kenya	271290 – Mineral waxes n.e.s	12	897	662
Mauritius	842959 – Earth moving/road making equipment, self-propelled ne	12	889	200
Egypt	731582 – Chain, welded link, iron or steel	12	880	13
Tunisia	848420 – Mechanical seals	12	780	12
Gabon	842131 – Intake air filters for internal combustion engines	12	665	12
Ghana	401019 – Conveyor belts n.e.s	12	603	80
Mauritius	390210 – Polypropylene in primary forms	12	540	88
Mozambique	630510 – Sacks and bags of jute or other bast fibres, used for packing of goods	12	525	56
Madagascar	860900 – Cargo containers designed for carriage	12	519	519
Zimbabwe	842139 – Filtering or purifying machinery for gases n.e.s	12	519	430
Tanzania	680223 – Cut or sawn slabs of granite	12	471	471
Mauritius	283319 – Sodium sulphates other than disodium sulphate	12	448	7
Mauritius	030420 – Fish fillets, frozen	12	430	347
Morocco	220870 – Liqueurs and cordials	12	428	8
Mali	852510 – Transmission apparatus for radio, telephone and TV	12	413	58
Seychelles	730690 – Tube/pipe/hollow profile of iron/steel, n.e.s	12	351	101
Djibouti	842959 – Earth moving/road making equipment, self-propelled ne	12	332	152
Cameroon	220429 – Grape wines, alcoholic grape must n.e.s	12	314	34
Kenya	080610 – Grapes, fresh	12	314	314

The product categories in Cells 11 to 15 that hold the highest potential export value are chemical and allied industries (cyanides, prepared explosives and pigment or colour for ceramics or glass), metals (circular cross bars and rods and iron or steel towers and lattice masts), wood and wood products (unbleached, uncoated paper and sack kraft, poles treated or painted with preservatives and paper and paper board) and transportation products (1000-1500 cc automobiles).

The export promotion organisation could use focused export promotion strategies and instuments to assist exporters that can produce this "low hanging fruit".

7.4   Conclusions

The main aim of this chapter was to identify export opportunities for South African products in the rest of the African continent.

The Department of Trade and Industry (DTI), as the government export promotion organisation (EPO) in South Africa, can, as a starting point, focus on gathering information on and deriving export promotion strategies for the countries, products and product-country combinations identified as priority export opportunities. Thereafter, the results of the top regions, countries, products and product-country combinations contained in this chapter can be analysed and more priorities can be established. This information can be very helpful in supplying foreign offices and export councils with specific export opportunities in their countries and/or sectors. If information on the products produced in every province in South Africa is available, the results per province can also be extracted from the results lists to provide the provincial trade promotion organisations in South Africa with the specific product-country combinations with high export potential in the world and in Africa.

As a final recommendation and analogue to the conclusions of Chapter 5 (see Chapter 5.9) it is highlighted that it is unwise to rest all export promotion decisions upon the DSM results alone (Cuyvers *et al.*, 1995:174). It is important not to use the results of the DSM in isolation. The model uses quantitative information to provide a limited list of identified export opportunities, but qualitative information concerning each product-country combination should also be taken into consideration in the export promotion activities and instruments. This information might include specific diplomatic and political issues between the exporting and importing countries, consumer tastes, product adaptation needs, packaging, labelling and a wide range of other factors. Product and country-specific research should, therefore, compliment the DSM approach to deliver optimal results (see Chapter 11 for exporters' information requirements).

References

Cuyvers, L. 1997. Export opportunities of Thailand: a decision support model approach. *CAS discussion paper, no. 9*. [Online.] Available from: http://webhost.ua.ac.be/cas/PDF/CAS09.pdf. Accecssed 17 January 2008.

Cuyvers, L., De Pelsmacker, P., Rayp, G. & Roozen, I.T.M. 1995. A decision support model for the planning and assessment of export promotion activities by government export promotion institutions: the Belgian case. *International Journal of Research in Marketing*, 12(2): 173-186.

DTI. *see* South Africa. Department of Trade and Industry.

Edwards, L. & Stern, M. 2007. Trade and poverty in South Africa: lessons and policy recommendations. *Journal for Studies in Economics and Econometrics*, 31(2): 1-22.

Papadopoulos, N. & Denis, J.E. 1988. Inventory, taxonomy and assessment of methods for international market selection. *International Marketing Review*, 5(3): 38-51.

Shankarmahesh, M.N., Olsen, H.W. & Honeycutt, E.D. 2005. A dominant product-dominant country framework of industrial export segmentation. *Industrial Marketing Management*, 34(3): 203-210.

South Africa. Department of Trade and Industry. 2006. Draft export strategy 2006-2009: Trade and Investment South Africa, Export development and promotion. (Internal unpublished document.) 101 p.

South Africa. Department of Trade and Industry. 2010. A South African trade policy and strategy framework. [Online.] Available from: http://www.thedti.gov.za/trade_policy/TPSF.htm. Accessed 9 March 2011.

Steenkamp, E.A. 2011. The identification of export opportunities for South African products with special reference to Africa. Unpublished doctoral thesis. Potchefstroom, NWU.

United Nations. 2010. World macro regions. [Online.] Available from: http://www.un.org/depts/dj/maplib/worldregions.htm. Accessed 15 Sep. 2010.

Part III

Strategic use of the DSM methodology and results

Chapter 8

The assessment of public export activities using DSM results: the case of Belgium[1]

Ludo Cuyvers & Michel Dumont

8.1   Introduction

Gathering information with regard to foreign markets, establishing (and maintaining) social networks and intermediaries necessary to enter foreign markets and the skills required for internationalisation activities may be subject to market failure (see for example BIS (2011) for an overview). Firms may be hesitant to incur research and marketing expenditures if these may also benefit their competitors. These market failures offer the the main rationale for government involvement in export promotion. However, public funding of an export promotion organisation (EPO) should be supported by an assessment of the social costs and benefits of export promotion activities (Lederman, Olarreaga & Payton, 2006:2). It should, therefore, be kept in mind that an increase in export (shares) does not necessarily imply an increase in welfare. Posen (2006) warns for faddish export promotion, pointing out that a focus on export competitiveness could erode living standards and distract policymakers from a more beneficial focus on productivity. Czinkota (2002:130) argues that EPOs in many instances have become a good idea gone bad, with goals becoming blurred and efficiency being low, EPOs becoming "grazing grounds for retired officials" and "havens for job generation" and trade missions being "tools to reward political friends".

1   We are grateful to Liesbeth Van Mol and Louise Blontrock for part of the data collection and data processing, and to Jan van Doren (VOKA), Wilma Viviers (North-West University, South Africa) and Christophe Crombez (KULeuven) for comments on an earlier draft. An earlier and abriged version of this paper was published in *Review of Business and Economics*, 2008, 53(1): 69-92.

Nothwithstanding some of these considerations with regard to the efficiency of national EPOs, their number has tripled over the last two decades. A World Bank estimation, using data on 119 countries, suggests that for the median EPO, one dollar of export promotion increases exports by 300 US dollars. This substantial overall result however conceals heterogeneity across countries (e.g. an additional impact of 490 US dollars for every US dollar of export promotion in Latin America but an additional impact of "only" 190 US dollars in OECD countries) and types of export promotion instruments (e.g. on-shore export support services seem to be more beneficial than country image building, marketing or market research activities). Results also suggest that there are decreasing returns to scale. Czinkota (2002) also pointed out that among industrialised countries there does not appear to be a link between export promotion expenditures and export success.

Most studies on EPOs are based on surveys of exporters (e.g. Kedia & Chhokar, 1986; Seringhaus & Botschen, 1991; Gencturk & Kotabe, 2001). These studies generally are critical with respect to the usage and efficiency of EPOs but do acknowledge their usefulness for (exporting) SMEs. A potential problem with these surveys is a selection bias (see e.g. Lederman, Olarreaga & Payton, 2006:4). In this chapter, rather than using surveys to establish the perception of EPO activities by exporters, we study the concordance between the major tenets of the export promotion policies of the public export promotion organisations in Belgium, i.e. Export Vlaanderen[2], AWEX and Brussels Export, in the period 1999-2003, on the one hand, and the most promising export opportunities, on the other hand, as they were derived using the decision support model (DSM) for the years 2000-2003.

Section 8.2 discusses these identified export opportunities, and which among these can be listed as realistic opportunities, as derived using the DSM based on various statistical data (for more detail on the DSM methodology, see Chapter 4).

In the next section, the export promotion activities of the three mentioned organisations, in the period 1999-2003, are reviewed, as these appear from the respective programmes and effectively implemented activities.

The third section analyses to which degree the export promotion activities of the three public export promotion organisations in Belgium can be associated with the realistic export opportunities, as reviewed in the first section.

---

2   In 2005, Export Vlaanderen was transformed into Flanders Investment and Trade (FIT) by the incorporation in one public institution with the functions of export promotion and of attracting foreign investment (previously the responsibility of Dienst Investeren Vlaanderen).

8.2   Realistic export opportunities for Belgium

The development of an export promotion strategy or the analysis of the effectiveness of existing export promotion programmes has to rely on hard quantitative data on foreign markets. As organisations are operating with scarce resources, a subsequent selection of opportune markets and product groups (product-country combinations) has to be made. For this purpose, the study makes use of the normative model, or decision support model, that was developed earlier (see Cuyvers, De Pelsmacker, Rayp & Roozen, 1995; Cuyvers, 1996; Cuyvers, 2004, for methodological details, see Chapter 4). This model endeavours to make a selection of possible export markets which, specifically from the Belgian point of view, are potentially profitable, from the set of all possible product-country combinations. Using macro-economic data and international trade statistics, available in 2003, the results of the decision support model was updated, which lead to the results summarised in Table 8.1.

As the aim is to determine for the Belgian exporting companies, in whatever industrial sector they are active, which products in which foreign markets should be considered as realistic export opportunities, and for an assessment of the activities of the export promotion organisations how far they promoted the exploration of these realistic export opportunities, thus determined, the use of these data, seem to be warranted. The disadvantage is that such statistical data are, by definition, never updated up to the present. This is not so much of a problem if we want to use these data for assessing export promotion activities of the past. However, if the model is used for the planning of export promotion activities, it needs to be supplemented with more qualitative data (e.g. survey data) on the business experts' judgments and prospects. If such qualitative data are used for assessing export promotion activities of EPOs in the past, when prospective events and developments are fully realised, such data might say more about the experts' expectations and biases, than that these events and developments are taken into account. Of course, assessing past export promotion activities against the expectations of business experts, who should be considered as the main benificiaries of such activities, is worthwhile, but is beyond the scope of this paper.

See Chapter 4, Figure 4.2 for a summary of the DSM process, the criteria used, as well as the number of countries, product groups and product-country combinations involved, and Table 8.1 for the categorisation of the realistic export opportunities, thus detected according to import market characteristics and relative market importance of the product-country combinations for the exports of the Belgium-Luxemburg Economic Union (BLEU).

It can be seen that the 2000-2003 run of the DSM allowed the detection of 3,902 realistic export opportunities for the BLEU[3]. Because detailed international trade statistics for Flanders, Wallonia and Brussels are not available, it is impossible to assess per region (e.g. using the so-called revealed comparative advantage indices, see Balassa, 1965), whether a realistic export opportunity is more suited to the situation of Flanders, Wallonia and Brussels. It should be emphasised that the model deals with numbers of product-country combinations, which precludes any judgment or assessment based on the size of these opportunities (e.g. in terms of import value in Euro). Table 8.1 also indicates that for the 2000-2003 period, almost 45% of the realistic export opportunities are in markets where the relative BLEU market share is small. However, 33.7% of the opportunities can be situated in markets where the BLEU market share is intermediately large or large.

Table 8.1. Distribution of the realistic export opportunities 2000-2003 with respect to the relative BLEU market share and import market characteristics.

	Market share of BLEU relatively small	Market share of BLEU inter-mediately small	Market share of BLEU inter-mediately large	Market share of BLEU relatively large	Total
Large product market	0	0	0	0	0
Growing (long- and short-term) product market	1,467	502	296	154	2,419
Large product market, short-term growth	68	106	106	134	414
Large product market, long-term growth	79	64	99	102	344
Large product market, short- and long-term growth	126	176	192	231	725
Total	1,740	848	693	621	3,902

The distribution of the detected realistic export opportunities at the SITC 2-digit product group level can be consulted in Annex 8.1. The numbers correspond to the number of product-country combinations, which are finally considered as realistic export opportunities. Two product-country combinations belonging to the same 2-digit SITC product group can

---

3   These product-country combinations are at SITC 4-digit level. More recent runs of the DSM for Belgium, South Africa and Thailand are based on HS 6-digit import data (for more detail see Chapter 6).

either refer to the same country, but belonging to a different product category at the 4-digit SITC level, or to product-country combinations in two different countries.[4]

Figure 8.1. Results of the filtering sequence of the decision support model.

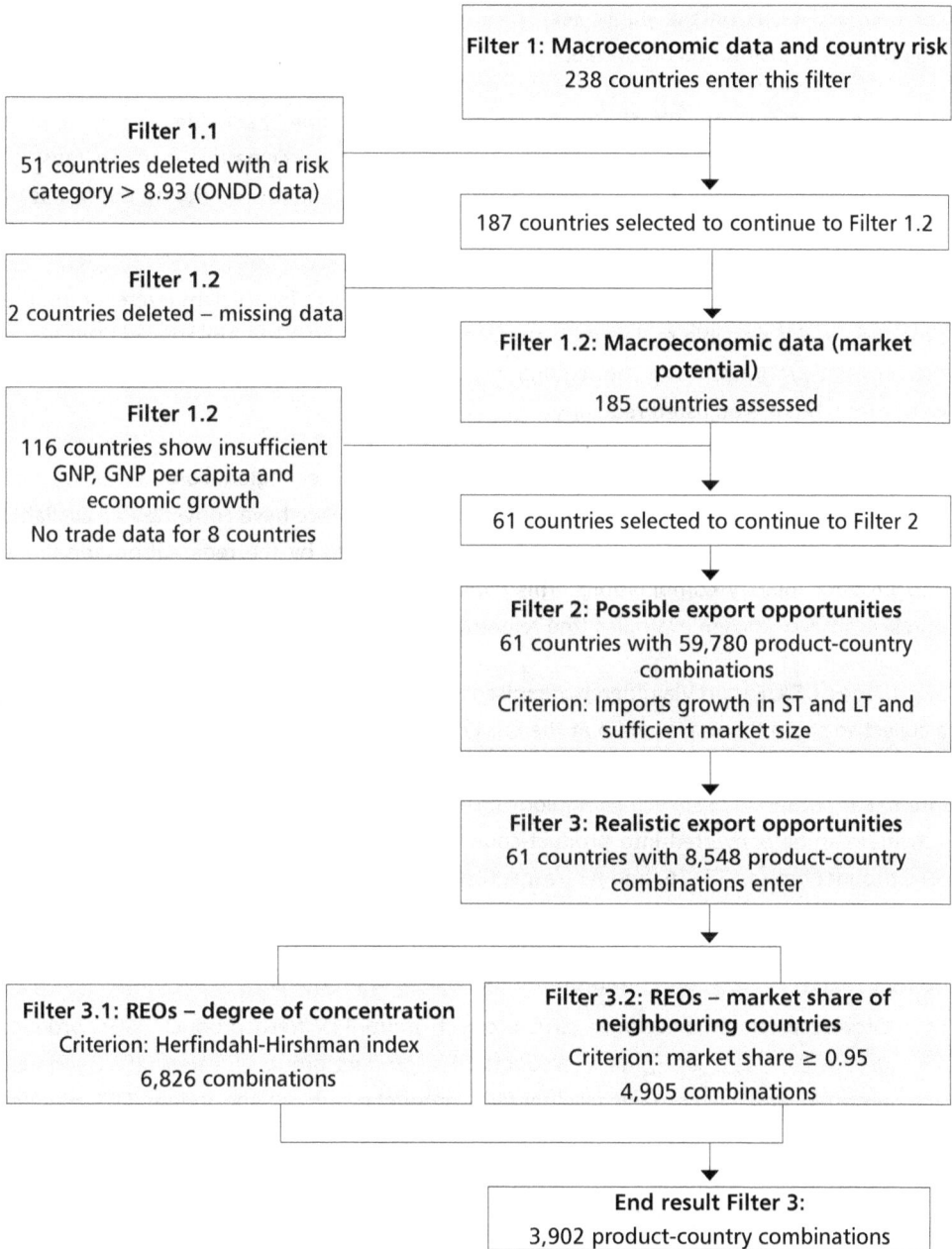

	Filter 1: Macroeconomic data and country risk 238 countries enter this filter
Filter 1.1 51 countries deleted with a risk category > 8.93 (ONDD data)	
	187 countries selected to continue to Filter 1.2
Filter 1.2 2 countries deleted – missing data	
	Filter 1.2: Macroeconomic data (market potential) 185 countries assessed
Filter 1.2 116 countries show insufficient GNP, GNP per capita and economic growth No trade data for 8 countries	
	61 countries selected to continue to Filter 2
	Filter 2: Possible export opportunities 61 countries with 59,780 product-country combinations Criterion: Imports growth in ST and LT and sufficient market size
	Filter 3: Realistic export opportunities 61 countries with 8,548 product-country combinations enter

Filter 3.1: REOs – degree of concentration Criterion: Herfindahl-Hirshman index 6,826 combinations	**Filter 3.2: REOs – market share of neighbouring countries** Criterion: market share ≥ 0.95 4,905 combinations

End result Filter 3: 3,902 product-country combinations

---

4   A list with the distribution of these opportunities over countries is available upon request from the authors.

8.3   The export promotion activities of the Belgian public export promotion organisations

In Belgium various organisations are active in the field of export promotion. This section, however, will focus on the public sector export promotion organisations, particularly the regional export promotion organisations, i.e. Export Vlaanderen[5], AWEX and Brussels Export.

These organisations annually prepare and publish a programme of activities relating among others to the organisation of trade missions abroad, of participation in trade fairs, of workshops and conferences, etc. The planned activities are announced during the course of the year (e.g. in the case of Export Vlaanderen through its weekly publication Exportbrief).

However, on occasion planned activities are abandoned due to insufficient interest from the exporters, and if possible replaced by alternative activities that are announced. Therefore, the activities programmes of the regional export promotion organisations are not a static instrument, but are adjusted regularly.

In order to compare the export promotion activities of the three regional organisations, with the detected realistic export opportunities of the DSM run, we have converted all available 1999-2003 information on the export promotion activities by the regional organisations into product-country combinations. This conversion can be illustrated by the following, purely arbitrarily chosen examples (the relevant SITC 2-digit codes are between brackets):

In Las Vegas, USA, Export Vlaanderen organised together with AWEX, its Walloon counterpart, a collective stand ("group stand") at the fair Comdex from 13 until 17 November 2000, for the exhibition of hardware and software products (SITC product groups 75 and 76) and for internet applications of speech technology (SITC product group 93). At the 2-digit level, the activities can be converted into product-country combinations relating to the USA and to SITC product groups 75, 76, and 93, respectively.

There was also participation in a fair in the Anaheim Convention Center (California) from 24 until 26 March 2000, in order to promote the following products:

(i)   Organic products: beverages (SITC product group 11), fresh products (SITC product groups 0, 1, 2, 3 en 5), dairy products (SITC product group 2), cereals (SITC product group 4), and even organic fertiliser (SITC product group 56) and fodder (SITC product group 8);

(ii)   Personal care: cosmetics (SITC product group 55), body and hair care (SITC product group 55) and soap (SITC product group 55);

---

5   After Export Vlaanderen became Flandes Investment and Trade (FIT) it also became responsible for inward FDI promotion in the Flemish region of Belgium.

(iii)   Food supplements: vitamins (SITC product group 54), minerals (SITC product group 54), herbs (SITC product group 9) en sportsmen food products (SITC product group 9);

(iv)   Herbs and medicinal products: aromatherapy (SITC product group 54), herb extracts (SITC product group 54) and essential oils (SITC product group 55);

(v)   Vegetarian and natural food products (SITC product group 9);

(vi)   Delicacies: soy products (SITC product group 5), tea (SITC product group 11), macrobiotic products (SITC product group 9), bakery products (SITC product group 9), flour (SITC product group 4), ready-made meals (SITC product group 9), rice products (SITC product group 9), sweets (SITC product group 6) and deserts (SITC product group 9); and

(vii)   Environmental products: household products (SITC product group 55), washing products (SITC product group 55), paper (SITC product group 64), clothes (SITC product group 84), books (SITC product group 64), magazines (SITC product group 64) and audiovisual products (SITC product group 76).

Export Vlaanderen also organised from 5 until 8 December 2000 a business trip for Flemish exporters from industrial sectors relating to equipment and investment goods (SITC product group 72, 74 and 77) to three German *Länder*: Hessen, Rheinland-Pfalz en Saarland. From 16 until 20 February 2000 Export Vlaanderen was present with a collective stand at the Berlin construction fair Bautec. This bi-annual fair is specialised in construction as such (SITC product group 81), but also in doors (SITC product group 89), windows (SITC product group 89), roll-down shutters (SITC product group 89) and gates (SITC product group 89), heating and ventilation systems (SITC product group 81), insulation (SITC product group 89), roof works (SITC product group 89), wall facing (SITC product group 89), electronic equipment (SITC product group 77), construction sites (SITC product group 53), construction chemistry (SITC product group 59), recycling of building material (SITC product group 93), specific software (SITC product group 76).

This study also convert international trade fair participation into product-country combinations, distinguishing between local, regional and international trade fairs, with due regard to the nationality of the visitors.[6] Only in case of local fairs, the conversion to product-country combinations is limited to the country at issue (e.g. Agrimaroc in Marocco, or Carrefour de Bois in France) and a "1" is assigned for the country and the relevant product group(s). For regional trade fairs (e.g. Bouwbeurs Utrecht, Netherlands) a "1" is

---

6   The best-known sources for nationality of exhibitors at trade fairs is *Le Moniteur du Commerce International, Ausstellungs- und Messe-Ausschuss der Deutschen Wirtschaft e.V., and. M+A Messeplanner.* These sources, however, do not provide sufficient information on nationality of visitors. We are indebted to Mr Marc Degraeve (export advisor of the regional export centre at Brugge), Mr André de Schryver (Manager Logistical Activities of Export Vlaanderen, Brussel) and Mr Jeroen de Vuyst (project manager, Export Vlaanderen, Brussel), for information allowing us to distinguish between local, regional and international trade fairs.

assigned per relevant product group to the country where the fair is organised (this is the Netherlands in the example of Bouwbeurs Utrecht), and a "0.5" per relevant product group, to each country from which visitors are coming (again in the case of Bouwbeurs Utrecht: Germany, Belgium and the United Kingdom). For the few truly international trade fairs (e.g. Anuga in Germany) a "1" is assigned per relevant product group to the country where the fair is organised, and a "0.5" to all other countries.

Annex 8.2 shows the thus coded export promotion activities of Export Vlaanderen, AWEX and Brussels Export during the period 1999-2003 per 2-digit product group and country respectively.

8.4. General assessment of the export promotion activities in Belgium, based on the BLEU's realistic export opportunities

In this section the study assesses globally the appropriateness and effectiveness of the export promotion activities of Export Vlaanderen, AWEX and Brussels Export with regard of the previously detected realistic export opportunities for the BLEU.

Although the international trade data used in the updating of the normative model are not going beyond the year 2000, they are the most recent ones for analysing the export promotion activities of the three Belgian regional organisations during the 1999-2003 period.

While interpreting the results reported below, one should keep in mind that the comparison is made with the BLEU's export opportunities, as detected using the decision support model, i.e. not specifically opportunities for Flanders, Wallonia or the Brussels region *per se*. It is also relevant to stress that the Flemish region accounted for 76.2 % of the Belgian exports in the period 2000-2002.

As the respective data sets are not normally distributed, we measure the degree of association between the export promotion activities in a specific target market abroad, and the realistic export opportunities, by Spearman's rank correlation coefficients. If both variables are quantitiave, a Pearson correlation coefficient can be computed which gives an indication of the degree of association between two variables. However, the Pearson correlation coefficient requires normality of the variables. If this is not the case, a nonparametric correlation coefficient (e.g. Spearman) can be estimated by ranking the observations of both variables and measuring the degree of association in ranking. For the degree of association between the export promotion activities and the realistic export opportunities in all relevant target markets Pearson correlation coefficients have been computed as in this case the normality condition appeared to be satisfied.

For the period 1999-2003, correlation coefficients were calculated between the export promotion activities of Export Vlaanderen, AWEX and Brussels Export, converted into product-country combinations at the 2-digit product group level, on the one hand, and the realistic export opportunities at the same level of aggregation. Starting from the data set of realistic export opportunities the study analyses to what extent the export promotion activities of the regional organisations are related to these opportunities.[7] The results can be found in the following Tables 8.2a, 8.2b and 8.2c, with the last column of each of these tables showing the correlation between the export promotion activities in the period 1999-2003 and the BLEU's realistic export opportunities for the most important countries.

Table 8.2a. Spearman correlation coefficients between the export promotion activities of Export Vlaanderen and all realistic export opportunities, SITC product groups (2 digit), by country (1999-2003).

Country	1999	2000	2001	2002	2003	1999-2003
Denmark	0.279*	0.252*	0.262*	0.303**	0.262*	0.313**
Germany	0.269*	0.251*	0.187	0.234*	0.131	0.216
Finland	0.093	0.219	0.148	0.065	0.129	0.214
France	0.191	0.449**	0.351**	0.445**	0.382**	0.396**
Greece	0.102	0.212	0.203	0.188	0.137	0.210
Ireland	0.409**	0.535**	0.292**	0.297**	0.316**	0.478**
Italy	0.379**	0.236*	0.325**	0.282*	0.287*	0.358**
Netherlands	0.199	0.364**	0.277*	0.320**	0.326**	0.356**
Austria	0.130	0.156	0.221	0.235*	0.234*	0.263*
Poland	0.103	0.289**	0.079	0.231*	0.153	0.255*
Portugal	0.179	0.192	0.232*	0.185	0.336**	0.275*
Spain	0.191	0.236*	0.200	0.350**	0.139	0.255*
United Kingdom	0.340**	0.338**	0.332**	0.435**	0.492**	0.486**
Sweden	0.136	0.182	0.330**	0.265*	0.271*	0.344**
Norway	0.246*	0.361**	0.248*	0.184	0.153	0.305**
Russia	0.124	0.175	-0.010	0.131	-0.061	0.071
Turkey	0.121	0.353**	0.269*	0.291**	0.297**	0.299**
South Africa	-0.068	-0.008	-0.115	-0.068	-0.110	-0.081
Canada	-0.157	0.044	0.085	0.020	-0.034	0.038
USA	0.264*	0.324**	0.289**	0.164	0.260*	0.358**
Brazil	-0.106	-0.157	-0.049	-0.025	-0.090	-0.103

7 Alternatively, the data on export promotion activities of the three regional organisations could be aggregated and correlated with the realistic export opportunities. This would provide a more general assessment of export promotion in Belgium, but at the price of losing the possibility of a comparison of the regional organisations' performance.

Country	1999	2000	2001	2002	2003	1999-2003
Mexico	0.197	0.271*	0.203	0.177	0.247*	0.295**
Uruguay	0.131	0.053	0.064	0.079	0.061	0.061
Venezuela	-0.092	-0.033	-0.074	-0.041	0.039	0.039
China	0.103	0.171	0.148	0.143	0.167	0.221*
Hong Kong	0.057	0.104	0.045	0.060	0.011	0.107
India	0.165	0.119	0.047	0.052	0.151	0.109
Indonesia	0.181	0.167	0.105	0.087	0.101	0.094
Japan	0.117	0.266*	0.234*	0.212	0.132	0.280*
Singapore	0.181	0.410**	0.291**	0.204	0.291**	0.424**
Taiwan	0.173	0.278*	0.216	0.249*	0.174	0.293**
Thailand	0.051	0.085	-0.061	0.045	-0.003	0.008
South Korea	-0.017	0.154	0.123	0.124	0.122	0.089
Australia	0.273*	0.132	0.280*	0.145	0.102	0.286*
Total	**0.168****	**0.201****	**0.139****	**0.158****	**0.169****	**0.215****

Note: significant at 1% ** , at 5% *.

Table 8.2b. Spearman correlation coefficients between the export promotion activities of AWEX and all realistic export opportunities, SITC product groups (2 digit), by country (1999-2003).

Country	1999	2000	2001	2002	2003	1999-2003
Denmark	0.362**	0.311**	0.325**	0.249*	0.338**	0.318**
Germany	0.393**	0.386**	0.373**	0.205	0.389**	0.387**
Finland	0.168	0.087	0.084	0.143	0.182	0.115
France	0.463**	0.426**	0.395**	0.449**	0.539**	0.523**
Greece	0.291**	0.284*	0.161	0.418**	0.303**	0.271*
Ireland	0.331**	0.337**	0.313**	0.399**	0.491**	0.408**
Italy	0.403**	0.421**	0.381**	0.319**	0.483**	0.529**
Netherlands	0.362**	0.386**	0.271*	0.498**	0.442**	0.454**
Austria	0.157	0.258*	0.173	0.378**	0.256*	0.253*
Poland	0.286*	0.265*	0.295**	0.335**	0.257*	0.315**
Portugal	0.370**	0.440**	0.265*	0.426**	0.396**	0.434**
Spain	0.311**	0.369**	0.225*	0.433**	0.400**	0.390**
United Kingdom	0.420**	0.443**	0.433*	0.558**	0.486**	0.479**
Sweden	0.283*	0.289**	0.299**	0.312**	0.259*	0.304**
Norway	0.285*	0.281*	0.313**	0.390**	0.313**	0.322**
Russia	0.150	0.263*	0.092	0.123	0.235*	0.231*
Turkey	0.267*	0.331**	0.267*	0.385	0.359**	0.347**

Country	1999	2000	2001	2002	2003	1999-2003
South Africa	0.058	-0.089	0.039	0.029	0.073	0.066
Canada	0.120	0.071	0.088	0.170	0.161	0.148
USA	0.332**	0.329**	0.298**	0.353**	0.268*	0.358**
Brazil	-0.088	-0.019	-0.073	-0.105	0.212	-0.012
Mexico	0.220	0.231*	0.305**	0.204	0.288*	0.243*
Uruguay	0.126	0.062	0.061	0.056	0.083	0.130
Venezuela	0.089	-0.103	0.014	-0.026	0.033	0.073
China	0.131	0.201	0.212	0.202	0.331**	0.296**
Hong Kong	0.096	0.089	0.061	0.189	0.170	0.126
India	0.119	0.050	0.128	0.129	0.265*	0.251*
Indonesia	0.088	0.144	0.132	0.262*	0.046	0.132
Japan	0.325**	0.183	0.310**	0.272*	0.245*	0.317**
Singapore	0.135	0.138	0.140	0.270*	0.293**	0.216
Taiwan	0.204	0.164	0.250*	0.153	0.195	0.203
Thailand	0.083	0.007	0.000	0.157	0.023	0.058
South Korea	0.121	0.130	0.214	0.102	0.306**	0.198
Australia	0.256*	0.211	0.249*	0.174	0.317**	0.289**
Total	0.222**	0.244**	0.292**	0.231**	0.359**	0.318**

Note: significant at 1% ** , at 5% *.

Table 8.2c. Spearman correlation coefficients between the export promotion activities of Brussels Export and all realistic export opportunities, SITC product groups (2 digit), by country (1999-2003).

Country	1999	2000	2001	2002	2003	1999-2003
Denmark	0.271*	0.284*	0.368**	0.213	-0.002	0.232*
Germany	0.256*	0.224*	0.302**	0.316**	0.263*	0.310**
Finland	0.069	0.009	0.009	0.044	0.230*	0.104
France	0.354**	0.325**	0.554**	0.378**	0.527**	0.535**
Greece	0.365**	0.203	0.340**	0.272*	0.360**	0.428**
Ireland	0.253*	0.268*	0.264*	0.310**	0.193	0.350**
Italy	0.285*	0.260*	0.416**	0.324**	0.460**	0.451**
Netherlands	0.197	0.223*	0.223*	0.281*	0.371**	0.374**
Austria	0.365**	0.197	0.243*	0.281*	0.155	0.366**
Poland	0.139	0.054	0.054	0.257*	0.193	0.229*
Portugal	0.377**	0.220	0.361**	0.253*	0.294**	0.406**
Spain	0.237*	0.181	0.391**	0.218	0.275*	0.370**
United Kingdom	0.383**	0.373**	0.374**	0.306**	0.374**	0.434**
Sweden	0.225*	0.162	0.333**	0.169	0.119	0.313**

Country	1999	2000	2001	2002	2003	1999-2003
Norway	0.376**	0.304**	0.304**	0.256*	0.222*	0.319**
Russia	-0.002	-0.068	-0.075	-0.014	0.120	0.030
Turkey	0.314**	0.409**	0.364**	0.367**	0.380**	0.390**
South Africa	0.079	0.083	0.039	0.023	0.017	0.093
Canada	0.084	0.054	0.084	0.079	0.093	0.074
USA	0.196	0.233*	0.243*	0.215	0.365**	0.380**
Brazil	-0.053	-0.079	-0.116	-0.105	0.101	-0.054
Mexico	0.119	0.070	0.054	0.069	0.159	0.127
Uruguay	0.074	0.032	-0.035	0.022	0.011	0.012
Venezuela	-0.039	-0.074	-0.082	-0.014	0.120	0.072
China	-0.063	-0.079	-0.109	0.004	0.091	-0.027
Hong Kong	-0.004	-0.041	-0.037	-0.048	0.041	-0.002
India	0.045	0.236*	0.022	0.182	0.186	0.217
Indonesia	0.320**	0.264*	0.253*	0.225*	0.070	0.263*
Japan	0.065	0.138	0.005	0.059	0.115	0.199
Singapore	0.082	0.114	0.116	0.112	-0.002	0.119
Taiwan	0.116	0.139	0.140	0.145	0.245*	0.258*
Thailand	0.160	0.113	0.106	0.102	0.034	0.126
South Korea	0.171	0.164	0.167	0.164	0.023	0.142
Australia	0.041	0.048	0.048	0.053	0.191	0.115
Total	0.154**	0.143**	0.170**	0.147**	0.266**	0.210**

Note: significant at 1% **, at 5% *.

The correlations for Export Vlaanderen, AWEX and Brussels Export are also depicted in Figures 8.2a, 8.2b and 8.2c, which will allow for a better visual inspection and assessment.

Whereas in the period 1990-1992 there was still somewhat more than a 60% probability that the export promotion activities of Export Vlaanderen exploited realistic export opportunities, and for AWEX 55% (Cuyvers and Rayp, 1993)[8], the planned and organised activities of the regional organisations for the 1999-2003 period show only a small, albeit a statistically significant relationship with the list of BLEU exports opportunities, with overall correlation of 0.215 for Export Vlaanderen, 0.318 for AWEX and 0.210 for Brussels Export.

8   There is no figure of reference for Brussels Export in the period 1990-1992.

Figure 8.2a. Spearman correlation coefficients between the export promotion activities of Export Vlaanderen and all realistic export opportunities, SITC product groups (2 digit), by country (1999-2003).

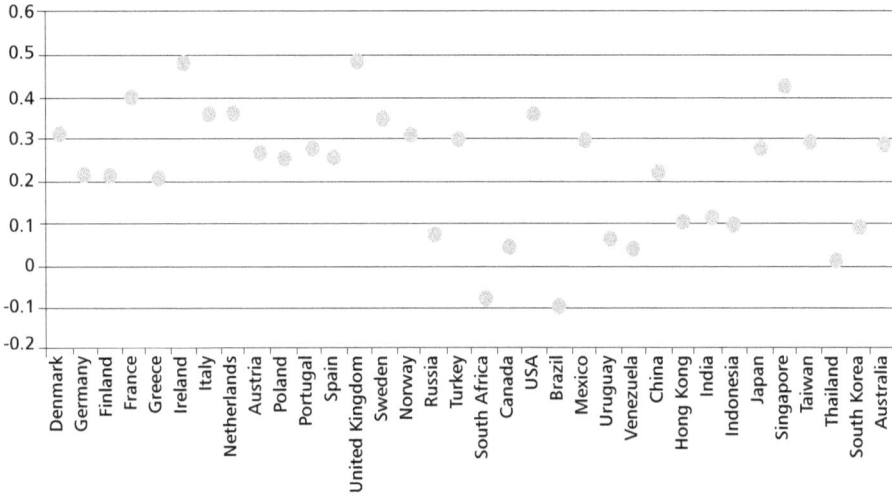

Figure 8.2b. Spearman correlation coefficients between the export promotion activities of AWEX and all realistic export opportunities, SITC product groups (2 digit), by country (1999-2003).

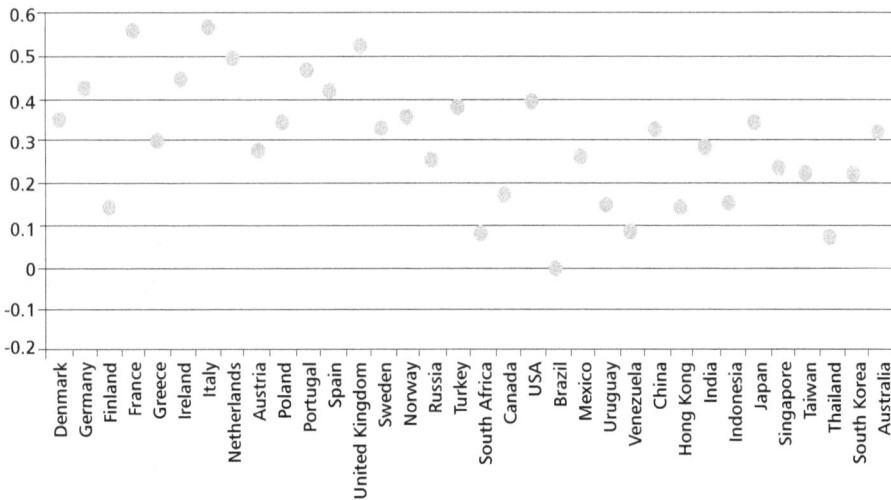

Figure 8.2c. Spearman correlation coefficients between the export promotion activities of Brussels Export and all realistic export opportunities, SITC product groups (2 digit), by country (1999-2003).

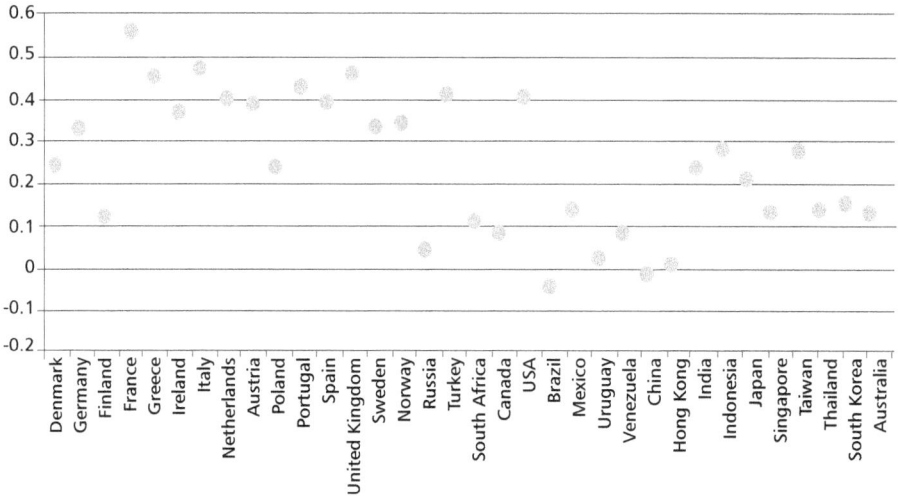

Moreover, it appears that the correlation coefficients remain in later years of the period 1999-2003 of the same order of magnitude (or improve sometimes). As the list op realistic export opportunities refers to 2000, this could lead to a cautious conclusion that the consideration of the BLEU export opportunities by the regional organisations, if at all, is done with considerable delay in time and/or inertia. This conclusion is supported by the higher correlation coefficients for AWEX activities than these of Export Vlaanderen, taking into account that Wallonia represented in the period 2000-2002 only 14% of the Belgian exports, against 76.2% for Flanders.

It also appears that the correlation coefficients are higher for the EU countries (e.g. even 0.478 for Ireland and 0.486 for the United Kingdom in the case of Export Vlaanderen; or 0.523 with France, 0.479 with the UK in the case of AWEX) than for countries outside the EU. However, for some important distant markets, the correlation coefficients are reasonable (e.g. de USA), but mostly low and not statistically significant.

The activities of Export Vlaanderen with respect to the BRIC countries are mostly poorly correlated with the realistic opportunities there. However, the correlation between the activities of AWEX and the BLEU's export opportunities is statistically significant for both China and India. In the most recent years, it seems that the three regional export promotion organisations have aligned their activities towards the emerging economies better with the opportunities detected, as compared with the earlier years.

8.5 Correlation between the export promotion activities of Export Vlaanderen, AWEX and Brussels Export, and the corresponding product-country combinations under the assumption of geographical focus

The Belgian regional export promotion organisations might well be focusing their export promotion geographically and/or sectorally, due to budget constraints, which would provide some explanation for the low correlation reported in the previous section. The 3,902 product-country combinations of realistic export opportunities are found in 61 countries. A policy of geographical concentration of export promotion activities will then, obviously, leave many opportunities untapped, which in turn will lead to low correlation with the full set op realistic export opportunities.

In order to test the relevance of this hypothesis, we have calculated the correlation between the export promotion activities and the corresponding product-country combinations from the complete set of realistic export opportunities. Stated more concretely, we deleted from the full list of realistic export opportunities, the product-country combinations with which no export promotion activity corresponds. This allows us to test whether realistic export opportunities are corresponding with the export promotion activities, whereas in the previous section we tested whether the export opportunities and the export promotion programmes correlate which create an upward bias in the correlation coefficients, due to the many combinations of product-country combinations, to which corresponds no realistic export opportunity, nor any public export promotion activity.

The new correlation coefficients are shown in Tables 8.3a, b and c, as well as in the following Figures 8.3a, b and c. From Tables 8.3a, b and c it clearly appears that the correlation coefficients, both in terms of value and significance, suffer from the data restrictions thus introduced. The results suffered least for AWEX, although the statistical significance has disappeared. For the full period 1999-2003 only some ten countries remain for which AWEX's export promotion activities and the realistic export opportunities are relatively strongly and significantly correlated (see Table 8.3b).

The value of the correlation coefficients for the export promotion activities of Export Vlaanderen and Brussels Export have decreased sharply and the statistical significance has vanished mostly. For the total period 1999-2003, for instance, Export Vlaanderen's situation shows only one correlation coefficient which is positive and significantly different from zero (see Table 8.3a): with the realistic export opportunities in France (notwithstanding correlation coefficients for the individual years that are not significant). Apart from this poor result, Table 8.3a, only shows significant coefficients for individual years, such as for Norway (1999 and 2001), Egypt (1999), Indonesia (2000) and Australia (1999).

Table 8.3a. Spearman correlation between export promotion activities of Export Vlaanderen and the corresponding realistic export opportunities, SITC product groups (2 digit) by country (1999-2003).

Country	1999	2000	2001	2002	2003	1999-2003
Denmark	Ct	0.071	0.394	0.210	0.154	0.246
Germany	-0.145	0.113	-0.050	0.079	0.124	0.199
Finland	Ct	-0.029	-0.121	0.090	-0.016	-0.113
France	0.025	-0.150	-0.130	0.182	0.027	0.443**
Greece	Ct	-0.048	-0.192	0.007	-0.415	-0.157
Ireland	-0.118	0.133	-0.201	-0.065	0.073	0.046
Italy	-0.045	0.266	-0.115	0.031	-0.097	0.054
Netherlands	Ct	0.113	-0.266	-0.036	-0.244	0.029
Austria	Ct	-0.376	-0.297	0.130	-0.081	-0.019
Poland	Ct	0.104	-0.426*	0.123	0.071	0.029
Portugal	0.261	-0.333	-0.076	0.090	-0.405	0.053
Spain	-0.052	0.295	0.117	0.029	-0.066	0.076
United Kingdom	0.125	0.074	-0.031	0.078	-0.092	0.185
Sweden	0.411	0.046	0.283	0.206	-0.158	-0.019
Norway	0.707**	-0.140	0.428*	-0.249	-0.121	0.165
Russia	-0.080	0.179	-0.093	-0.025	-0.289	0.072
Turkey	-0.183	0.239	0.188	-0.283	-0.078	0.284
South Africa	-0.151	-0.187	Ct	-0.068	-0.221	-0.070
Canada	0.136	-0.305	Ct	0.116	0.059	-0.255
USA	0.249	0.053	-0.087	-0.229	-0.132	0.026
Brazil	-0.048	-0.076	-0.188	0.272	-0.078	-0.045
Mexico	0.159	-0.198	-0.106	0.040	0.146	0.216
Uruguay	-0.048	-0.149	0.098	-0.066	-0.069	0.122
Venezuela	Ct	-0.132	Ct	0.056	-0.202	-0.331
China	-0.268	0.037	-0.247	-0.278	0.031	-0.096
Hong Kong	-0.305	-0.074	-0.010	0.101	0.125	-0.194
India	0.003	-0.178	-0.142	0.156	-0.213	-0.019
Indonesia	Ct	0.475*	Ct	-0.249	-0.263	0.330
Japan	-0.322	-0.253	Ct	-0.166	-0.041	-0.395
Singapore	Ct	-0.044	0.295	-0.189	0.396	-0.066
Taiwan	Ct	0.181	Ct	0.261	0.396	0.069
Thailand	0.466	0.237	-0.125	0.226	-0.253	0.278
South Korea	0.009	Ct	Ct	-0.071	-0.078	0.138
Australia	0.512*	-0.271	0.325	-0.376	-0.280	-0.114
Total	**0.194****	**0.199****	**0.122****	**0.160****	**0.157****	**0.127****

Note: significant at 1% **, at 5% * ; Ct: at least 1 variable constant

Table 8.3b. Spearman correlation between export promotion activities of AWEX and the corresponding realistic export opportunities, SITC product groups (2 digit) by country (1999-2003).

Country	1999	2000	2001	2002	2003	1999-2003
Denmark	0.092	0.668**	0.385*	0.344	0.220	0.389*
Germany	-0.226	-0.152	-0.015	0.146	0.244	0.268
Finland	-0.046	0.120	0.060	-0.016	-0.025	0.127
France	0.564**	0.380*	0.470**	0.252	0.308	0.468**
Greece	0.266	0.372	0.164	-0.050	0.253	0.469**
Ireland	-0.094	0.217	0.366*	-0.034	-0.219	0.234
Italy	0.253	0.069	0.298	0.068	0.286	0.488**
Netherlands	0.467*	0.376	0.357*	-0.019	0.089	0.437**
Austria	-0.055	0.363	0.064	0.432*	0.242	0.355*
Poland	0.087	-0.323	0.150	0.029	0.179	0.148
Portugal	0.242	0.158	0.338	0.020	0.492**	0.441**
Spain	0.128	0.047	0.370*	-0.109	0.064	0.244
United Kingdom	0.343	0.105	0.281	0.054	0.221	0.433**
Sweden	0.066	0.577**	0.143	0.127	0.270	0.290
Norway	-0.151	0.251	0.453*	0.303	-0.029	0.385*
Russia	0.074	0.242	0.161	-0.266	0.267	0.101
Turkey	0.173	0.135	0.491**	0.259	0.090	0.277
South Africa	-0.255	-0.403	-0.079	0.197	-0.133	0.093
Canada	-0.068	0.074	-0.066	0.025	0.204	0.047
USA	-0.326	-0.195	-0.027	-0.380	0.189	0.042
Brazil	-0.034	-0.174	-0.074	-0.028	0.325	0.016
Mexico	0.105	0.009	0.224	-0.198	0.375	0.251
Uruguay	-0.042	0.067	0.010	0.142	-0.240	0.003
Venezuela	-0.132	0.034	0.175	-0.03	0.204	-0.195
China	-0.370	-0.200	-0.002	-0.512*	-0.061	0.054
Hong Kong	0.001	-0.039	0.128	-0.478*	-0.102	0.067
India	0.221	0.188	0.132	-0.230	0.025	-0.125
Indonesia	-0.207	-0.138	0.277	0.413	-0.240	0.159
Japan	-0.183	-0.027	0.318	-0.626**	0.238	0.182
Singapore	0.122	-0.181	0.343	0.027	0.293	0.319
Taiwan	0.356	0.264	0.401*	-0.061	0.188	0.284
Thailand	-0.232	-0.115	-0.252	0.465	-0.234	0.098
South Korea	0.237	0.168	0.213	0.053	-0.034	0.256
Australia	-0.030	0.079	0.152	-0.409	0.216	0.194
Total	0.196**	0.237**	0.353**	0.195**	0.384**	0.301**

Note: significant at 1% **, at 5% *; Ct: at least 1 variable constant.

Table 8.3c. Spearman correlation between export promotion activities of Brussels Export and the corresponding realistic export opportunities, SITC product groups (2 digit) by country (1999-2003).

Country	1999	2000	2001	2002	2003	1999-2003
Denmark	Ct	0.244	-0.135	0.348	Ct	0.469*
Germany	-0.418	-0.526	-0.692**	0.203	-0.047	-0.112
Finland	Ct	0.345	0.345	0.043	Ct	0.037
France	0.118	-0.175	-0.663**	-0.081	-0.200	-0.129
Greece	Ct	0.157	-0.236	-0.604*	-0.08	-0.108
Ireland	Ct	0.228	-0.228	-0.415	0.604	0.040
Italy	-0.358	-0.159	-0.457	-0.177	0.213	-0.076
Netherlands	Ct	0.076	0.076	-0.124	0.038	-0.248
Austria	-0.028	Ct	Ct	-0.112	Ct	0.101
Poland	Ct	Ct	Ct	-0.095	0.227	-0.101
Portugal	Ct	0.383	-0.416	-0.265	0.115	0.032
Spain	-0.122	-0.129	-0.489*	-0.396	0.073	-0.199
United Kingdom	-0.350	-0.086	-0.115	-0.144	0.233	0.049
Sweden	Ct	0.470	-0.238	-0.163	-0.100	0.074
Norway	Ct	0.632*	0.632*	-0.542*	0.255	0.298
Russia	Ct	Ct	-0.346	-0.430	Ct	-0.322
Turkey	Ct	-0.053	0.000	-0.054	0.136	0.276
South Africa	Ct	0.209	0.285	-0.371	Ct	-0.078
Canada	0.376	-0.243	0.376	0.277	0.110	0.493
USA	-0.734*	-0.477	0.593*	-0.533	-0.072	0.282
Brazil	-0.258	-0.059	Ct	1.000**	Ct	-0.098
Mexico	Ct	0.350	-0.350	0.352	Ct	0.057
Uruguay	Ct	0.285	Ct	-0.191	Ct	0.008
Venezuela	Ct	0.222	-0.222	-0.545	Ct	-0.356
China	Ct	0.165	0.285	0.145	Ct	-0.066
Hong Kong	Ct	Ct	0.222	-0.289	Ct	-0.123
India	Ct	Ct	-0.093	-0.163	Ct	-0.227
Indonesia	Ct	Ct	-0.350	-0.402	Ct	-0.110
Japan	Ct	0.604*	-0.356	0.767**	-0.671	-0.259
Singapore	Ct	Ct	0.087	-0.076	Ct	-0.019
Taiwan	Ct	Ct	0.043	0.261	0.180	0.051
Thailand	Ct	Ct	-0.285	-0.371	Ct	-0.203
South Korea	Ct	Ct	0.167	-0.036	Ct	0.329
Australia	Ct	Ct	0.000	0.181	Ct	-0.102
Total	0.198**	0.264**	0.120**	0.175**	0.219**	0.123**

Note: significant at 1% **, at 5% *; Ct: at least 1 variable constant.

Figure 8.3a. Spearman correlation between export promotion activities of Export Vlaanderen and the corresponding realistic export opportunities, SITC product groups (2 digit) by country (1999-2003).

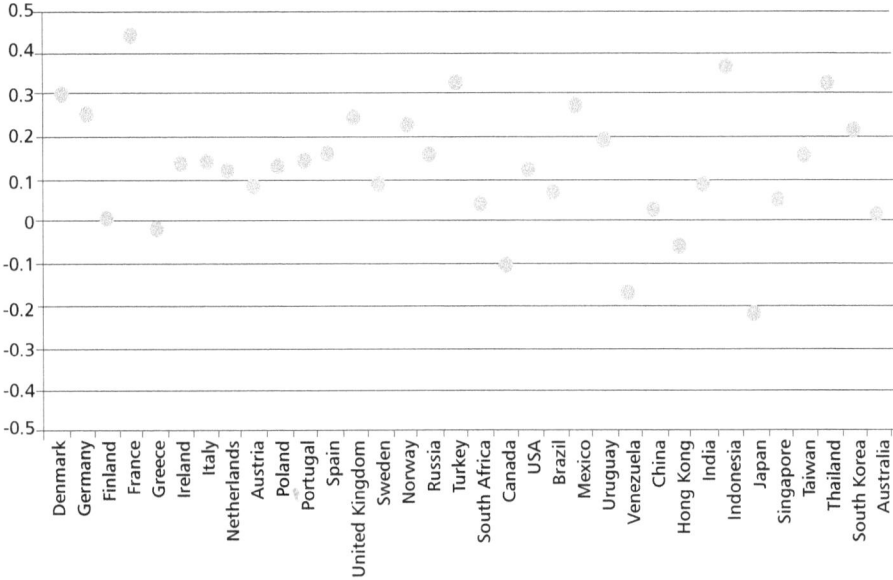

Figure 8.3b. Spearman correlation between export promotion activities of AWEX and the corresponding realistic export opportunities, SITC product groups (2 digit) by country (1999-2003).

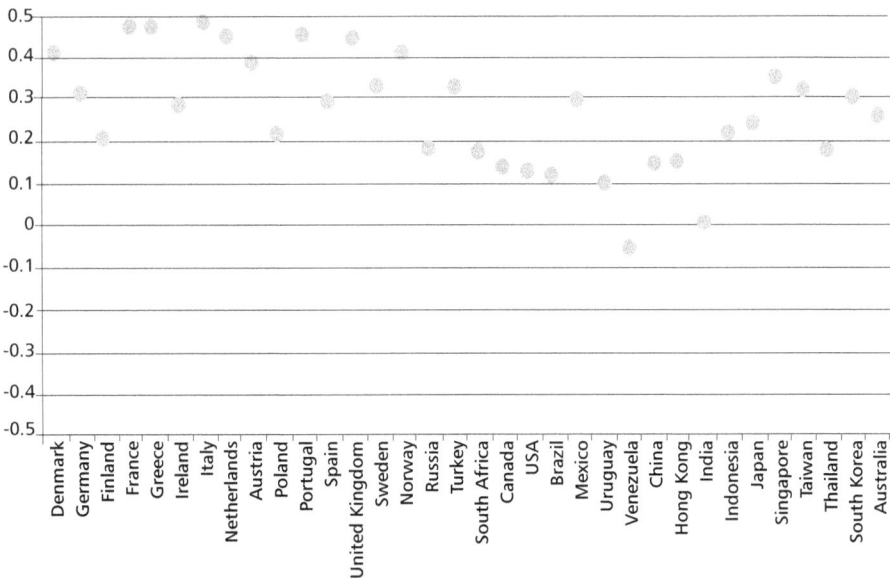

Figure 8.3c. Spearman correlation between export promotion activities of AWEX and the corresponding realistic export opportunities, SITC product groups (2 digit) by country (1999-2003).

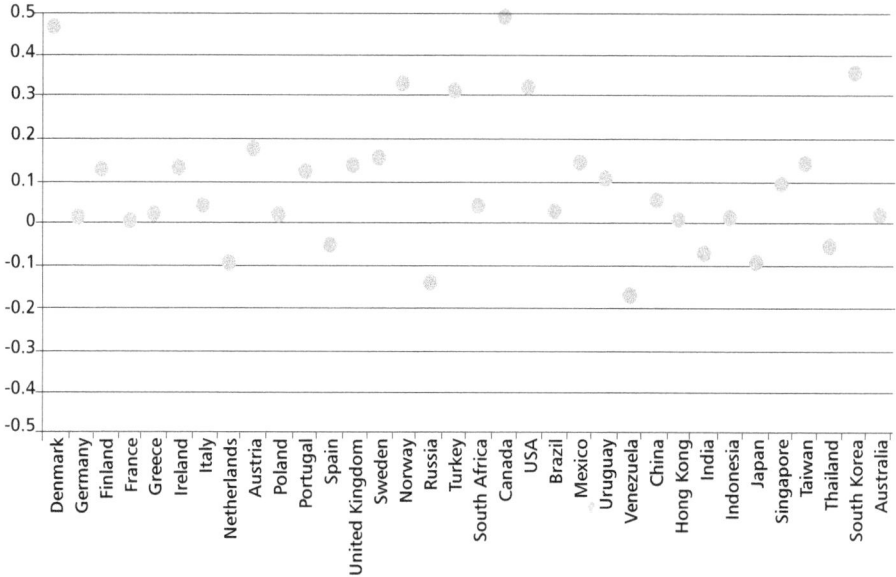

8.6   Conclusion

This chapter assessed the degree of correspondence, for the period 1999-2003 between the export promotion activities of the main public export promotion organisations in Belgium (Export Vlaanderen, AWEX and Brussels Export) and the realistic export opportunities of the BLEU.

There is hardly any evidence that in the period studied, export promotion activities were sufficiently geared to realistic export opportunities. These opportunities, as detected using an updated DSM, correlate most of the times only weakly with the export promotion activities. When due account is taken of a hypothetical export promotion focus (which is not corroborated by our results) on a selective number of countries and opportunities, or opportunities in countries where the BLEU's market position warrants more success, due to e.g. a budget constraint, the average correlation coefficients are even lower (and not significantly different from zero).

As a matter of fact, AWEX seems to score highest of the three organisations. When correlation coefficients are calculated for a limited data set from which the product-country combinations are deleted to which no export promotion activity corresponds, a number of coefficients for AWEX remain at about 0.30 and 0.50, and are significantly different from zero, in contrast to these for Export Vlaanderen and Brussels Export.

Obviously, the existing processes of identification, formulation and planning of export promotion activities within the three regional organisations must be held responsible for the poor correlation with export opportunities. It is possible that, particularly in the case of Export Vlaanderen and Brussels Export, the organisations hardly used hard and quantitative data during these processes. This, in turn, implies that too much is relied on subjective and possibly strongly personal information about developments in foreign markets. An alternative explanation is the existence of interference in the processes of identification, formulation and planning from directly interested exporters and their professional organisations.

A potential problem of export promotion in Belgium is the finding of the aforementioned World Bank study that "A single and strong EPO should be preferred to the sometimes observed proliferation of organisations within countries" (Lederman, Olarreaga & Payton, 2006:5). Not only are there three regional EPOs in Belgium but also numerous private and semi-private organisations take on the role of export promotion. The expenditures of the Belgian regional EPOs are well above the level resulting in a maximum impact on exports, estimated by Lederman, Olarreaga and Payton (2006) to lie between 0.6 and 2.7 dollar per capita. The best performing EPO in the world appear to be publicly funded but with a large share of the executive board in the hands of the private sector (Lederman, Olarreaga & Payton, 2006:5). If for political reasons a single publicly funded EPO is not possible in Belgium, the established diminishing returns to scale of export promotion call for strategic choices. We believe that determining realistic export opporunities is a valuable instrument to put public funds for export promotion to good use.

References

Balassa, B. 1965. Trade liberalisation and revealed comparative advantage. *Centre Paper 63*, Yale University Economic Growth Centre, New Haven.

BIS. 2011. International trade and investment: the economic rationale for government support. *BIS Economics Paper 13*, The Department for Business, Innovation and Skills, May 2011.

Czinkota, M. 2002. National export promotion: a statement of issues, changes, and opportunities. In: Kotabe, M. and Aulakh, P. (eds). *Emerging issues in international business research.* Cheltenham (UK): Edward Elgar.

Cuyvers, L. 1996. Export opportunities of Thailand: a decision support model approach. *Journal of Euro-Asian Management*, 2(2): 71-97.

Cuyvers, L. 2004. Identifying export opportunities: the case of Thailand. *International Marketing Review*, 21(3): 255-278.

Cuyvers, L., De Pelsmacker, P., Rayp, G. & Roozen, I.T.M. 1995. A decision support model for the planning and assessment of export promotion activities by government promotion institutions: the Belgian case. *International Journal of Research in Marketing*, 12(2): 173-186.

Cuyvers, L. & Rayp, G. 1993. Handelspolitiek in België: een poging tot evaluatie van het institutioneel kader en de getroffen maatregelen. *De onderneming en de dynamiek van de economische orde* (Papers 21st Vlaams Wetenschappelijk Economisch Congres), Vereniging voor Economie, 1993, pp. 239-289.

Gencturk, E. & Kotabe, M. 2001. The effect of export assistance program usage on export performance: a contingency explanation. *Journal of International Marketing*, 9(2): 51-72.

Kedia, B. & Chhokar, J. 1986. An empirical investigation of export promotion programs. *Columbia Journal of World Business*, 21: 13-20.

Lederman, D., Olarreaga, M. & Payton, L. 2006. Export promotion agencies: what works and what does not. *Trade Note 30*, World Bank group, Washington D.C.

Posen, A.S. 2006. Faddish export promotion is a heavy burden for any economy. *Financial Times* (9 August).

Seringhaus, F. & Botschen, G. 1991. Cross-national comparison of export promotion services: the views of Canadian and Austrian companies. *Journal of International Business Studies*, 22(1): 115-133.

Annexures

Annex 8.1. Export opportunities according to the normative model (SITC 2-digit).

	2000	2001	2002	2003
00 Live animals other than fish, crustaceans, mollusks and aquatic invertebrates of division 03	12	13	13	15
01 Meat and meat preparations	41	37	36	37
02 Dairy products and birds' eggs	30	30	35	32
03 Fish (not marine mammals), crustaceans, mollusks and aquatic invertebrates, and preparations thereof	21	23	17	21
04 Cereals and cereal preparations	47	34	30	38
05 Vegetables and fruit	49	48	30	43
06 Sugars, sugar preparations and honey	18	22	19	20
07 Coffee, tea, cocoa, spices and manufactures thereof	14	14	20	16
08 Feeding stuff for animals (not including unmilled cereals)	21	22	23	21
09 Miscellaneous edible products and preparations	5	7	8	5
11 Beverages	18	18	16	16
12 Tobacco and tobacco manufactures	17	17	15	16
21 Hides, skins and fur skins, raw	10	8	12	9
22 Oil seeds and oleaginous fruits	16	16	14	12
23 Crude rubber (including synthetic and reclaimed)	6	8	8	7
24 Cork and wood	18	21	20	18
25 Pulp and waste paper	8	7	8	9
26 Textile fibers (other than wool tops and other combed wool) and their wastes (not manufactured into yarn)	19	19	17	18
27 Crude fertilizers (imports only), except those of division 56, and crude minerals (excluding coal, petrol)	24	30	31	23
28 Metalliferous ores and metal scrap	16	16	16	14
29 Crude animal and vegetable materials, n.e.s.	29	37	35	31
32 Coal, coke and briquettes	7	9	9	8
33 Petroleum, petroleum products and related materials	15	17	21	17
34 Gas, natural and manufactured	0	0	0	0
35 Electric current	1	1	1	1
41 Animal oils and fats	7	5	8	nvt
42 Fixed vegetable fats and oils, crude, refined or fractionated	16	21	16	17
43 Animal or vegetable fats and oils processed; waxes and inedible mixtures or preparations of animal or vegetables	13	14	13	12
	0	0	0	0
51 Organic chemicals	15	13	17	17
52 Inorganic chemicals	17	16	24	18
53 Dyeing, tanning and coloring materials	8	12	14	8
54 Medicinal and pharmaceutical products	19	23	23	21
55 Essential oils and resinoids and perfume materials; toilet, polishing and cleansing preparations	12	13	14	13
56 Fertilizers (exports include group 272; imports exclude group 272)	6	11	7	7
57 Plastics in primary forms	0	0	0	0
58 Plastics in nonprimary forms	0	0	0	0
59 Chemical materials and products, n.e.s.	15	15	18	17

	2000	2001	2002	2003
61 Leather, leather manufactures, n.e.s., and dressed fur skins	2	2	5	2
62 Rubber manufactures, n.e.s.	12	14	12	11
63 Cork and wood manufactures other than furniture	9	16	15	9
64 Paper, paperboard, and articles of paper pulp, paper or paper board	27	31	29	29
65 Textile yarn, fabrics, made-up articles, n.e.s., and related products	36	44	48	29
66 Nonmetallic mineral manufactures, n.e.s.	39	50	49	37
67 Iron and steel	35	45	39	38
68 Nonferrous metals	25	40	38	24
69 Manufactures of metals, n.e.s.	42	53	45	44
71 Power generating machinery and equipment	14	19	17	16
72 Machinery specialised for particular industries	46	55	45	42
73 Metalworking machinery	17	29	24	24
74 General industrial machinery and equipment, n.e.s., and machine parts, n.e.s.	39	52	43	47
75 Office machines and automatic data processing machines	11	14	14	13
76 Telecommunications and sound recording and reproducing apparatus and equipment	19	16	19	19
77 Electrical machinery, apparatus and appliances, n.e.s., and electrical parts thereof	45	43	37	43
78 Road vehicles (including air-cushion vehicles)	21	24	20	17
79 Transport equipment, n.e.s.	0	0	0	0
81 Prefabricated buildings; sanitary, plumbing, heating and lighting fixtures and fittings, n.e.s.	20	27	22	20
82 Furniture and parts thereof; bedding, mattresses, mattress supports, cushions and similar stuffed furnishing	0	0	0	0
83 Travel goods, handbags and similar containers	9	11	12	10
84 Articles of apparel and clothing accessories	74	66	61	76
85 Footwear	9	7	9	10
87 Profssional, scientific and controlling instruments and apparatus, n.e.s.	18	19	27	20
88 Photographic apparatus, equipment and supplies and optical goods, n.e.s.; watches and clocks	30	40	37	31
89 Miscellaneous manufactured articles, n.e.s.	49	66	60	47
93 Special transactions and commodities not classified according to kind	7	7	8	9
95 Coin, including gold coin; proof and presentation sets and current coin	7	9	6	8
96 Coin (other than gold coin), not being legal tender	0	0	0	0
97 Gold, nonmonetary (excluding gold ores and concentrates)	5	7	3	5
98 Estimate of items valued under $251 and of other low valued items nonexempt from formal entry	0	0	0	0
99 Estimate of non-canadian low value shipments; compiled low value shipments to Canada; and various shipment	0	0	0	0

Annex 8.2. Activities Export Vlaanderen (SITC 2-digit).

	2000	2001	2002	2003
00 Live animals other than fish, crustaceans, mollusks and aquatic invertebrates of division 03	2	26	17	1
01 Meat and meat preparations	16	34	17	7
02 Dairy products and birds' eggs	17	33	17	4
03 Fish (not marine mammals), crustaceans, molluscs and aquatic invertebrates, and preparations thereof	14	33	17	1
04 Cereals and cereal preparations	15	33	17	1
05 Vegetables and fruit	16	33	17	8
06 Sugars, sugar preparations and honey	16	33	18	3
07 Coffee, tea, cocoa, spices and manufactures thereof	13	33	17	1
08 Feeding stuff for animals (not including unmilled cereals)	1	0	17	3
09 Miscellaneous edible products and preparations	31	33	18	34
11 Beverages	7	30	2	3
12 Tobacco and tobacco manufactures	0	0	0	0
21 Hides, skins and fur skins, raw	0	0	0	0
22 Oil seeds and oleaginous fruits	0	0	0	0
23 Crude rubber (including synthetic and reclaimed)	0	0	0	0
24 Cork and wood	1	0	1	6
25 Pulp and waste paper	0	0	2	8
26 Textile fibers (other than wool tops and other combed wool) and their wastes (not manufactured into yarn)	0	13	0	0
27 Crude fertilizers (imports only), except those of division 56, and crude minerals (excluding coal, petrol)	0	0	0	0
28 Metalliferous ores and metal scrap	0	0	0	0
29 Crude animal and vegetable materials, n.e.s.	6	0	0	1
32 Coal, coke and briquettes	1	0	0	1
33 Petroleum, petroleum products and related materials	1	8	3	2
34 Gas, natural and manufactured	1	0	3	1
35 Electric current	1	4	6	5
41 Animal oils and fats	0	0	0	0
42 Fixed vegetable fats and oils, crude, refined or fractionated	0	0	0	0
43 Animal or vegetable fats and oils processed; waxes and inedible mixtures or preparations of animal or vegetables	0	0	0	0
51 Organic chemicals	0	1	4	1
52 Inorganic chemicals	0	1	4	2
53 Dyeing, tanning and coloring materials	2	0	1	0
54 Medicinal and pharmaceutical products	6	10	6	11
55 Essential oils and resinoids and perfume materials; toilet, polishing and cleansing preparations	9	0	1	6
56 Fertilizers (exports include group 272; imports exclude group 272)	1	0	2	0
57 Plastics in primary forms	0	0	0	0
58 Plastics in nonprimary forms	1	0	0	0
59 Chemical materials and products, n.e.s.	9	2	0	18
61 Leather, leather manufactures, n.e.s., and dressed furskins	1	0	2	0
62 Rubber manufactures, n.e.s.	0	0	1	0

	2000	2001	2002	2003
63 Cork and wood manufactures other than furniture	0	0	0	1
64 Paper, paperboard, and articles of paper pulp, paper or paper board	5	2	0	9
65 Textile yarn, fabrics, made-up articles, n.e.s., and related products	20	0	6	16
66 Nonmetallic mineral manufactures, n.e.s.	0	0	2	2
67 Iron and steel	0	4	3	5
68 Nonferrous metals	0	0	0	0
69 Manufactures of metals, n.e.s.	1	0	1	4
71 Power generating machinery and equipment	11	0	4	1
72 Machinery specialised for particular industries	5	4	10	21
73 Metalworking machinery	1	4	7	0
74 General industrial machinery and equipment, n.e.s., and machine parts, n.e.s.	8	10	6	6
75 Office machines and automatic data processing machines	8	10	5	5
76 Telecommunications and sound recording and reproducing apparatus and equipment	21	16	13	16
77 Electrical machinery, apparatus and appliances, n.e.s., and electrical parts thereof	23	22	7	11
78 Road vehicles (including air-cushion vehicles)	9	9	6	9
79 Transport equipment, n.e.s.	3	4	15	20
81 Prefabricated buildings; sanitary, plumbing, heating and lighting fixtures and fittings, n.e.s.	17	13	12	25
82 Furniture and parts thereof; bedding, mattresses, mattress supports, cushions and similar stuffed furnishing	5	5	6	18
83 Travel goods, handbags and similar containers	0	0	1	0
84 Articles of apparel and clothing accessories	5	8	0	2
85 Footwear	2	0	0	0
87 Profssional, scientific and controlling instruments and apparatus, n.e.s.	3	0	0	1
88 Photographic apparatus, equipment and supplies and optical goods, n.e.s.; watches and clocks	1	1	0	2
89 Miscellaneous manufactured articles, n.e.s.	11	0	4	12
93 Special transactions and commodities not classified according to kind	9	10	0	9
95 Coin, including gold coin; proof and presentation sets and current coin	0	0	0	0
96 Coin (other than gold coin), not being legal tender	0	0	0	0
97 Gold, nonmonetary (excluding gold ores and concentrates)	1	0	0	0
98 Estimate of items valued under $251 and of other low valued items nonexempt from formal entry	3	1	3	1
99 Estimate of non-canadian low value shipments; compiled low value shipments to Canada; and various shipment	0	0	0	2

Chapter 9

Developing strategies for export promotion using a decision support model: South African case studies

Ludo Cuyvers, Wilma Viviers, Noleen Sithole-Pisa & Marié-Luce Kühn

9.1 Introduction

It can be assumed that export promotion organisations (EPOs) are increasingly facing diminishing returns in the use of export promotion instruments, particularly the more traditional and most widely used instruments, such as the participation in trade missions, the participation in trade fairs and exhibitions, etc. Empirical support for this assumption can be found in studies such as Alvarez (2004), De Wulf (2001), and others, including for the existence of diminishing returns to scale of the export promotion budgets (see e.g. Lederman, Olarreaga & Payton, 2006). On the other hand, with the success of the export strategies of a number of Newly Industrialising Countries and emerging exporting countries, export promotion organisations in both the developed and the developing countries are facing an urgent need of enhancing the efficiency of their export promotion activities, the more so as many of these EPOs are confronted with constraints in the available financial and other resources. From this it follows that EPOs are in need of criteria to prioritise their activities to the markets and products that are offering the most promising export results for the countries which they represent, and to develop the most appropriate export promotion strategies for the products and the markets which they prioritised. The present chapter deals with the latter issue.

In previous studies, we have developed and applied a decision support model (DSM) for the planning and implementation of export promotion activities towards realistic export opportunities (REOs) of countries as diverse as Belgium, Thailand and South Africa (Cuyvers *et al.*, 1995; Cuyvers, 1996; Cuyvers, 2004; Pearson *et al.*, 2010; see also Chapters 5-7). In this chapter we endeavour to define concrete export promotion strategies for public export promotion organisations based on the characteristics of individual REOs as derived from this decision support model (DSM). These export promotion strategies will be illustrated in their application by investigating a limited number of case studies of South African REOs.

It should be stressed from the outset that we are using the concept "export promotion strategy" in a restrictive way. Strategy evidently refers to a plan of action designed to achieve a particular goal. Contrary to a country's export strategy, in which current and future export targets for the country at large are defined at a macro-level, an export promotion strategy of an EPO relates to achieving the goal of tapping an individual REO in a specific country, such as e.g. the South African Department of Trade and Industry (DTI) aiming at increasing market penetration for South African macadamia nuts in the German market or in the European Union at large. These export promotion strategies are designed by the EPO such that the most appropriate export promotion instruments are used and coordinated with the other relevant private or public "players" of the country in the field of export promotion, fully taking the concrete market characteristics for the individual REO considered and the competitive situation of the exporters in the given market into account.

In the next section we briefly review the results of the decision support model (DSM), which are used for defining export promotion strategies. Section 3 discusses such export promotion strategies according to market share of the exporting country and major market characteristics of the importing country. Section 4 provides details on three South African REOs as case studies in applying DSM results and supplementary market research results in the design of suitable export promotion strategies for the EPO.

9.2   The identification and categorisation of realistic export opportunities using a decision support model (DSM)

Numerous studies have been conducted in order to prioritise or segment export markets, or to investigate companies entering export markets (For a literature review on export segmentation studies, see Chapter 3). The DSM, which was presented in Cuyvers *et al.* (1995), the methodology of which is outlined in Chapter 4, introduced four filters that sequentially eliminate less interesting markets. The filtering process leads to a list of product-country combinations, which we call realistic export opportunities (REOs). These REOs are further categorised, as explained in Chapter 4 and illustrated in Chapter 5, according to the market characteristics and the exporting country's market share (Filter 4).

The results of the application of the DSM for South Africa using data up to 2007 are summarised in Table 9.1, which shows the number of REOs based on this categorisation according to the import market characteristics and South Africa's respective market shares.

Table 9.1. Categorisation of the 2007 REOs of South Africa according to South Africa's market share and import market characteristics (number of REOs).

	Market share of South Africa relatively small	Market share of South Africa intermediately small	Market share of South Africa intermediately large	Market share of South Africa relatively large	Total
Large product market	9,279 (Cell 1)	1,272 (Cell 6)	1,104 (Cell 11)	569 (Cell 16)	12,224
Growing (long- and short-term) product market	44,037 (Cell 2)	531 (Cell 7)	442 (Cell 12)	1,771 (Cell 17)	46,781
Large product market, short-term growth	4,558 (Cell 3)	516 (Cell 8)	455 (Cell 13)	241 (Cell 18)	5,770
Large product market, long-term growth	3,066 (Cell 4)	275 (Cell 9)	262 (Cell 14)	177 (Cell 19)	3,780
Large product/market short- and long-term growth	7,717 (Cell 5)	723 (Cell 10)	707 (Cell 15)	396 (Cell 20)	9,,543
Total	68,657	3,317	2,970	3,154	78,098

To illustrate the use that can be made of Table 9.1, we list an example of a REO for each cell, as taken randomly from the list of REOs:

(i)   Cell 1: HS 310530 – Diammonium phosphate, in packs >10 kg to Argentina;

(ii)   Cell 2: HS 200990 – Mixtures of juices not fermented or spirited to Qatar;

(iii)   Cell 3: HS 847920 – Machines to process animal or fixed vegetable fats or oils to Tunisia;

(iv)   Cell 4: HS 720250 – Ferro-silico-chromium to the United Kingdom;

(v)   Cell 5: HS 030372 – Haddock, frozen, whole to China;

(vi)   Cell 6: HS 290219 – Cyclanes, cyclenes and cycloterpenes nes to Belgium;

(vii)   Cell 7: HS 060290 – Plants live, mushroom sp. to Czech Republic;

(viii) Cell 8: HS 950720 – Fish-hooks, whether or not snelled to Thailand;

(ix)   Cell 9: HS 710231 – Diamonds (jewellery) unworked or simply sawn, cleaved to Hong Kong;

(x)   Cell 10: HS 200520 – Potatoes, prepared or preserved, not frozen/vinegar to Germany;

(xi)   Cell 11: HS 711319 – Jewellery and parts of precious metal except silver to the United Kingdom;

(xii)   Cell 12: HS 090940 – Caraway seeds to China;

(xiii) Cell 13: HS 411330 – Leather further prepared after tanning/crusting, incl. parchment-dressed leather, etc. to Italy;

(xiv)   Cell 14: HS 381230 – Anti-oxidisers and stabilisers for rubber or plastics to India;

(xv)   Cell 15: HS 780420 – Lead powders and flakes to France;

(xvi)   Cell 16: HS 590390 – Fabric impregnated, coated, covered with plastic nes to the United States;

(xvii) Cell 17: HS 902290 – Parts and accessories for radiation apparatus to Thailand;

(xviii) Cell 18: HS 790200 – Zinc waste or scrap to India;

(xix)   Cell 19: HS 680421 – Grindstones, etc. of synthetic or natural diamond to Ireland; and

(xx)   Cell 20: HS 281119 – Inorganic acids n.e.s. to Brazil.

9.3   Defining export promotion strategies (EPS) according to the DSM results

The characteristics of the REOs in Table 9.1, which are the result of the data filtering process described in Chapter 4, can now be used in order to design appropriate, though still, broadly defined export promotion strategies (EPS).

In a previous study (Cuyvers *et al.*, 1995), it was suggested to distinguish the export promotion strategies for the REOs according to the market share of the exporting country, i.e. based on the columns of Table 9.1, as follows:

(i)   the realistic opportunities in Cell [1] to [10] show a low market share for various reasons, and an offensive market exploration EPS is appropriate for products where a comparative advantage exists or can be developed;

(ii)   the realistic opportunities in Cell [11] to [15] show relatively medium large market share and are situated in large and/or growing market segments; therefore an offensive EPS of market expansion can be advocated; and

(iii)   the realistic opportunities in Cell [16] to [20] are situated in market segments where the exporting country has already gained an important market share and a defensive EPS of market maintenance seems appropriate.

Application of these broad strategies implies the utilisation of a specific 'policy instruments mix' and a specific mode of cooperation between the EPO and the private sector. An offensive market exploration EPS entails the active exploration of each detected export opportunity, in co-ordination with the EPO's offices abroad. As the relative market share is small, but the country is already exporting the products to other markets, the EPO should seek to develop export promotion activities in these markets such as general trade missions, financial support of local media campaigns, communication of market potentials to the exporters, the general follow-up of detected realistic opportunities by the diplomatic missions or foreign economic representatives (FERs) in the target countries, etc. A different mix of export promotion instruments is needed to conduct an offensive EPS of market expansion, together with a larger involvement of the private sector (export councils, sectoral/industry associations, exporter's clubs, Chambers of Commerce, etc.) Other examples of instruments are incentives for participants in sectoral trade fairs and exhibitions, and targeted press campaigns in the local press. Finally, an EPS of market maintenance (Cells 16-20) will imply minimal involvement of the EPO. Rather, it should be largely left to the exporters how to further tap these REOs, as they know best how to keep their market share up. The role of the EPO will be restricted to follow-up concrete market conditions in these market segments and support exporters whenever sudden severe or unfair competition is encountered, by e.g. supplying competitive export credits or high-level diplomatic support during negotiations.

In addition to the above export promotion strategies for the REOs according to the market share of the exporting country, a further EPS categorisation can be made according to the characteristics of the import market, i.e. based on the rows of Table 9.1. Neglecting the REOs in the last column of Table 9.1, for which we advocate minimal EPO involvement, this tentatively might lead to the following broadly defined types of EPS:

(i)   Tapping the realistic export opportunities in Cell [1], [6] and [11] imply an EPS of "breaking in" into a large market, especially when the market share of the exporting country is still small. Also in large markets where the market share of the exporting country is relatively large, the EPS type can be labelled "breaking in", but the instruments used to achieve this goal will be different.

(ii)   An EPS of "taking advantage of a growing market" relates to the REOs in Cell [2], [7] and [12], i.e. opportunities in import markets that are growing in the long and the short period. The EPS type will also involve the use of other instruments when the market share of the exporting country is already relatively large.

(iii)   An EPS of "growing and consolidating" applies to the REOs in Cell [3], [8] and [13], as they are about the imports of large volumes which have experienced important growth in the recent past. The EPO hopes to contribute to the rise of the country's exports of the given product to the target country by benefiting from the expected rise of the already high demand.

(iv) In large import markets that show important growth in the long run, but not in the recent past, i.e. the import markets relating to [4], [9] and [14], the EPO should rather follow an EPS of "leapfrogging". This might be a continuation of the "growing and consolidating" EPS, but there is no immediate reason to expect further growth of the market, which evidently creates some uncertainty about the future.

(v) An EPS of "jumping on the bandwagon" applies to Cell [5], [10] and [15]. The target country is importing large volumes of the product and these imports show important growth, both in the long and short run.

We can now combine the EPS categories of both rows and columns of Table 9.1, as is illustrated in Table 9.2.

Table 9.2. Export promotion strategies categorisation based on REOs.

	Small market share: offensive market exploration EPS	Medium large market share: offensive market expansion EPS
Large market	Breaking in into a large market: Niche market approach based EPS Supportive media campaign…	Breaking in into a large market: Invest in future growth Improve presence (e.g. support representation office)…
Growing market	Taking advantage of a growing market: Better exploit competitive advantage (price, service, delivery) Supportive media campaign…	Taking advantage of a growing market: Better exploit existing presence Go to the customer…
Large and growing market	Combined EPS of growing and consolidating, leapfrogging or jumping on the bandwagon	Combined EPS of growing and consolidating, leapfrogging or jumping on the bandwagon

This will lead to the following examples of EPSs in which the following instruments are used:

(i) An offensive market exploration EPS of breaking in into a large market: as the imports are large and the exporting country's market share small, it is appropriate for the EPO to help exporters in finding a market niche in the target country. The potential exporters are receiving market information which intends to make them aware of the market potentials. The potential exports are incited to join high-profile trade missions which are also supported by media campaigns in the target country.

(ii) An offensive market expansion EPS taking advantage of a growing market: the exporting country has already achieved a medium large market share. The existing exporters have experience in the target country. The EPO should help the exporters to better exploit their presence and their image, by e.g. giving financial support for developing or improving publicity material, improving product design and quality, to conduct detailed market research, etc.

(iii)   An offensive market exploration EPS of jumping on the bandwagon: the import market is large and growing, but the exporters' presence is small, if at all. Here the EPS should combine elements that will allow the potential exporters to enter the market or increase their market presence. The dissemination of market information and participation of the potential exporters in high-profile trade missions, supported by media campaigns, has to be combined with more aggressive instruments, among which financial, which will allow the potential exporters to improve their competitive advantage further (e.g. official loans to the target country, improved credit insurance conditions, but also matchmaking with exporters of complementary products and giving incentives for piggy-back export systems). Also inviting key-decision makers in the target country (major importers or distributors) or facilitating outgoing foreign direct investment to the target economy can be an effective instrument.

(iv)   An offensive EPS of market expansion of leapfrogging: the EPO should design an EPS which will allow the exporters to increase their sales to the target country (by improving financial conditions by e.g. official loans and development aid to the target country, improved credit insurance conditions, etc. but also by giving incentives for participation in specialised trade fairs and exhibitions which attract importers of the target country) and/or to improve their presence by finding synergy with other exporters (setting up or supporting a joint representation office in the target country, matchmaking with other producers/exporters for piggy-back exporting).

It will be clear, however, that not every possible combination makes much sense and can be defined. For instance, consider in Table 9.1 Cell [11] and [14]. It is far from evident how different the instrument mix will be for an "offensive market expansion EPS of breaking in into a large market" from the mix for an "offensive market expansion EPS of leapfrogging", as the exporting country has already a relatively important market share and thus will probably benefit from both the large size and the growth of the import market of the given product in the target country. However, one can easily see that an offensive market exploration EPS of jumping on the bandwagon, applicable to a REO in Cell [5], is different from an offensive market expansion EPS of jumping on the bandwagon, applicable to a REO in Cell [15], as in the latter situation the EPO can rely much more on e.g., the experience and co-operation of its exporters than in the former situation.

Our categorisation of export promotion strategies according to the cell in Table 9.1 where a given REO is located, seems a useful tool for defining such strategies in broad terms, but evidently needs to be supplemented with a list of concrete and detailed steps and instruments, which also take into account other information and data that can be derived from the output of the filtering process, such as quantitative data on market concentration and market accessibility/trade barriers. Figure 9.1 below lists tentatively supplementary export promotion instruments according to the combination of market concentration and market accessibility. However, much more concrete and detailed information is required for designing an appropriate export promotion strategy, than the statistics which are used in detecting REOs by a decision support model, such as the one described in section 9.2. Such detailed information should rather come from market research, both desk and field research, and from further competitive intelligence (CI) on the REOs (for more detail, see Chapter 11). Although there exists an abundant literature on export management strategies, the topic of defining export promotion strategies based on market performance and import market characteristics, has remained uncharted territory.

Figure 9.1. Export promotion instruments according to concentration and accessibility of the import market.

		Trade barriers	
		Low	High
Concentration	Low	Inform exporters on market potentials	Inform exporters on trade barriers
		Create awareness	Organise product-country focused seminars
		Create exposure for exporters	Create exposure for exporters
	High	Create awareness	Facing scarce resources, should the EPO bother about these REOs?
		Convince the market	
		Develop EPOs with sufficient scale and synergy	

In the following sections we will, therefore, rather rely on a thorough discussion of appropriate EPSs, using the above categorisation, but applying these to well-identified and concrete case studies of some selected realistic export opportunities of South Africa, as follows:

(i)   Macadamia nuts to Germany (Cell 2).

(ii)   Extruders for rubber and plastic to Tunisia (Cell 2).

(iii)   Jewellery of precious metals (except silver) to the United Kingdom (Cell 11).

9.4   South African case studies

9.4.1   Macadamia nuts to Germany

According to the results of the DSM to identify REOs for SA, the German import market of macadamia nuts is a large and growing market, both in the short and long term, with South Africa having only a relatively small market share (Cell 2). Based on our previous categorisation, an offensive EPS of market exploration is appropriate, and will allow South African macadamia nut growers and exporters to "jump on the bandwagon" of that sizable and growing market, which also would establish South Africa's presence.

The main players in the South African macadamia nuts industry with regards to export promotion are the Department of Trade and Industry (DTI) and the Southern African Sub-Tropical Growers Association (SA-SubTrop). The DTI's Sector Specific Assistance Scheme (SSAS) and Export Marketing and Investment Assistance (EMIA) individual support schemes provide support for individual participants as well as industry organisation's participation at trade shows. However, exporters and the industry association are not well informed of the existence of the DTI's export support programs. In order for the South African macadamia nut industry to realise its full export potential in the German market, which is essentially a new market, it is vital for the DTI, to provide extensive export support to individual exporters. This can be in the form of general support, which includes availing publications such as market guides or market profiles to specific geographic locations, market opportunity studies, "how-to" booklets about trips, market surveys, reference sources, setting up an export business, and domestic and international sources of export financing (Seringhaus & Mayer, 1988). Additionally, the DTI needs to raise awareness of its assistance toward participation in trade fairs. It is important to note that the impact of trade missions on export performance can be most appropriately measured by "soft" management dimensions rather than "hard" performance measures as noted by Seringhaus and Botschen (1991:3).[1]

The DTI's existing foreign offices can also be used to provide exporters with real time intelligence from the German market and assistance about exporting. Foreign offices can provide market reports, maintain close contact with government and regulatory bodies and increasingly offer export seminars to assist exporters (Seringhaus & Botschen, 1991:3). The foreign offices can be a source of overall industry intelligence. In particular the use of voluntary and non voluntary standards is increasingly becoming more significant in international trade. Although these standards are not always mandatory they now serve as barriers to market accessibility and without conformance to the standard's requirements, exporters may find it difficult to do business in those markets. In the German market the Global GAP standard applies to imports of macadamia nuts. It is a business-to-business (B2B) standard making it a voluntary standard. However, some of the largest retailers in Europe only purchase goods that are Global GAP certified (Standards Map, 2011). The foreign offices in the German market can provide South African exporters of macadamia nuts with such real time intelligence and improve market accessibility as well as enhance the profitability of exporters.

Furthermore, the DTI can provide an export information telephone service or web-based information provision portals. This portal or telephone service would provide South African

---

1 Soft management dimensions refer to the intangible benefits that accrue to the firm's foreign market development such as increased knowledge and competence. On the contrary, hard management measurement dimensions would include tangible factors such as sales (Seringhaus & Mayer, 1988).

macadamia nut exporters (and other exporters alike), with information relating to the markets with the highest possible export potential, for their products. This is particularly important as firms often lack the time and resources to do in-depth market studies on export opportunities. Alternatively, following the Californian Almond Board website, the export help desk can create a web link to the South African Macadamias Growers' Association (SAMAC) website, which would be strongly consumer focused and offer consumers more detailed information about the macadamia nuts, the associated health benefits from consumption as well as recipes and ingredient measures to suit each culture.

Consumption of edible nuts in Germany amounted to 319,000 tons and accounted for 16% of total EU consumption in 2006, making it the leading edible nut consumer (FAO, 2008). The consumption of edible nuts increased by 4% in Germany in 2008 (FAO, 2008). Most edible nuts are consumed as part of confectionary products. Groundnuts were the most consumed edible nut in Germany accounting for 31% of the volume of Germany's total edible nut consumption, whilst almonds are also widely consumed in Germany (20% of total volume) (CBI, 2007). Macadamia nut consumption was still relatively low and it constituted only 0.7% of the total German consumption of edible nuts. In this case promoting macadamia nut exports in Germany can be achieved by jumping on the bandwagon since the import market is large and growing, but the South African exporters' presence is small. Hence an increase in consumer awareness of the product can be achieved through brand and generic advertising, in-store promotions and public relations (Kinnucan, Xiao & Yu, 2000:560).

The consumption of luxury nuts has gained popularity in the EU market and in Germany in particular. This is mainly as a result of the consumers becoming more health conscious and the ability of nut packers to successfully market newly-developed nut mixtures. Consumption of edible nuts is rising and is increasingly becoming an alternative source of protein due to the prevalence of diseases such as foot-and-mouth disease in cattle. Due to the change in lifestyles, more German consumers spend less time preparing meals and this has led to the rise in consumption of healthy snacks that contain protein, for example, edible nuts. Consumer awareness on the associated health benefits from consuming macadamia nuts can be raised in the German market through in-store promotions and tasting of the product. Furthermore, information dissemination through the distribution of leaflets and booklets to consumers can also enhance consumer awareness and shift attitudes towards the product. Alternatively, South African macadamias can be branded with other high quality products and promoted through joint marketing groups. This will entail generating complementary synergies with other industries. This can be through branding with South African wines or dried fruit and targeted to the high quality conscious consumer. These products can be branded together and promoted through booklets, paper and media advertisements and displayed at national pavilions and trade fairs.

The distribution channel for food and beverages in Germany is mainly characterised by retailers importing from a central buyer or an importer. Importers act as intermediaries between suppliers abroad and customers in Germany (BGA, 2008). Retailers seldom import directly from suppliers, especially those that are not in the EU. Central buyers or traders or importers handle large orders that consist of a variety of products in large volumes and are responsible for distribution to the various retailers. Retailers import directly only if the products possess special qualities, price or promotional support (FAS, 2008). The Southern African Macadamia Growers Association (SAMAC) offers its members assistance on trade statistics, documentation and market specific research. This role, however, can further enhanced by increasing cooperation with the DTI to support the SAMAC to be better equipped to provide exporters with up to date and relevant information. This is mainly because interviews with members of the industry association revealed that there is little or no co-operation between the industry association and the DTI (Sithole & Viviers, 2010).

Furthermore, export promotion can be targeted to magazines, where the product can be featured as a high end, healthy gourmet product. Such a feature would assist to justify the high prices for which the product fetches (McKinna et al., 2007:48). Consumer awareness can also be raised by television advertisements. Television is the most effective media to raise awareness. However, this will require a high investment and as a result, the television advertisements can initially be limited to one city and then be increased as consumer awareness and market share increases (McKinna et al., 2007:48).

The export promotion strategy can take advantage of economies of scale or scope in export promotion by linking macadamia nut-related products or potentially-related products for which South Africa has already acquired a reasonable degree of comparative advantage, as well as their promotion. These products can be promoted as South African health foods with proven health benefits. Mention can be made here of:

(i)   080440 – Avocados, fresh or dried (Cell 6)

(ii)   200811 – Groundnuts, otherwise prepared or preserved (Cell 16)

(iii)   080810 – Apples, fresh (Cell 11)

(iv)   081350 – Mixtures of edible nuts, dried and preserved fruits (Cell 20)

Furthermore, there are also South African REOs for products in the German market that can be related or complimentary to macadamia nuts, especially fresh or dried fruit, but for which South Africa has not sufficient comparative advantage, but which might be followed up as well in developing an export promotion strategy for macadamia nuts and related products, such as e.g.:

(i)   220421 – Grape wines n.e.s., fortified wine or must, pack < 2l (Cell 15)

(ii)   080610 – Grapes, fresh (Cell 10)

(iii) 080620 – Grapes, dried (Cell 15)

(iv) 200190 – Vegetables, fruit, nuts n.e.s. prepared or preserved by vinegar (Cell 14)

(v) 200850 – Apricots, otherwise prepared or preserved (Cell 16)

(vi) 080290 – Nuts edible, fresh or dried, n.e.s. (Cell 10)

(vii) 200892 – Fruit mixtures, otherwise prepared or preserved (Cell 6)

(viii) 080430 – Pineapples, fresh or dried (Cell 15)

(ix) 220410 – Grape wines, sparkling (Cell 11)

(x) 081320 – Prunes, dried (Cell 3)

The next section will describe the possible instruments for an EPS for extruders for rubber and plastics to Tunisia.

9.4.2   Extruders for rubber and plastic to Tunisia

Similar to the performance of macadamia exports to Germany, the results of the DSM, indicate that the export opportunity for extruders to Tunisia fall in Cell 2, which represents a short- and long-term growth market for extruders and indicates that South African-exported extruders have a negligibly small or no market share in Tunisia. Based on the previous categorisation, an offensive EPS of market exploration would be appropriate, allowing South African manufacturers to extruders to exploit the opportunities that are present by taking a combined EPS of growing and jumping on the bandwagon.

There are mainly two EPOs relevant to manufacturers of capital equipment, and specifically extruders, in South Africa, namely the South African Capital Equipment Export Council (SACEEC) and the Department of Trade and Industry (DTI). The SACEEC represents companies in the business of manufacturing equipment of a fixed capital nature. The SACEEC organises, amongst others, inward-buying missions and its mandate is to promote mining and capital equipment buying internationally (SACEEC, 2009). The promotion of local products in the international marketplace forms the driving force behind the activities of the SACEEC. Specifically, the role of the SACEEC is to identify foreign markets for South African capital equipment exporters and to market South Africa to capital equipment dealers, manufacturers and investors globally directed at attracting investment into the South African capital equipment industry.

The DTI has an Export Promotion Directorate responsible for developing and promoting South African manufactured goods and services. The SACEEC is one of twenty industry export councils to which DTI provides financial support. Previous research has determined that there is no specific trade-promotion strategy followed by either the DTI or the SACEEC with regard to promoting export of extruders or other products in the capital equipment industry to Tunisia.

In order to capitalise on the said export opportunity, the DTI and the SACEEC need to adopt certain offensive actions in their export-promotion strategy to enable exporters to take advantage of the growing market both in the short and long term, and to gain successful entry into this significant market. Previous research determined that a degree of market concentration and certain trade barriers (that also include NTBs) exist (Kühn, 2010). Therefore, it is recommended that an offensive export-promotion strategy be selected that actively pursues the opportunities available.

Part of the offensive export promotion strategy could be to piggy-back onto other products in the capital equipment industry that can be targeted for export-promotion activities. Other elements of an offensive export-promotion strategy could include closer co-operation and establishment of partner relationship between EPOs and potential extruder exporters in order to assess the information needs of such exporters and to inform them of the export potential and on the market characteristics: Such a partnership between the EPOs and the potential exporters will enhance the export opportunity and will ensure that the correct export-promotion activities are arranged or provided by the EPOs for extruders exporting to Tunisia using the most appropriate and available export-promotion instruments.

Detail on issues related to the market in Tunisia can be gathered, analysed and made available to extruder manufacturers. Such market information is typically required by exporters (whether new or more experienced) and could include information on institutions that could be involved in the export promotion of extruders both in South Africa and Tunisia, e.g. export-promotion organisations in Tunisia, banks and relevant government bodies. This information offering should be tailored to the needs of the exporters and the stage of export of the exporter.

Focused communication is another element of an EPS that can be considered by EPOs. Exporters could be communicated with regarding the status of the export opportunity and Tunisia as an export destination and the DTI commercial attaché based in Tunis could be communicated with regarding the status of the REO and Tunisia as an export destination. Furthermore, extruder manufacturers and perhaps also exporters of extruder components could be invited to participate in general trade missions, and local and regional trade fairs, in addition to the traditional fairs organised by the DTI and the SACEEC. An example is the METEF-FOUNDEQ 2010 trade show held in Italy which focuses on the Middle Eastern and North African market, which will give greater prominence to the aluminium extrusion production chain (METEF-FOUNDEQ, 2010). Present at this event are typically the main extruders users and leading global manufacturers of extruder machinery, plants and components. In addition, foreign Tunisian industry decision-makers and major importers could be invited to networking events organised by the DTI commercial attaché based in Tunisia.

EPOs can also consider developing and presenting tailored advanced export training and technical assistance with a particular focus on trade in North Africa and specifically Tunisia. Financial support for in-market marketing campaigns targeting the food-processing, plastics, and mechanical and metal works (especially aluminium) industries can be considered while an assessment of the trade barriers can be made and presented to inform local extruder manufacturers of these trade barriers and the way to manage them. Workshops and seminars on results of market research and recommendations on possible steps of action: E.g. a workshop for extruder manufacturers and in particular new exporters, focusing specifically on the export of extruders to Tunisia and by extension the Middle East and North Africa, could be organised. Such a workshop could be expanded to also include the wider capital equipment industry and the users of extruders in South Africa and Tunisia. One of the main purposes should be to determine the information needs of exporters and specifically new exporters and to assess whether the EPO could assist in providing such information (and also communicate the areas in which the EPO cannot assist). Previous research indicates that there are gaps between what exporters' needs are in terms of information and what EPOs provide in terms of advice, services, publications, and other trade promotion initiatives. It was found that EPOs provide a general and wide range of export-promotion services, including information that could be useful to exporters, yet the latter were unaware of these products and services. Making available all this relevant information to exporters in the identified product sectors would enhance the potential success of export ventures to identified markets, as it would enable exporters to develop detailed marketing and export plans based on the provided analysed information. It would also support the assessment of strategies, enhance competitor perceptions and efficacy of export operations, provide insights into competitor capabilities, and enhance long-term market prospects.

EPOs could offer a networking opportunity for companies that export to Tunisia inviting delegates from the DTI, the SACEEC and the Department of Foreign Affairs (DFA), and perhaps banks and logistics companies to provide relevant information. Tunisian commercial attachés should also attend such networking events. EPOs could provide information to extruder manufacturers on exhibits, trade shows and pavilions. The DTI identified Tunisia and Egypt as key destinations for South African exports for growth in the Middle East and North Africa. EPOs could contact their Tunisian counterparts in order to assess the level of support available to South African exporters of extruders. These EPOs can also be valuable sources of Tunisian trade and industry information.

EPOs could investigate the advantages of promoting other products that fall under HS Chapter 84, together with extruders in Tunisia. Such products include rubber or plastic vacuum moulders, thermo-formers (HS 847740); parts of machines for working rubber or plastic (HS 847790); moulds, injection and compression, for rubber or plastic (HS 848071); and metal treating machines, electric wire coil-winders (HS 847981). Currently, South Africa does not export to or has limited exports of any of these products to Tunisia.

EPOs could start market development activities in Tunisia in the form of introductions of the product. This could include the gathering of local market information by the South African embassy staff based in Tunis. This competitive intelligence input from either the EPO and/or external organisations of information that has been synthesised, analysed, evaluated and contextualised must be used by the EPO in its export-promotion strategy formulation, and disseminated to the exporters. This would assist EPOs in achieving the export-promotion differentiation required for this particular market type (growing short and long term, and relatively small or no market share) and differentiation according to trade barriers and market concentration.

Enhancing the capacity of the SACEEC can be a further recommendation. This can be done by providing for additional information and analysis specialists for the capital equipment industry. At present, the SACEEC has no analysis capability and, therefore, no capacity to determine the key intelligence needs for its industry. Finally, an EPS could include market profiles of the markets that show the most potential for specific products produced and manufactured in South Africa be compiled under the auspices of the DTI, using the structure of the case study presented in this chapter, and that these profiles be regularly updated and made available to exporters.

The next section will describe the possible instruments for an EPS for jewellery of precious metals (except silver) to the United Kingdom.

9.4.3 Articles of jewellery to the United Kingdom

The realistic export opportunity (REO) for "Articles of jewellery in the United Kingdom" is found in Cell 11 of the categorisation matrix (Table 9.1) and thus relates to a large import market with a market share of South Africa which is relatively large. Moreover, according to the information from filter 3 of the DSM, the UK market for these articles does not seem to be very concentrated with a Hirschman-Herfindahl index of 0.132 and relatively high market accessibility.

Based on interviews, it was discovered that the South African jewellery exporters to the UK market are not sufficiently taking care of the market trends and the consumer preferences.

Therefore, as the UK market of jewellery is large, there is scope for more South African exports by both actual and new exporters.

Small scale jewellers in South Africa do not always have access to private loans to buy equipment needed for overseas orders. It is thus important for the DTI to assist these small and medium enterprises in providing financial assistance to get their export initiative off the ground. The DTI has financial programmes that assist first time exporters such as the EMIA scheme. This scheme provides the necessary financial assistance that South African jewellery exports need to enhance their presence in the UK. Other export promotion programmes include trade lead facilitation, In-market support, facilitating exports by matching potential exporters with foreign buyers and the EMIA financial assistance scheme.

Due to the financial crisis, there was a declining production in metal jewellery, especially gold. On the contrary, the production and consumption of jewellery made from platinum increased. The DTI can, through their foreign offices and foreign desks, assist new exports of jewellery by providing real time intelligence to exporters to keep them informed of new trends in target markets. The DTI can, therefore, advise South African jewellery manufacturers to focus on platinum jewellery even if it is only for a short time period until gold prices are stabilised.

The Jewellery Council of South Africa (JCSA) is the industry association for jewellery in South Africa. The vision of the JCSA is to create an environment for the South African Jewellery industry to become a successful trading hub for the continent Africa (Chikane, 2006). Communication between the DTI and the JCSA is very limited. The problem extends to the absence of communication between Gauteng and Cape Town jewellery manufacturers thus constraining the awareness of export opportunities. It is essential that governments develop effective communication programmes. Jewel City is an industry cluster in Johannesburg and is providing training schools; serves as an empowerment incubator and supports manufacturers. The main advantage of this industry is their focus on exports; they raise awareness of the jewellery industry and their financing arrangements. Although they are more focused on diamonds, there is an opportunity for other precious metals to collaborate with and this increasing the export potential (Kaiser Associates, 2001).

It is important that the jewellery industry must strengthen and widen their cooperation to enter in export markets. Exports of South African jewellery can be effectively promoted through joint marketing. There are limited efforts between players and small manufacturers as they have limited marketing resources. Joint marketing could be considered with the fashion industries to collaborate with a variety of successfully exported fashion products for instance clothing, shoes, watches and arts and craft. This will increase the awareness of articles of jewellery as a complementary product even though jewellery can be substituted with the other fashion items. Such joint marketing ventures can be targeted at prestigious fashion events such as London fashion week. This event is hosted twice yearly and it is one of the world's biggest fashion shows (UK Trade & Investment, 2009). Exhibiting South African jewellery at such an event will increase consumer awareness of the product and also target high-end consumers. The JCSA and the DTI can collaborate to assist exporters by providing financial assistance as well as providing information on possible clothing designers with which South African jewellery producers can collaborate.

The consumption preferences of jewellery in the UK according to Kaiser Associates (2001) were characterised of earrings (31%), rings (25%), neckwear (21%) and wrist wear (14%). The UK is a traditionally 9-carat market and thus important for South Africa to emphasise their on 9-carat precious metal jewellery. The UK is one of the largest import markets of jewellery in Europe and for the past years. Bilateral trade in gold jewellery between the UK and South Africa has been stable in the past. It is essential to continuously promote these exports and this can be done through trade fairs in South Africa in the UK, to ensure future development in gold jewellery (Kaiser Associates, 2001).

Platinum jewellery imports are also a prominent component of the UK's trade inflows, mainly the bridal sector. Industry experts recommend that South Africa must focus on platinum manufacturing and exporting as great opportunities exist in this sub-sector for South Africa. This also creates an opportunity to jointly promote platinum jewellery bridal wear at bridal expos for instance. Platinum jewellery is a more innovative and dynamic market than gold jewellery in the UK.

Unfortunately there are negative perceptions of South African jewellery. South African jewellery is regarded as too exotic and "chunky" (Kaiser Associates, 2001). A major retail chain in the UK has the opinion that the UK needs more conservative and small designs of jewellery. SA exporters can benefit from the DTI's trade lead facilitation, which offer market information from foreign economic representatives in the various target export markets. These trade leads should provide exporters with insight into the consumer preferences and consumption trends. The DTI can also assist jewellery exporters through their scheme to match buyers and sellers. This will facilitate easier market access for South African exporters and enable exporters to communicate and adapt their product to meet the buyer's needs. Lastly, the DTI and the JCSA can provide technical support as well as in market support to assist exporters to adapt their product to meet the UK consumer's preferences and to sell their product successfully.

In addition, it is perceived that the price and quality ratio of South African jewellery is too high. It is thus essential that exporters receive financial information from the DTI in order to price the traded jewellery competitively. To conclude in this regard it important for South

Africa to approach the UK jewellery market in a unique, but conservative style of jewellery. Although the market share of South African exports of jewellery is growing it is important to attend trade shows. Kaiser Associates (2001) enlighten the importance of South Africa attending trade shows, in order to get the jewellery in front of a lot of buyers and these trade shows are the most effective way. There are six major trade shows which South Africa can attend to namely in Basel, Vicenza, Hong Kong, Las Vegas, Birmingham Spring Fair and the International Jewellery London show. The DTI should promote specifically participation of South African exporters these trade shows, both for existing and new exporters to the UK market.

There is also potential to have economies of scale or scope in export promotion by linking jewellery to related or potentially related products for which South Africa has already acquired a reasonable degree of comparative advantage, as well as their promotion. Mention can be made here of:

(i)   330430 – Manicure or pedicure preparations (Cell 16)

(ii)   330590 – Hair preparations, n.e.s. (Cell 11)

(iii)   710239 – Diamonds (jewellery) worked, but not mounted or set (Cell 6)

However, there are also South African REOs for women or fashion products in the UK market that can be related to jewellery, for which South Africa has not sufficient comparative advantage, but which might be followed up as well in developing an export promotion strategy for jewellery and related products, such as e.g.:

(iv)   330300 – Perfumes and toilet waters (Cell 11)

(v)   330410 – Lip make-up preparations (Cell 11)

(vi)   330420 – Eye make-up preparations (Cell 16)

(vii)   610413 – Women's, girls' suits, synthetic fibres, knit (Cell 5)

(viii) 610419 – Women's, girls' suits, of material n.e.s. knit (Cell 5)

(ix)   610433 – Women's, girls' jackets, blazers, synthetic fibres, knit (Cell 20)

(x)   610439 – Women's, girls' jackets and blazers, material n.e.s. knit (Cell 3)

(xi)   610442 – Women's, girls' dresses, of cotton, knit (Cell 6)

(xii)   610452 – Women's, girls' skirts, of cotton, knit (Cell 8)

(xiii) 610453 – Women's, girls' skirts, synthetic fibres, knit (Cell 6)

(xiv)   610459 – Women's, girls' skirts, of material n.e.s. knit (Cell 1)

(xv)   610462 – Women's, girls' trousers and shorts, of cotton, knit (Cell 6)

(xvi)   610469 – Women's, girls' trousers and shorts, material n.e.s. knit (Cell 4)

Among the above REOs those in Cells 16 and 20, but also those in Cell 11, should catch our special attention, as in spite of a low degree of comparative advantage South African producers are exporting these products to the UK market.

The list of related products above shows some of the potentials for economies of scale and scope in export promotion. However, with due regard of South Africa's present share in the UK market for jewellery, the promotion of jewellery products per se should not be diluted unnecessarily. In contrast, the present market share would warrant a market expansion EPS of "breaking in" into a large market, with instruments that are somewhat different from these used in order to tap into REOs of other large markets such as cells 1 and 6. This can be done by investment in future growth, e.g. by setting up a marketing and design advisory division in London. This division could then also be involved in market information and dissemination, the organisation of workshops and seminars, own exhibitions, etc. which are instruments that should be used in case of low barriers to trade and low market concentration.

9.5   Conclusions

Apart from being an instrument to identify export opportunities, export promotion organisations can also use the DSM results in the preparation and assessment of export promotion activities. In filter 4 of the DSM, the export opportunities detected are grouped according to the respective market shares of the exporting country in the various target markets and according to some general import market characteristics at the level of the respective products. Obviously, export promotion strategies will differ, and hence the export promotion activities required, between e.g. a yet to tap relatively small export opportunity which shows long-term growth in the past, and a large and relatively stable export opportunity in a country where the exporting country has already achieved a relatively strong market position. Appropriate export promotion strategies at product level can thus be designed, by taking this into account. In this chapter, we have explored this in some detail and attempted to make the strategic considerations based on DSM results as concrete as possible by illustrating the choices made in three detailed case studies of South African export opportunities. If one lesson can be drawn from this exercise it is that the DSM results provide input in this process of concrete strategy formulation, but that much more concrete and detailed information is required for designing an appropriate export promotion strategy. This important input should come from market research, both desk and field research, and from further competitive intelligence on given export opportunities.

References

Alvarez, R. 2004. Sources of export success in small- and medium-sized enterprises: the impact of public programs. *International Business Review*, 13: 383-400.

Chikane, A. 2006. Jewellery Council of South Africa Strategic Plan. [Online.] Available from: http://www.jewellerysa.com/index2.php?option=com_docman&task=doc_view&gid=27&Itemid=99999999. Accessed 23 August 2010.

Cuyvers, L., De Pelsmacker,P., Rayp, G. & Roozen, I.T.M. 1995. A decision support model for the planning and assessment of export promotion activities by government promotion institutions: the Belgian case. *International Journal of Research in Marketing*, 12(2): 173-186.

Cuyvers, L. 1996. Export opportunities of Thailand: A decision support model approach. *Journal of Euro-Asian Management*, 2(2): 71-97.

Cuyvers, L. 2004. Identifying export opportunities: the case of Thailand. *International Marketing Review*, 21(3): 255-278.

De Wulf, L. 2001. Why have trade organizations failed, and how they can be revitalized? *PREM Notes, 56*, World Bank.

Foreign Agricultural Services (FAS). 2008. A guide to exporting food and beverage products to Germany. Report prepared by FAS staff in Germany. United States Department of Agriculture. [Online.] Available from: http://www.fas.usda.gov/info/agexporter/1997/January&201997/germany. Accessed 29 March 2008.

Kaiser Associates. 2001. Programme, development, management and evaluation. [Online.] Available from: http://www.kaiseredp.com/new/proj_programme.htm. Accessed 24 August 2010.

Kinnucun, H.W., Xiao, H. & Yu, S. 2000. Relative effectiveness of USDA's non-price export promotion instruments. *Journal of Agricultural and Resource Economics*, 2592: 559-577.

Kühn, M-L. 2010. Exporters' information requirements: The role of Competitive Intelligence in the export promotion of extruders. Unpublished doctoral thesis. North-West University, Potchefstroom.

Lederman, D., Olarreaga, M. & Payton, L. 2006. Export promotion agencies: what works and what doesn't. *Policy Research Working Paper Series: 4044*. The World Bank.

McKinna *et al.* 2007. Strategic insights: horticulture Australia Ltd – Macadamia review HAL 0291. [Online.] Available from: http://www.mckinna.com.au/case.html. Accessed 14 May 2010.

Metef-Foundeq. 2010. Expectations for METEF-FOUNDEQ 2010 exhibition. [Online.] Available from: http://www.metef.com/ENG/home.asp. Accessed 14 May 2010.

Pearson, J., Viviers, W., Cuyvers, L. & Naudé, W. 2010. Spotting opportunities for international entrepreneurship in the southern engines: a DSM approach. *International Business Review*, 19(4): 345-359.

Seringhaus, F.H.R. & Botschen, G. 1991. Cross-national comparison of export promotion services: the views of Canadian and Austrian companies. *Journal of International Business Studies*, 22(1).

Seringhaus, F.H.R. & Mayer, S.F. 1988. Different approaches to foreign market entry between users and non-users of trade missions. *European Journal of Marketing*, 22(10): 7-18.

Sithole, N.M. & Viviers, W. 2010. The export potential of South African edible nuts with special reference to the export of macadamia nuts to Germany. *Agrekon*, 49(4): 484-504.

South African Capital Equipment Export Council (SACEEC). 2009. General information on website. [Online.] Available from: http://www.saceec.org.za. Accessed 14 February 2010.

Standards Map. 2011. Global GAP. [Online.] Available from: http://www.standardsmap.org/assets/media/Fairtrade/Final_FLO.pdf. Accessed 13 June 2011.

Chapter 10

Adaptation and application of the DSM for services in South Africa

Sonja Grater & Wilma Viviers

10.1   Introduction

World trade in services has increased dramatically in recent years. The total exports of services globally constituted 22% of total world exports during 2009, with an average growth rate of 7.6% since 1980 (UNCTAD, 2010). The Uruguay Round of the General Agreement on Tariffs and Trade (GATT) in 1993 initiated the global drive to liberalise services trade through the establishment of the General Agreement on Trade in Services (GATS). The GATS negotiations have driven the global process of opening markets for services trade that were previously protected by domestic government policies and other barriers (WTO, 2005). Countries now face various challenges, such as introducing healthy competition to the local services sector, building sufficient regulatory institutions that support the local services sectors and establishing effective export promotion mechanisms (Mattoo & Stern, 2008).

The services sector in South Africa has played a more considerable role in the economy and is becoming one of South Africa's significant export sectors (Steuart & Cassim, 2005). In the period from 2005 to 2009 the services sector contributed on average 65% to the GDP of South Africa (SARB, 2010). In 2010 a total of 79% of the labour force in South Africa was employed in the services sector (STATSSA, 2010). However, the exports of services only contributed 19% to the total exports of South Africa from 2005 to 2009 (ITC, 2010a). The largest services export sectors for South Africa over the five-year period were travel (63%), transportation (11%), and other business services (9%). This indicates that South Africa's service exports are mostly concentrated in one sector, travel, which constitutes 63% of services exports. Therefore, South Africa has potential to diversify service exports into other sectors. Hausmann and Klinger (2008) indicated South Africa needs a much faster growth rate in exports and this can be achieved by moving exports into more non-resource based exports that do not need expensive resource inputs. Services are one of these non-resource based sectors that could contribute to the potential growth.

In the South African Trade Policy and Strategy Framework (TPSF), the Department of Trade and Industry (DTI), expresses the need for well-considered research that identifies the related development and export potential of key service sectors. It is further stated that South Africa needs to use scientific research to identify the development and export potential of key services sectors (DTI, 2010b).

Cuyvers, De Pelsmacker, Rayp and Roozen (1995) indicated that export promotion instruments should be aimed at identifying potential export opportunities in order to allocate scarce resources in government to the active promotion of those sectors that hold the greatest potential. In their study a decision support model (DSM) was developed in order to determine potential export opportunities in a scientific manner. This model addresses the need of governments to use a scientific method to identify export potential (see Chapter 4 for more detail).

This DSM approach has been adopted for the South African products in 2007 (Viviers & Pearson, 2007) and again in 2009 and 2010 (Viviers, Rossouw & Steenkamp, 2009; Viviers, Steenkamp, Rossouw & Cuyvers, 2010) to cater for the needs of the South African government. However, this model was only applied to products and the model does not identify export opportunities for services. Therefore, this chapter is aimed at identifying a methodology to develop a decision support model (DSM) for services, based on the same principles as the DSM for products. No other models for services could be found in the literature that performs the same function.

The following section of the chapter aims to create an understanding of the services sector. This is followed by an outline of the methodology of the DSM for services and subsequently a discussion of the results of the model.

10.2 Understanding services and the GATS negotiations

Due to the nature of services it is not possible to state one definition that captures the essence of the services sector as a whole (Fieleke, 1995; McLachlan, Clark & Monday, 2002). Traditionally services were defined as the "residual" economic sector (ASR, 2007). This term describes services as all economic activities other than mining, manufacturing, agriculture, forestry and fishing, therefore, defining services by what they are not. Services were also seen as "non-tradable" and that services could only be delivered as it is produced, such as a hairdresser that gives a customer a haircut (Francois, 1990; Grönroos, 1999, Oyewole, 2001). Therefore, policymakers did not view services, as an integral part of the economy and services was associated with the informal sector of the economy, consisting of part-time and low-skilled jobs.

The perception of services has changed dramatically as the policymakers have realised the role that services actually play in an economy. Services can act as a support industry to the manufacturing and other sectors and Warren and Findlay (1999) described services as an economic activity that adds value to another "economic unit" or product. For example, financial services and transportation services are crucial to the manufacturing process and also to the exports of products.

However, Howells (2000) found that services cannot only be regarded as a support industry, but should also be recognised as an industry on its own. For instance, the banking sector acts as a support service to many other industries, but the banking sector in itself is also a tradable service and produces a "product" of its own (Daniels, 2000). This is the reason why it is difficult to develop one definition to describe the nature of service delivery.

The concept of classifying services evolved in the 1980s and under GATS the most well-known classification system was developed (WTO, 1991). This classification system divides services into 12 main-sector classifications. Each classification entails a group of services that perform similar functions, such as business services, communication services, construction services or financial services. These main sectors are then further divided into 160 sub-sectors, for example business services are divided into professional services, computer-related services, research and development services, and some other sub-sectors (WTO, 1991).

The GATS agreement also established the modes of supply, which represents the different methods by which a services trade transaction can take place. The modes of supply are summarised in Table 10.1. The modes of supply show that a service can be delivered to its end-user within the exporters' own market, within the importer's market, or without any contact between either of the two parties. This depends on the specific transaction and means that each mode of supply has different criteria and different challenges.

As part of the GATS framework, WTO member countries negotiate with each other to open markets for certain services sectors and these negotiations are captured by each country in a set/schedule of commitments. The commitments are made on a sub-sector level for all four modes of supply and the commitments in essence show to what extent market access is given for a specific services sector, as well as any restrictions that governments may impose on the sector. For example, a country may only wish to issue a limited amount of licenses for foreign banks in the financial sector and this is captured as a "commitment" that will apply to all WTO member countries. The country cannot decrease the amount of licenses issues without informing all WTO member countries and officially making changes to their schedules of commitments. These commitments are made available publically (WTO, 2009). An example of a set of commitments is shown in Table 10.2.

Table 10.1. GATS modes of supply.

Mode of supply	Supplier's presence	Criteria
Mode 1: Cross-border supply	Service supplier is not present within the import country.	The exporter of the service provides the service to the importer without leaving the exporting country.
Mode 2: Consumption abroad	Service supplier is not present within the import country.	The exporter of the service provides the service to the importer in the exporting country.
Mode 3: Commercial presence	Service supplier is present within the import country.	The exporter provides the service to the importer by creating a commercial presence in the importing country.
Mode 4: Presence of natural person	Service supplier is present within the import country.	The service is exported by a natural person that enters the importing country to deliver the service.

Source: Author's own interpretation of WTO (1991); Hoekman (1996)

In order to increase exports of services and diversify exports into different sectors, the South African government needs to be actively involved in the export promotion of services. One of these activities includes negotiating with different WTO member countries to lift some of the barriers that are in place in order to South African services firms to gain entrance into those markets. To negotiate for all 160 sub-sectors of services is a great task, and therefore, it is advisable to select specific markets and services sectors that hold the greatest export potential for South African services.

Export promotion of services can take on many forms. Some guidelines are discussed in the following section.

10.3   Export promotion of services in South Africa

Export promotion organisations (EPOs) aim to stimulate exports by a variety of export promotion instruments, such as trade fairs, training and financial assistance. These instruments assist firms to market their products more successfully in other countries (Gillespie & Riddle, 2004). If export promotion is successfully enforced it should ultimately lead to export market diversification and provide a more balanced export platform (Martincus & Carballo, 2008).

According to the ITC (2010b) the main challenge services firms face when exporting are to convince foreign buyers to use a service from a source they have never engaged before. Usually new services firms are only contracted if they were referred on the recommendation of other firms that used the same services, and services firms that do not have an established reputation are avoided. Therefore, EPOs need to play a role in establishing the credibility of local service firms in foreign markets. The ITC also suggests that a successful EPO should select priority services sectors in which the country may have a competitive edge, sufficient capacity in the sector to support increased exports and a sector where there may be potential for synergy among the services (ITC, 2010b). The support instruments for services should be grouped into four categories, namely market understanding by means of field based studies, organising trade missions in target countries, assisting with focussed marketing projects and providing quality assurance for services firms to enhance their reputation (CDC, 2006). These instruments should be directed at those specific services sectors that hold the greatest export opportunities for South Africa.

The export promotion activities for services in South Africa are limited to only a few industry associations and export councils that are focussed on sub-sectors of services. The DTI in South Africa is the government institution that is responsible for export promotion and within the DTI structure the ITED (International Trade and Economic Development) and TISA (Trade and Investment South Africa) divisions are both involved in the services sector (DTI, 2010a). ITED is involved in the trade negotiations processes in order to open markets and lower barriers for South Africa's services. TISA is the division that performs most of the export promotion activities.

TISA has been involved in the development of a strategy to prioritise specific markets for South African exports as part of the process to more effectively allocate their resources (DTI, 2006). The DTI has limited capacity and therefore a need exists to have a scientific selection process by which realistic export opportunities could be identified for South Africa. A decision support model (DSM) is currently in use and identifies potential export opportunities for South African products by means of a scientific method (see section 1). This model was only applied to products and the aim of the following section is to develop a similar model that can be applied to the services sector in South Africa. The results of the new decision support model (DSM) for services can be used to formulate a more scientific-based approach to export promotion for services in South Africa, as well as provide guidelines to diversify exports of services. The DSM for services is explained in the following section.

10.4   The development of a decision support model (DSM) for services

The DSM for products was based on a four filter process by which all possible product-country combinations were analysed and the combinations that showed the least potential were eliminated in each filter (see Chapter 4, also Viviers *et al.*, 2010). The same principle could be applied to services; however, the methods behind some of the filters have to be adjusted to account for the nature of services as well as the limited data availability. The aim of this section is to explain the methodology that was developed for each filter of the decision support model (DSM) for services.

10.4.1 Decision support model for services: Filter 1

The first filter of the DSM for products evaluated macro-economic data for 240 countries. The first part of the filter, known as Filter 1.1, analyses the political and commercial risk that a South African exporter would face in a foreign country. The credit risk ratings from the Belgian public credit insurance agency (ONDD, 2009) were used to calculate a compound risk rating for each country. The scores were weighed equally for all 240 countries and a cut-off value was determined to eliminate those countries that had a risk score higher than the cut-off value. The less interesting markets within the group of 240 were eliminated if they exceeded the cut-off value for the risk ratings and a total of 209 countries' risk scores were below the cut-off value and could be considered for further analyses in Filter 1.2. Of the 209 countries only 196 could be used in the next stage of Filter 1 due to insufficient data (Steenkamp *et al.*, 2009; Viviers *et al.*, 2010).

Filter 1.2 used the 196 countries continuing from Filter 1.1 and evaluated macro-economic indicators to determine if these markets were sizable or have been growing sufficiently in the short and long term. As per Cuyvers *et al.* (1995) and Cuyvers (2004) the GDP and GDP per capita would indicate of the country's economy is too small or do not show enough potential for growth and would therefore not be deemed as viable markets to export to. The nominal GDP and GDP per capita as well as GDP and GDP per capita growth rates were used. Again a cut-off value was determined and the markets with insufficient growth were eliminated. A total of 101 countries complied with the set conditions and continued to the second filter of the model (Steenkamp et al., 2009; Viviers et al., 2010).

The same methodology for Filter 1.1 and 1.2 was used for the DSM for services as this filter is applied to country-level data and no adjustments were necessary.

10.4.2 Decision support model for services: Filter 2

The aim of the second filter of the DSM for products was to determine possible export opportunities for South Africa based on import data that would indicate market potential. Therefore, the same principle could be applied to the data for services. This section explains how Filter 2 was applied for services.

Filter 2 assessed the services sector-level data for each country. Data was extracted from the ITC Trade Map database for the 101 countries for the 61 sub-sectors for the period 2003 to 2007 (ITC, 2010b). This period's data was used in order to have comparable results with the DSM for products. Two countries, Turkmenistan and Uzbekistan, had no services trade data available and were eliminated immediately. This filter used the services import data for 99 countries for each of the 61 services sectors as a proxy for market size. Therefore, a total of 6,039 services-country combinations entered into this filter.

Within this filter the revealed comparative advantage (RCA) for South Africa is used to determine a cut-off point for each services sector. The assumption is made that if South Africa is relatively specialised in a particular product, i.e. RCA ≥ 1, then one can be less strict in the selection of interesting countries than if South Africa is not specialised in the service, i.e. RCA < 1 (see Steenkamp et al., 2009; Viviers et al., 2010).

The model then further considered the import data for each services sector in the 99 countries continuing from Filter 1. The second filter determines whether the 6,039 services-country combinations had sufficient short- and long-term growth or a sufficient import market size. Countries were then categorised according to their potential short-term growth, long term growth and market size (see Steenkamp et al., 2009; Viviers et al., 2010) and the services-country combinations that showed sufficient growth were selected to continue to the next filter.

After applying this process to the 6,039 service-country combinations that entered the filter, a total of three countries were eliminated completely showing no export potential based on import growth or size. These countries were Bahamas, Bhutan and Brunei. A total of 96 countries showed possible export potential in at least one service sector or more. A total of

1,843 service-country combinations from the original 6,039 combinations showed possible export potential and could continue to Filter 3.

10.4.3 Decision support model for services: Filter 3

The third filter of the DSM for products used specific calculations for market concentration in Filter 3.1 that could not be applied to the available data for services, due to the fact that bilateral trade data is not available for services. For market accessibility in Filter 3.2 the DSM for products uses various variables that are specific to product trade such as tariffs, shipping costs and other logistics issues related to products. These variables are not applicable to services as services trade occur much differently to products trade, and no tariffs can be raised on services. Therefore, this study developed a new methodology for the third filter for services, as will be explained in this section.

10.4.3.1 Filter 3.1 of the DSM for services

Filter 3.1 of the DSM for products is based on the assumption that if a market for a specific product is very concentrated, i.e. there are only one or two major exporters to that market, access for new exporters will be very difficult (see Chapter 4, also Cuyvers *et al*, 1995; Steenkamp *et al.*, 2009; Viviers *et al.*, 2010). The same concept was applied to the DSM for services by creating a proxy for trade openness based on the level of imports of a specific services sector. For the purposes of the DSM for services, the term "openness for services imports" (OSI) was used to describe the level of access for the market based on the ratio of imported services to the total services used in the specific market on a sector level. This proxy should be a relative guideline to show whether a market is easy to access or not.

The assumption was that if a country has high imports of services in relation to the total use or demand of services in the market, then the market is relatively open and there is scope to export services to that market. However, if a country has low imports of services in relation to the total use or demand of services in the market, then it is assumed that the market produces many services locally and the market is not very open or easily accessible for trade. Therefore, it would be more difficult to enter the market with new service exports. The assumption has its limitations, as a high imports of services in a market could still mean that the services in that market are imported only from one or two large suppliers, which means the market is still very concentrated and difficult to access. However, due to the lack of bilateral data it is not possible to determine the amount of exporters that supply a specific market and the current available data cannot prove otherwise.

Firstly in order to determine the amount of services used or demanded in a market, the amount of services produced locally was calculated. This was done by using the GDP figures for each country (UNCTAD, 2010). These figures are broken down into agriculture, industry and services (which is further divided into wholesale, retail trade, restaurants and hotels, transport, storage, communication and other service activities). Therefore, to determine the total amount of services locally produced or supplied within the market, the total amount reported for the services sector as part of GDP was used and will be further referred to as "Services Produced (SP)". To calculate the total services demanded (SD) within the market, the following calculation was made:

$$SD_j = SP_j + Z_j - X_j$$

where:

j = importing country/market

SD = services demanded within the importing country

SP = services produced within the importing country

Z = services imported

X = services exported

The results of this calculation were used in order to determine the ratio of imported services to the total services demanded, which would determine the openness of the specific service in that market. This calculation was made as follows:

$$OSI_j = \frac{Z}{SD_j}$$

where:

j = importing country/market

OSI = openness for services or demand for services in the importing country

Z = services imported

SD = services demanded in the importing country as calculated for SD_j above.

These calculations were made for all 61 sub-sectors of services and the results of OSI_j were percentages of market openness for services for each of the services-country combinations that continued from Filter 2. A cut-off value was determined in order to identify the services-country combinations that were sufficiently "open" to continue to the next filter. Filter 3.1 was, therefore, aimed at creating an index for market concentration or trade openness for the 1,843 service-country combinations continuing from Filter 2. After applying the methodology of Filter 3.1 a total of 961 service-country combinations had an OSI percentage above the cut-off value[1] and were selected to continue to the final section of Filter 3.

10.4.3.2   Filter 3.2 of the DSM for services

Filter 3.2 of the DSM for products eliminated product-country combinations on the basis of market accessibility. This filter for the DSM for services was developed to perform the same function, given the available data on services barriers. This study considered the methodology behind various techniques used in the literature to measure market accessibility (MA) or market access barriers in services. The broad categories of methods can be grouped into frequency measurements, price-based measurements, quantity-based measurements, gravity-model estimates and financial-based measurements. After reviewing the various methods it was found that the first methodology known as frequency measurements is the most applicable to Filter 3.2 of the DSM for services.

Hoekman (1996) was one of the first researchers to develop a method to quantify the barriers to trade in services, which became known as frequency measures. As part of the GATS agreement, participating countries list their individual schedules for all sectors for which they are prepared to make commitments, and any barrier that they wish to still apply to a part thereof. An example of a set of GATS commitments are provided in Table 10.2.

---

1   The calculation of the cut-off values in the different filters was done in the same manner as in the original DSM models. For a detailed description on the formulas used to determine the cut-off values, see Chapter 4, also Cuyvers (1997, 2004).

2   The limitations on market access are a set of restrictions that a government applies to national as well as foreign suppliers and relates to the specific operations of the services sector firms (WTO, 2006).

3   The limitations on national treatment implies that a government will not treat foreign services suppliers differently to national suppliers and are granted equal opportunities to compete. Under the GATS commitments a country would, therefore, indicate whether foreign suppliers would be treated differently or not (WTO, 2006).

Table 10.2. Example of a schedule of GATS commitments.

Sector or sub-sector	Mode of supply	Limitations on market access[2]	Limitations on national treatment[3]
Horizontal commitments (across all sectors)	Cross-border supply (Mode 1)	None	None other than tax measures that result in differences in treatment with respect to R&D services.
	Consumption abroad (Mode 2)	None	Unbound for subsidies, tax incentives, and tax credits.
	Commercial presence (FDI – Mode 3)	Maximum foreign equity stake is 49%	Unbound for subsidies, under a specific law, approval is required for equity stakes over 25%; new investment that exceeds a specific amount.
	Temporary entry of natural persons (Mode 4)	Unbound except for the following: intra-corporate transferees of executives and senior managers; specialist personnel subject to economic-need test for stays longer than one year; service sellers (sales people) for up to three months.	Unbound except for categories of natural persons mentioned referred to in the market-access column.
Specific commitments (for specific sector e.g. legal)	Cross-border supply (Mode 1)	Commercial presence required	Unbound
	Consumption abroad (Mode 2)	None	None
	Commercial presence (FDI – Mode 3)	25% of senior management should be nationals	Unbound
	Temporary entry of natural persons (Mode 4)	Unbound, except as indicated in horizontal commitments.	Unbound, except as indicated in horizontal commitments.

(Source: Hoekman, 1996; WTO, 2009)

Similar commitments to the ones shown in the table above are made by the WTO member countries for those services sectors that they are willing to open their markets. Under each sector that a country commits to, they have to specify one of three entries, namely none, bound with restrictions or unbound (WTO, 2009). Hoekman (1996) used these entries in his frequency measurements to quantify barriers to access for services by applying a weighting method for each commitment in each country. This was done as follows:

(i)   **None:** this indicates that a country commits not to place any limitations on market access or national treatment for a specific sector/mode of supply combination. National treatment indicates that treatment of a foreign supplier is no less favourable than that of domestic services and service providers. Therefore, **a value of 1** was allocated for each "none" commitment made.

(ii) **Bound with restrictions:** this indicates that a country sets a specific restriction on that specific sector, and this restriction is listed in their schedules of commitment. **A value of 0.5** was allocated in this instance.

(iii) **Unbound:** No commitment has been made for a particular sector/mode of supply combination. A **value of 0** was allocated for each sector where a country is not willing to commit, and therefore, Hoekman (1996) viewed these as a market that is completely blocked against trade in that sector.

These scale values were allocated so that all the commitments from each country could be added together in order to provide a total value in the form of an index. The assumption was that the higher the total value, the greater the extent of market accessibility for the sector in the specific country, i.e. the more liberal the country was towards services trade (Hoekman, 1996). It is important to note that this methodology provides an indication towards the relative degree of restriction, and should not to be taken literally as indicators of ad valorem tariff equivalents.

The same concept was applied to Filter 3.2 in the DSM for services. The scale values were calculated for all of the services-country combinations continuing from Filter 2. A calculation was made of the maximum amount of commitments a country can make under each sector, assuming that if a country made the maximum amount of commitments that the market for that specific service sector had no trade restrictions or was completely accessible. Therefore, for each of the countries continuing from Filter 2, the total amount of commitments could be evaluated for each sector and a scale value of 0, 0.5 or 1 be applied as per the methodology by Hoekman (1996). This was done for each country for commitments on market access as well as national treatment, for each of the four modes of supply. Therefore, for each sector one set of commitments had to be made, with a minimum of four commitments for market access and four commitments for national treatment (see Table 10.2).

For each country the total commitments for market access and national treatment respectively could receive scale values on a sector level and then be compared to the total or maximum amount of commitments that can be made under each sector. These two percentages then form the level of openness under each sector and the average of the two percentages were used to determine the total level of openness or market access. Therefore, the overall level of market access (MA) for each services-country combination was calculated as follows:

$$MA_j = \text{Average} \left(\frac{LMA_j}{LMA_t} + \frac{LNT_j}{LNT_t} \right)$$

where:

MA = Market Access

j = importing country

t = total/maximum amount of commitments that can be made for the sector

LMA = total score for Limitations on Market Access as per the country's GATS commitments

LNT = total score for Limitations on National Treatment as per the country's GATS commitments

For the set of results a cut-off value was determined in order to identify which services-country combinations are sufficiently accessible (with low barriers) to continue to the next filter. By applying this methodology to the 1,843 services-country combinations continuing from Filter 2, it was possible to eliminate the services-country combinations that had very low market accessibility. A total of 666 services-country combinations had a market access value above the cut-off value and was selected to continue to the final selection in Filter 3.

10.4.3.3   Final Filter 3 selection

From Filter 3.1 and 3.2 two sets of data were now available to analyse in further detail. As per the methodology used in the DSM for products in South Africa (Steenkamp et al., 2009; Viviers et al., 2010), a services-country combination had to comply with the cut-off values of both Filter 3.1 and Filter 3.2 in order to continue to Filter 4.

The same method was followed for the DSM for services. The 961 services-country combinations from Filter 3.1 and the 666 services-country combinations from Filter 3.2 were compared and if a services-country combination was selected in both filters it could continue to the next filter. Therefore, a total of 578 services-country combinations were selected to enter into Filter 4, which is discussed in the following section.

10.4.4 Decision support model for services: Filter 4

No further services-country combinations were eliminated in this filter. The 578 services-country combinations were grouped into cells that differentiate the opportunities according to market size and growth (Filter 2) as well as market access characteristics (Filter 3). The aim of the cell classification was to provide a method by which the results of the DSM for services could be interpreted in order to differentiate between the different export promotion strategies. A cell classification (see Table 10.3) was constructed by which the services-country combinations were grouped according to the size or growth in the market (as per calculations from Filter 2) as well as the level of market openness for service imports (OSI) (as per Filter 3.1) and market accessibility (as per Filter 3.2).

The rows in the cell classification in Table 10.3 indicate the size of the import market as per the calculations from Filter 2. Therefore, it indicates whether the opportunity falls in a large services market, a market which is growing over the short term and long term, a market which is large in size and is growing over the short term, a large market that is growing over the long term or a large market that is growing in the short and long term. The last cell classification is the optimal opportunity for exports as there is growing opportunity within an already large market. The columns in the cell classification in Table 10.3 are divided according to the market accessibility that was calculated in Filter 3.1 and 3.2, with either low or high openness for services imports (as per Filter 3.1) and either low or high market accessibility (as per Filter 3.2).

Table 10.3. Cell classification for the DSM for services.

Market size	Low OSI & Low MA	Low OSI & High MA	High OSI & Low MA	High OSI & High MA
Large services market	Cell 1	Cell 6	Cell 11	Cell 16
Short-term and long-term growth	Cell 2	Cell 7	Cell 12	Cell 17
Large services market, short-term growth	Cell 3	Cell 8	Cell 13	Cell 18
Large services market, long-term growth	Cell 4	Cell 9	Cell 14	Cell 19
Large services market, short-term & long-term growth	Cell 5	Cell 10	Cell 15	Cell 20
Total				

The optimal combinations of export opportunities lie in the fourth column where the markets are open for services imports and easily accessible with low trade barriers. It is also important to note that columns 2 and 3 are interchangeable as both have one positive and one negative value incorporated. Allocating the results of the DSM for services according to these cells provides a method by which an export promotion strategy for services in South Africa can be formulated. The following section provides a summary of the filters and results of each filter of the DSM. This is followed by a discussion of the results of the model in more detail with some policy recommendations that were derived.

10.5   A summary of the DSM for services for South Africa

Figure 10.1 below shows a summary of the filters that was applied in the DSM for services. The figure also shows the results of applying each filtering process to the available services data.

Figure 10.1. A summary of the application of the DSM for services for South Africa.

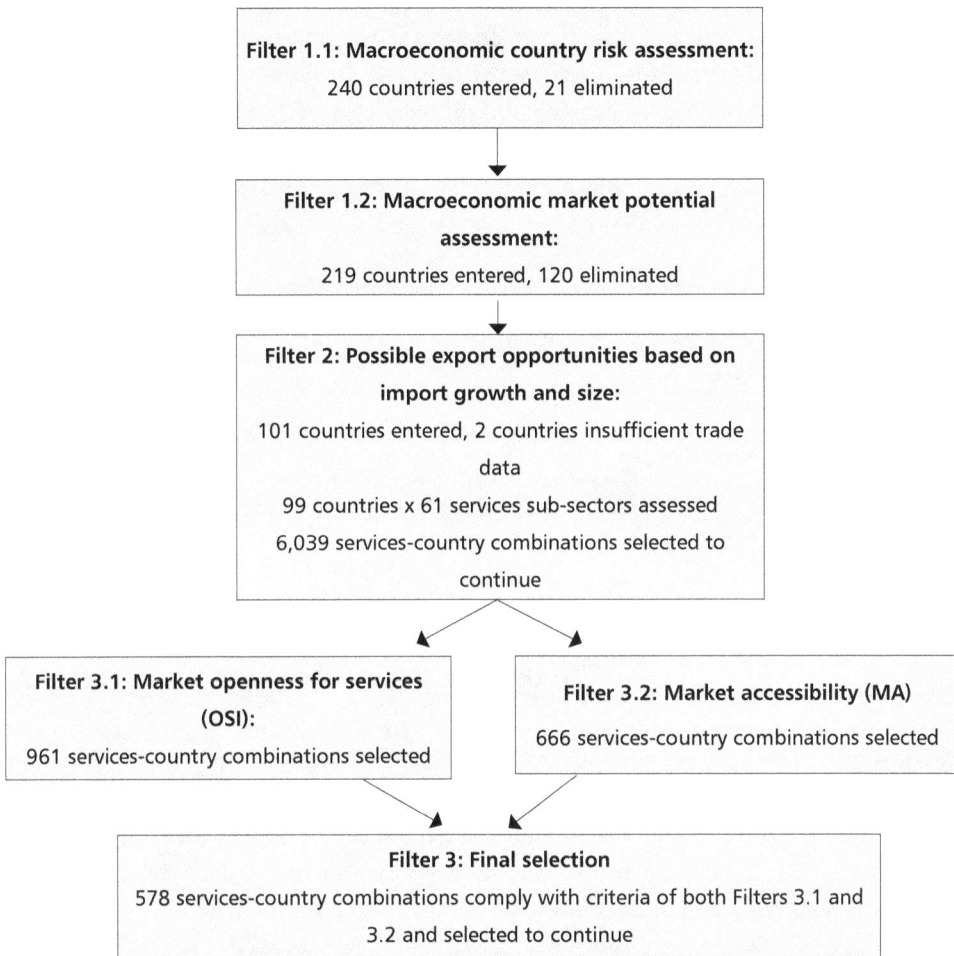

Filter 1.1: Macroeconomic country risk assessment:
240 countries entered, 21 eliminated

Filter 1.2: Macroeconomic market potential assessment:
219 countries entered, 120 eliminated

Filter 2: Possible export opportunities based on import growth and size:
101 countries entered, 2 countries insufficient trade data
99 countries x 61 services sub-sectors assessed
6,039 services-country combinations selected to continue

Filter 3.1: Market openness for services (OSI):
961 services-country combinations selected

Filter 3.2: Market accessibility (MA)
666 services-country combinations selected

Filter 3: Final selection
578 services-country combinations comply with criteria of both Filters 3.1 and 3.2 and selected to continue

10.6   An analysis of the results of the DSM for services

After applying the filtering process discussed in section 4, a total of 578 services-country combinations were identified that had realistic export opportunities (REOs) for South African services. The results are analysed in two sections, firstly the results according to the cell classification, and secondly the results according to sectors, countries and regions.

10.6.1 Results according to cell classifications

The 578 services-country combinations were firstly clustered according to the cells as explained in section 4.4. The total number of opportunities per service does not show the size of the market, which is important in determining whether the export opportunity is viable or not. A market may show high numbers of realistic export opportunities for a service, but the value of the opportunities may be very small. Therefore, in order to create a proxy for the market size, the total import demand for each sector was used for 2007. For the EU countries the intra-EU service trade data was taken out of the total imports for each country as many of these countries might show high imports, but it is mostly from other EU countries. These markets are less inaccessible for South African exporters. Due to data limitations unfortunately South Africa's bilateral trade could not be incorporated into these figures. The results were classified into cells, as can be seen in Table 10.4 below.

Table 10.4. Cell classifications of REOs based on the total import demand for each export opportunity in USD.

Market size	Low OSI & Low MA	Low OSI & High MA	High OSI & Low MA	High OSI & High MA
Large services market	160,084,540	158,688,749	39,455,027	49,050,145
Short-term and long-term growth	13.655.732	37,829,747	11,167,786	4,422,767
Large services market, short-term growth	14,389,582	102,435,938	10,099,651	30,670,944
Large services market, long-term growth	12,288,370	28,136,120	8,746,579	1,622,176
Large services market, short-term & long-term growth	56,530,626	62,007,274	4,101,128	38,691,540
Total	256,948,851	389,948,827	73,470,171	124,457,572

According to Table 10.4 the cell with the largest value of potential exports is Cell 1 where the markets are large in size, but the market openness for services and market access is low in comparison to the average of all the services-country combinations. Thereafter, there are also a large value of potential export opportunities in Cells 6 and 8. Each cell classification could have a different interpretation when it comes to export promotion.

The rows of the cell structure show the size of the import markets, varying from large service markets to growing markets. The majority of the number of export opportunities was in Rows 1 and 2. The first row indicates that the potential markets are already large in size and show very little additional extension/growth. However, these markets are settled and the demand for the service is constant. The second row is markets that have been growing in the short term and long term. These are also very good markets to enter due to the growing demand for these services in these markets.

The columns in the cell classifications indicate how easy these large and growing markets are to enter. If the opportunities fall in the first column, then the markets have low market accessibility. These markets need intervention from the government to reduce barriers to entry. The export promotion organisations should be involved in these markets to negotiate easier access for South Africa's service firms.

The second column indicates export opportunities in markets that have low market openness for services as they import very little in comparison to domestic supply of the service. This is a great barrier for exporters as this indicates that the domestic firms in these markets are very competitive. Therefore, EPOs need to be involved in the South African firms to indentify means of ensuring they are very competitive before entering these markets. The services provided by the South African firms have to be on the same competitive level as the domestic and international firms in that market, with similar price ranges and providing the same quality service, if not better.

The third column shows export opportunities that have high market openness for services in terms of exports but are difficult to access due to stringent policies. Here the EPOs need to ensure they are involved in the negotiation processes to lower these barriers and ease access into these markets.

The fourth column indicates export opportunities that need very little export promotion intervention. These are opportunities with high openness for services as well as high market access. The exporters should have no trouble entering these markets themselves and may only need some supportive assistance if they are new exporters and have little export experience. The following section discusses the regional and sector results of the model for services.

10.6.2 Results according to region, country and sector

The following table shows the results of the DSM for services as allocated geographically in each region. The United Nations world regions were used to allocate the results regionally (UN, 2002). According to the number of opportunities identified in the model, the majority lies in Western Europe, Northern Europe and Eastern Europe. However, when analysing the total import demand for the identified export opportunities in each region, Eastern Asia shows the highest potential value for exports of services from South Africa.

Table 10.5. Geographical distribution of export opportunities.

Region	Sub-region	Number of opportunities	Total import demand 2007 in USD
Caribbean	Latin America	7	56,309
Central America	Latin America	2	758,090
Eastern Africa	Africa	1	282,400
Eastern Asia	Asia	41	214,505,347
Eastern Europe	Europe	63	72,399,922
Middle Africa	Africa	2	261,550
Northern Africa	Africa	2	391,823
Northern America	Northern America	21	59,270,475

Region	Sub-region	Number of opportunities	Total import demand 2007 in USD
Northern Europe	Europe	97	112,780,181
Oceania	Oceania	13	24,229,920
South America	Latin America	10	6,612,300
South-Central Asia	Asia	19	12,413,208
South-Eastern Asia	Asia	48	68,455,352
Southern Europe	Europe	93	62,257,510
Western Africa	Africa	10	600,157
Western Asia	Asia	45	59,960,357
Western Europe	Europe	104	148,739,521

For the purposes of diversifying South Africa's exports away from the travel sector (see section 10.1), it is necessary to show the results of the DSM per sector, based on the number of opportunities identified for each sector. Table 10.6 below indicates various sectors that hold potential for South Africa to diversify exports of services.

Table 10.6. Top 20 services sectors according to the number of export opportunities.

Services sector	EBOPS code	Number of opportunities	Total import demand 2007 in USD
Travel Personal – Health-related	241	39	2,962,487
Travel Personal – Other	243	38	250,780,485
Travel Business – Expenditure by seasonal & border workers	238	29	4,305,250
Travel Personal – Education-related	242	29	17,715,945
Travel Business – Other	239	27	59,934,743
Communications Services – Telecommunication services	247	19	18,099,223
Air Transport – Other	213	16	20,633,456
Air Transport – Passenger	211	15	34,497,114
Construction Services – Construction in the compiling economy	251	15	22,735,754
Advertising, market research, and public opinion polling	278	15	18,499,281
Road Transport – Freight	225	14	15,348,593
Franchises and similar rights	891	14	18,354,752
Sea Transport – Other	209	13	30,418,609
Services between affiliated enterprises, n.i.e.	285	13	24,466,759
Other personal, cultural and recreational services	897	13	3,168,628
Air Transport – Freight	212	12	12,671,646

Services sector	EBOPS code	Number of opportunities	Total import demand 2007 in USD
Rail Transport – Other	222	12	374,466
Computer services	263	12	14,560,542
Legal services	275	12	3,130,370
Architectural, engineering and other technical services	280	12	16,234,796

In Table 10.6 many travel and transport sectors are indicated, together with various other sectors, namely telecommunication services, construction services, advertising and market research, franchising, personal, cultural and recreational services, computer services, legal services as well as architectural and engineering services.

The following table provides the top 20 country-services combinations that were identified by the DSM for services, according to total import demand figures for each export opportunity.

Table 10.7. Top 20 country-services combinations according to the total import demand.

Country	EBOPS code[4]	Services sector	Total import demand 2007 in USD
China	208	Sea Transport – Freight	35,132,100
United Kingdom	243	Travel Personal – Other	26,068,016
Japan	208	Sea Transport – Freight	25,313,076
China	243	Travel Personal – Other	23,299,199
Canada	243	Travel Personal – Other	19,242,650
Russia	243	Travel Personal – Other	18,488,611
Saudi Arabia	243	Travel Personal – Other	15,972,559
Germany	243	Travel Personal – Other	15,092,160
Romania	243	Travel Personal – Other	14,790,889
France	243	Travel Personal – Other	12,857,572
South Korea	208	Sea Transport – Freight	12,828,300
South Korea	243	Travel Personal – Other	12,337,900
Hong Kong	243	Travel Personal – Other	11,766,150
Australia	243	Travel Personal – Other	11,267,072
Norway	243	Travel Personal – Other	11,163,100
China	277	Business and management consultancy and public relations services	10,856,400

4   The ITC (2010b) reports trade data for services according to the Extended Balance of Payments for Services (EBOPS) classification developed by the United Nations (UN, 2002).

Country	EBOPS code	Services sector	Total import demand 2007 in USD
South Korea	209	Sea Transport – Other	10,765,900
Japan	211	Air Transport – Passenger	10,703,481
Singapore	243	Travel Personal – Other	9,755,525
Japan	209	Sea Transport – Other	9,332,815

This table indicates mostly European and Asian countries and the services sectors are mostly transportation-related and travel (tourism)-related. These sectors usually entail transactions of high value, which would motivate the reason why these sectors are in the list of top combinations.

These countries and services sectors can be used as key strategic sectors by the DTI in South Africa for the purposes of increasing and diversifying exports of services.

10.7 Conclusion

The aim of this chapter was to identify a methodology for a decision support model (DSM) for services, based on the same principle as the DSM for products. The chapter firstly described what is meant by the services sector in section 2 with a brief discussion on the GATS classification system and modes of transport. This was followed by a brief explanation of the export promotion of services in South Africa.

The fourth section discussed the methodology of the four filters of the DSM for services and a new methodology was developed for Filters 3.1, 3.2 and the cell structure in Filter 4. The result of the model was a list of the most realistic export opportunities for South African services that could be used by the DTI to make informed decisions and have a scientific base for strategic policy making. No other model for services could be found in the literature that performs the same function.

The results of the model indicated that the highest values of export opportunities for services are allocated in the European and Eastern Asian regions. Various sectors hold potential for South Africa to diversify exports of services. Many travel and transport sectors are indicated as those sectors with the highest potential export value based on import demand. Other services sectors also show high export potential for South African services, namely telecommunication services, construction services, advertising and market research, franchising, personal, cultural and recreational services, computer services, legal services as well as architectural and engineering services. These sectors can be used as key strategic sectors by the DTI in South Africa for the purposes of increasing and diversifying exports of services.

Further research on this model for services is necessary. It should be possible to link the results of the DSM for services with the DSM for products in order to identify synergetic export promotion opportunities for South Africa. Further research could also look at alternatives to refine the third filter that identifies export opportunities for services based on market accessibility as the GATS negotiations are expanded in the coming years. Currently the biggest problem is data availability for services trade. As the data for services become more readily available in the future, the DSM for services could be adapted accordingly. The results of the model could also be used in further research that is sector-specific and country specific to evaluate the selected export opportunities from Filter 4 in more detail.

References

ASR. *see* Australian Services Roundtable.

Australian Services Roundtable. 2011. Events. [Online.] Available from: http://servicesaustralia.co/events/. Accessed 13 April 2011.

CDC. *see* Consultancy Development Centre.

Consultancy Development Centre. 2006. *Export promotion of consultancy and management services from India.* Report prepared for Ministry of Commerce and Industry, March 2006.

Cuyvers, L. 1997. Export opportunities of Thailand: a decision support model approach. Centre for Asean Studies (CAS), *Discussion Paper no. 9*, January.

Cuyvers, L. 2004. Identifying export opportunities: the case of Thailand. *International Marketing Review*, 21(3): 255-278.

Cuyvers, L., De Pelsmacker, P., Rayp, G. & Roozen, I.T.M. 1995. A decision support model for the planning and assessment of export promotion activities by government export promotion institutions: the Belgian case. *International Journal of Research in Marketing*, 12: 173-186.

Daniels, P.W. 2000. Exports of services or servicing exports? *Human Geography*, 82(1): 1-15.

Department of Trade and Industry. 2006. *National Export Strategy 2006-2009*. Division: Trade and Investment South Africa (TISA). Chief Directorate: Export Development and promotion. Pretoria, March 2006.

Department of Trade and Industry. 2010a. *Export promotion directorate*. [Online.] Available from: http://www.dti.gov.za/exporting/resourcebasedindustries.htm. Accessed 23 February 2011.

Department of Trade and Industry. 2010b. *A South African Trade Policy and Strategy Framework*. The DTI Campus, Pretoria. 64 p.

DTI. *see* Department of Trade and Industry.

Fieleke, N. 1995. The soaring trade in "non-tradeables". *New England Economic Review*, Nov/Dec: 25-36.

Francois, J. 1990. Trade in producer services and returns due to specialization under monopolistic competition. *The Canadian Journal of Economics*, 23(1): 109-124.

Gillespie, K. & Riddle, L. 2004. Export promotion organisation emergence and development: a call to research. *International Marketing Review*, 21(4/5): 462-473.

Grönroos, C. 1999. Internationalization strategies for services. *Journal of Services Marketing*, 13(4/5): 290-297.

Hausmann, R. & Klinger, B. 2008. South Africa's export predicament. *Economics of Transition*, 16(4): 609-637.

Hoekman, B. 1996. Assessing the general agreement on trade in services. In: W. Martin and L.A. Winters. *The Uruguay Round and the developing countries*. Cambridge: University Press.

Howells, J. 2000. Innovation and Services: New conceptual framework. *CRIC Discussion Paper, 38*, August.

International Trade Centre. 2010a. *Trade Map: existing and potential trade*. [Online.] Available from: http://www.trademap.org/. Accessed 6 April 2010.

International Trade Centre. 2010b. *Trade promotion approaches for services exports*. [Online.] Available from: http://www.intracen.org/servicexport/. Accessed:5 February 2010.

ITC. *see* International Trade Centre.

Martincus, C.V. & Carballo, J. 2008. Is export promotion effective in developing countries? Firm-level evidence on the intensive and the extensive margins of exports. *Journal of International Economics*, 76: 89-106.

Mattoo, A. & Stern, R.M. 2008. Overview. In: A. Mattoo, R.M. Stern and G.A. Zanini. *A handbook of international trade in services*. New York: Oxford University Press.

Office National du Ducroire. 2009. *Country risk ratings*. [Online.] Available from: http://www.ondd.be/WebONDD. Accessed 27 October 2009.

ONDD. *see* Office National du Ducroire.

Oyewole, P. 2001. Prospects for developing country exports of services to the year 2010: Projections and public policy implications. *Journal of Macromarketing*, 21(1): 32-46.

SARB. *see* South African Reserve Bank.

South African Reserve Bank. 2010. National accounts. *Quarterly bulletin,* 257, Sept. [Online.] Available from: http://www.resbank.co.za/Publications/QuarterlyBulletins. Accessed 11 April 2011.

Statistics South Africa. 2010. *Quarterly labour force survey, quarter 3*. [Online.] Available from: http://statssa.gov.za. Accessed 6 December 2010.

STATSSA. *see* Statistics South Africa.

Steenkamp, E., Rossouw, R., Viviers, W. & Cuyvers, L. 2009. Export market selection methods and the identification of realistic export opportunities for South Africa using a decision support model. [Online.] Available from: http://www.sadctrade.org/node/281. Accessed 17 December 2009.

Steuart, I. & Cassim, R. 2005. *Opportunities and risks in liberalising trade in services: country study of South Africa*. International Centre for Trade and Sustainable Development (ICTSD), Feb 2005.

UN. *see* United Nations.

UNCTAD. *see* United Nations on Trade and Development.

United Nations. 2002. *Manual on statistics of international trade of services*. New York: United Nations Publications.

United Nations Commission on Trade and Development. 2010. *Handbook of Statistics*. [Online.] Available from: http://unctadstat.unctad.org/. Accessed 16 February 2011.

Viviers, W. & Pearson, J.J.A.P. 2007. *The construction of a decision support model for evaluating and identifying realistic export opportunities in South Africa*. Report prepared for the Department Trade and Industry, South Africa, May, 92 p.

Viviers, W., Rossouw, R. & Steenkamp, E.A. 2009. *The sustainability of the DSM for identifying realistic export opportunities for South Africa: 2007-2008*. Report prepared for the Department Trade and Industry, South Africa, February, 105 p.

Viviers, W., Steenkamp, E.A., Rossouw, R. & Cuyvers, I. 2010. *Identification realistic export opportunities for South Africa: application of a decision support model (DSM) using HS 6-digit level product data.* Report prepared for the Department of Trade and Industry, South Africa, September. 57 p.

Warren, T. & Findlay, C. 1999. Measuring impediments to trade in services. *CIES Discussion Paper,* 99(19): 1-25.

World Trade Organisation. 1991. *Services sectoral classification list.* [Online.] Available from: http://www.wto.org/english/tratop_e/serv_e/mtn_gns_w_120_e.doc. Accessed 27 May 2008.

World Trade Organisation. 2005. *A handbook on the GATS agreement: prepared by the WTO Trade in Services Division.* Cambridge, UK: Cambridge University Press.

World Trade Organisation. 2006. *Introduction to GATS.* [Online.] Available from: http://www.wto.org/english/tratop_e/serv_e/serv_e.htm. Accessed 15 November 2009.

World Trade Organisation. 2009. *Services database: schedules of commitments.* [Online.] Available from: http://tsdb.wto.org/default.aspx. Accessed 15 November 2009.

WTO. *see* World Trade Organisation.

Chapter 11

Exporter's information requirements: competitive intelligence as an export promotion instrument

Marié-Luce Kühn[1] & Wilma Viviers

11.1 Introduction

Many firms regard exporting as a means to counter and monitor growing foreign competition, enlarge their market base, and augment profitability. However, despite the financial implications of selling to foreign markets, the process is uncertain and has many potential pitfalls. Exporting requires detailed knowledge of various factors (e.g. foreign business practices, cultures, competition) that could affect a small firm's ability to be successful in foreign markets (Belich & Dubinsky, 1999:45). It is, therefore, clear that if an increasing number of firms move into export operations, gathering and processing the right information will be of critical importance.

All companies require information upon which to make informed business decisions. In the case of exporters, the importance of acquiring the correct information is even greater due to the complexities of exports (Denis & Depelteau, 1985; Benito, Solberg & Welch, 1993; Souchon & Diamantopoulos, 2000). The export environment is politically, economically and socially complex, and lack of knowledge about these complexities, increases uncertainty about the target market and possibly leads to lost opportunities (Douglas & Craig, 1983; Douglas & Craig, 1989). Another complicating factor affecting upon exports is the economic volatility in certain export markets. Export decision support has, therefore, become important in monitoring competitive drivers in export markets and making appropriate management decisions (Richey & Myers, 2001). A decision support model (DSM) developed by Cuyvers (Cuyvers *et al.*, 1995) is one such support instrument from an export information

1   The chapter resulted from the PhD study by ML Kühn at the School of Economics, North-West University.

requirement perspective. The DSM provides indications on the types of export information that is required by exporters of both products and services (see Chapters 4 and 10).

Export information as a field considers what information is required (the types of information) for successful exporting of products and/or services, the way/methods in which it is acquired, the sources and quality of information and the way in which interpreted information is applied in strategic export decisions. One of the challenges an exporter faces is finding the right export market for his product and/or service and once a realistic export opportunity or a market presents itself, exporters need to determine which types of information they require. The various types of information need to be gathered, analysed and interpreted in order to inform the important business decisions. Information can be gathered using a variety of methods and using a variety of sources of information.

Decision-makers in companies and governments are increasingly aware of the need to manage and use information strategically to maintain or increase organisational competitiveness and innovation. With Competitive Intelligence (CI) as an instrument to achieve this, managers are increasingly recognising the importance of CI as a key asset and source of competitive advantage (Darling, 1996). Yet, information gathering and the process of making sense of the information, is often a time and cost intensive activity and therefore, from a competitiveness perspective, it is important that exporters to focus on gathering the right information and then make optimal use of gathered information.

This chapter firstly examines exporters' need for information, the types of information considered important by exporters and the sources consulted for gathering information. Secondly, this chapter considers the manner in which exporters can use CI as an instrument to assist them in identifying the information they need to collect from the available sources and eventually making strategic business decisions based on the results of the CI process.

Finally, this chapter will indicate that the DSM can be used in conjunction with the CI process to provide exporters of products and/or services with an indication of potential markets and therefore the types of market information required, thereby enhancing export promotion activities and export success.

11.2   Exporters' need for information

Export information plays an important role in enhancing a company's internationalisation and competitiveness. An absence or lack of the right information could be a barrier to embarking on exporting and in export expansion (Souchon & Diamantopoulos, 1996; Chetty & Blankenburg-Holm, 2000). The taking of sound business decisions requires that export managers are aware of their export information requirements and the information available to them. Informed export decision-making is also dependent on the availability and use of the right information in sound export plans and decisions (Zaltman & Moorman, 1988; Menon & Varadarajan, 1992; Crick & Chaudhry, 2010).

In a competitive business environment in which much of the same information is often equally available to all companies, a key source of competitive advantage lies in the manner in which the information types are identified and applied (Zaltman & Moorman, 1988). As the number of companies participating in export activities increases, information regarding the international environment becomes critical to effectively managing corporate ventures.

The importance of access to and use of the right information for export success is highlighted in Leonidou and Katsikeas (1997). This importance has also been recognised by governments through the establishment of export promotion organisations that assist exporters in acquiring the desired information about potential markets for products and/ or services (Cuyvers, De Pelsmacker, Rayp & Roozen, 1995; Craig & Douglas, 2000). These organisations focus on export development and export promotion (Craig & Douglas, 2000).

11.3   Types of export information

Based upon existing studies, the types of information exporters perceive to be important and the sources consulted depend upon such factors as organisational characteristics and the availability of resources (Walters, 1983; Makinen, 1986; Woods & Goolsby, 1987). The extent of export experience also has a direct influence on the types of information exporters perceive to be important and the sources they consult (Walters, 1983; Makinen, 1986; Woods & Goolsby, 1987; Mohamad, Ahmed & Honeycutt, 2001).

Broadly, types of information can be categorised into distinct categories. In a study of US exporters, Woods and Goolsby (1987) distinguished amongst five types of information used by US exporters: political information, economic information (its effect on lifestyles), macro-economic information relating to market potential, export restrictions (tariff, non-tariff, and transportation barriers), and legal information.

In terms of the importance of the various types of information, exporters ranked market information and export restrictions as most important. Literature on the types of information used by UK exporters revealed a similar pattern. Market feasibility information (market competition, buyers' preferences and price trends), adaptation information (product and other marketing adaptation issues), and background information (such as social, political, and economic background, transport infrastructure, and government assistance) were rated as important types of information (Hart, Webb & Jones, 1994; Williams, 2003; Cavusgil, 1984a). This general information about foreign markets ranked as an important area of information (Benito, Solberg & Welch, 1993).

Based on the literature, seven types of information were identified. They are: macro-economic information, political information, regulatory information, market information, export marketing information, competitor information, and information on market-access barriers (Klein, 2000; Toften & Rustad, 2005; Moser, Nestmann & Wedow, 2006; Viviers & Calof, 2002; Julien & Ramangalahy, 2003). These types are summarised in Table 11.1.

Table 11.1. Types of exporter information.

Types of information	Sources
Market information	
Market attractiveness/feasibility as indicated by the ranking of market potential, customer information (buyer preferences, lifestyles and culture) and price levels of products and/or services, product and other marketing adaptation issues (advertising and promotions):	
• Typical profit margins for similar products and/or services;	
• Market trends regarding market growth or decline;	
• Technology trends;	
• Number of potential customers;	
• Market(s) size of the market (value and volume);	
• Percentage of imports in relation to total market;	Cavusgil, 1984a; Cavusgil, 1984b; Hart *et al.*, 1994; Wright *et al.*,
• Key countries exporting to target country in this market.	2002; Leonidou & Katsikeas, 1997;
List and description of all potential marketing channels;	Leonidou & Adams-Florou, 1999; Woods & Robertson, 2000; Julien
• Geographic areas with high concentrations of potential customers;	& Ramangalahy, 2003; Williams, 2003.
• Key drivers and challenges including delivery times, level and type of service expected;	
• If the proposed product is unique, how is the problem it solves handled currently?;	
• Issues of importance to customers when purchasing the particular product/assessment of satisfaction with current supplier or the product and price trends;	
• Customer culture: Attitude of buyers to imported products in this market and factors that encourage buyers to switch suppliers; and	
• Expected credit and payment terms.	
Export marketing information	
Marketing or strategic partner.	
Market presence including independent sales office, partnership with a local company for an independent sales office, purchase a local company in the target country, agencies.	Deshpandé & Zaltman, 1982; Elbashier & Nicholls, 1983; Kohli &
Trade exhibitions and conferences.	Jaworski, 1990; Leonidou, 1995a; Souchon & Diamantopoulos, 1996;
Trade associations and their recent and service offering, e.g. publications.	Leonidou & Theodosiou, 2004; Hart *et al.*, 1994; Koksal, 2008.
Advertising and PR agencies.	
Export incentives.	

Types of information	Sources
Macro-economic information	
Background on economic conditions, economic indicators information. Potential investors (names of companies in the particular field that may be open to investment opportunities, venture capital companies that are active in the industry). Infrastructure (financial, roads, rail, sea and airports). Financial incentives.	Woods & Goolsby, 1987; Hart et al., 1994; Cavusgil, 1984a; Cavusgil, 1984b; Wright, Pickton & Callow, 2002; Klein, 2000; Williams, 2003; Toften & Rustad, 2005.
Political information	
Government assistance, political stability. Security matters.	Woods & Goolsby, 1987; Hart et al., 1994; Cavusgil, 1984a; Cavusgil, 1984b; Wright et al., 2002; Williams, 2003; Moser, Nestmann & Wedow, 2006.
Legal/regulatory information	
Standards approvals and licenses required selling the products in the target export market. Labour issues. Issues regarding starting a business, regulations on local shareholding, taxes. Legal system.	Woods & Goolsby, 1987; Hart et al., 1994; Cavusgil, 1984a; Wright et al., 2002; Williams, 2003.
Competitor information	
Identification of key competitors and profiles on each including key indicators. Competitor strengths and weaknesses. Competitor pricing. Competitor customers: positioning, segmentation, prices offered. Competitor marketing strategy and where they advertise: trade show participation. Competitor distribution, i.e. locations and channels (dealers, agents, direct, wholesalers). Copies of printed materials of competitors (brochures/technical data sheets).	Klein, 2000.
Information on market-access restrictions	
Tariff and non-tariff barriers. Transport barriers. Barriers of entry.	Woods & Goolsby, 1987; Hart et al., 1994; Cavusgil, 1984a; Cavusgil, 1984b; Leonidou & Katsikeas, 1997; Sandrey, 2003; Klein, 2000; Williams, 2003; Heritage Foundation, 2010.

Various factors influence the types of export information exporters gather as well as the processing of that information. These are export dependence, the extent of export operations, the stage of export, and export complexity (Belich & Dubinsky, 1999; Souchon, Diamantopoulos, Holzmueller, Axinn, Sinkula, Simmer & Durden, 2003). Given the above information needs of exporters, one of the instruments that exporters could use to assist in focusing on gathering the right information, interpret, apply and making optimal use of the gathered information is Competitive Intelligence (CI). Decision-makers in small and medium-sized enterprises, large companies and governments are also increasingly aware of the need to manage and use information strategically to maintain or increase organisational competitiveness and innovation. CI as an instrument will be subsequently discussed.

Taking a step back, however, even before the types of information are identified and before CI can be used, it is important for exporters to take strategic decisions on export growth including exploring new export markets and expanding existing export markets. In this regard, the DSM becomes important as it provides exporters and EPOs with information on realistic export opportunities (REOs) that could be explored further.

The next section will investigate CI as an instrument to determine, gather and process important export information.

11.4 Competitive Intelligence (CI)

The basis for CI revolves around decisions made by managers about the positioning of a business to maximise the value of the capabilities that distinguish it from its competitors. Failure to collect, interpret or analyse and act upon competitive information in an organised way can lead to the failure of an organisation. Having the capability to determine the types of information required and then accessing and acquiring the right types of information and making sense of the information is therefore advantageous for exporters. De Oliveira and Vieira (2006) argue that companies that intend exporting or that endeavour to grow their exports often lack the instruments to help them in decision support. There is a basic understanding that CI is a focused and comprehensive approach to information that helps companies gain a better understanding of their business environment, including competitors, suppliers, customers and regulatory matters. It also helps exporters to focus on these issues. CI is, therefore, suggested as a process that could assist especially exporters in obtaining the information they require (Rouach & Santi, 2001; De Oliveira & Vieira, 2006).

11.4.1 Definition of Competitive Intelligence (CI)

CI as a strategic management instrument has been researched by many authors under many different labels including environmental scanning, Business intelligence (BI) strategic intelligence (SI), competitor analysis and market[ing] intelligence (Saxby, Parker, Nitse & Dishman, 2002). Most of these terms have positioned intelligence as the necessary (and sometimes assumed) prerequisite for strategic planning (Porter, 1980). In essence, CI is aimed at gaining strategic competitive advantage (Porter, 1980).

CI is not just about monitoring competition, but also about scanning the entire business environment in which firms have to function. Herring (1998) states the objective of CI as "being able to predict competitors' moves, customers' moves, government moves and so forth." CI, according to the Society of Competitive Intelligence Professionals (2011) is "a systematic and ethical programme for gathering, analysing and managing external information that can affect the company's plans, decisions and operations." The ultimate aim of CI is "being able to predict competitors' moves, customers' moves, government moves and so forth" (Gilad, 1996) in order to reduce managerial decision uncertainty. The advantages of using the process of CI in order to identify key information requirements are well-documented. It provides the means to gain and sustain a competitive advantage (Calof & Breakspear, 1999; Herring, 1999) and improves insight into competitors, accurate market predictions and accurate monitoring of trends with significant impact on a company's future (Fuld, 1995).

11.4.2 The Competitive Intelligence cycle

From the perspective of export information types, CI is not about all information but about information that affects or potentially affects an organisation's competitiveness. CI is more specifically concerned with turning information into intelligence through a continuous process in a company present in all of the functions of business of the organisation.

Kahaner (1996:23) recommends that companies structure a formal programme of CI internally that includes a formal unit and a systematic CI process. A number of researchers (Calof & Breakspear, 1999; Elizondo & Glitman, 2003) go on to describe CI as comprising various sequential phases whereby raw information is accessed, gathered, transmitted, evaluated, analysed and made available to various users of CI as finished intelligence for use in business planning. Each phase is essential and employs established techniques that are applied to specific questions or issues.

Calof and Breakspear (1999) identified six key activity areas or constructs that collectively form the CI model. These constructs were confirmed by Saayman, De Pelsmacker, Viviers, Cuyvers, Muller and Jegers (2008). Calof and Dishman (2003) acknowledged that the CI process is affected by certain contextual influences, namely organisational culture/awareness, the formal infrastructure available as well as employee involvement. The CI cycle contributes towards this distinction between the CI process and contextual influences (see Figure 11.1).

Figure 11.1. The Competitive Intelligence cycle.

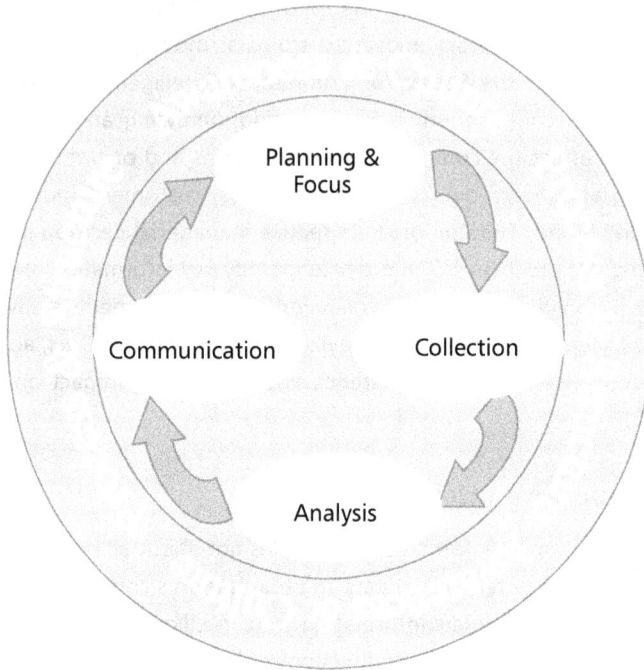

Source: Adapted from Kahaner (1996) and Fleisher & Bensoussan (2003)

The various constructs and contextual influences are subsequently discussed.

11.4.2.1 Planning and focus

CI is not concerned with simply collecting information, but it focuses on gathering information on issues of highest importance to senior management (Herring, 1999). For exporters these Key Intelligence Needs (KIN) or intelligence types are typically the types of information they require to successfully export (see Table 11.1). Klein (2000) found that exporters invest many resources worldwide to determine their CI needs. For exporters, meticulous attention to compiling a list of types of information required is a key element in a business strategy designed for the company's success in export markets (Klein, 2000; Elizondo & Glitman, 2003).

According to Herring (1999) a company's intelligence needs can generally be assigned to one of three functional categories namely strategic actions and decisions, e.g. the development of strategic plans and strategies; early warning intelligence e.g. competitor initiatives, technological surprise, and governmental actions; and intelligence on key players in the relevant marketplace or export market including competitors, customers, suppliers, regulators, and potential partners. Although gathering information from foreign markets significantly raises exporters' probability of succeeding in the export market, the acquisition of foreign knowledge also contributes to exporters' innovation strategies, such as where to allocate research and development (R&D) resources (Wakasugi, Todo, Sato, Nishioka, Matsuura & Ito, 2008).

During the planning and focus component, and guided by the types of information that is sought, resources are allocated for the CI project or process, and the purpose and result of the findings is established. Different types of KINs, therefore, require different types of intelligence operations (Herring, 1999). For example, intelligence to support decision-making usually requires secondary source research with current human-source collection inputs. Early-warning intelligence is critically dependent on human-source collection and monitoring, with analysis serving as the detection mechanism that "signals" possible future development that an exporter should be prepared to act on. Player-oriented intelligence usually takes the form of analytical profiles, sometimes tailored to specific user questions or planned actions.

11.4.2.2 Collection

Information gathering concerns three aspects namely the way in which relevant information is gathered, the sources that are accessed, and how this information flows from the supplier to the user who should use the information in business decisions (Souchon & Diamantopoulos, 1997; Menon & Varadarajan, 1992; Garvin, 1993; Maltz & Kohli, 1996). Once the type of information that is required is determined, that information must be gathered from a variety of sources for examination during the CI process (Lenz & Engledow, 1986a; 1986b). This systematic secondary and primary intelligence collection using various means of collection including environmental scanning is a key element in a business strategy designed for the company's success in export markets (Klein, 2000; Elizondo & Glitman, 2003).

Various gathering methods are discussed in the literature and are summarised in Souchon et al., (2003), Souchon and Diamantopoulos (1997) and Cavusgil (1984a) as comprising mainly formal marketing research, export market research and export assistance (often provided by official EPOs) and export market intelligence. Marketing research and market intelligence as collection methods can entail all aspects of information collection (Kohli & Jaworski, 1990) because export marketing sources often overlap (Diamantopoulos & Souchon, 1999; Williams, 2003). Cavusgil (1984b:262) defines export marketing research as "the research activities of companies carried out either in the home market or in foreign markets for the purpose of reducing uncertainty surrounding international marketing decisions"; it is distinct from other information acquisition modes because it is formalised, systematic, and objective. Finally, export market intelligence is an informal and ongoing information acquisition mode that includes approaching potential customers, distributors, and competitors and that Kotler (1991:91) defines as reflecting, "a set of procedures used by managers to obtain their everyday information about pertinent developments in the marketing environment."

A variety of sources are accessed to gather information. The choice of sources is influenced by the nature of the information that needs to be gathered. These sources are both within the organisation and external to it. Some examples are sales representatives, research of new patent filings and competitor websites. A survey of Norwegian companies found that exporters place their main emphasis on informal contacts as a basis for information sources. These include customers (external) and sales people (internal) (Benito, Solberg & Welch, 1993). Information can also be found on the Internet itself – most companies are now advertising their services and some specialise in offering information that can be used for competitor research. Other sources include trade shows and conferences.

11.4.2.3 Analysis

The mere fact that a company like an exporter possesses information or has access to information does not automatically translate into competitive advantage. Information gathered must be subjected to a process of analysis and interpretation in order to develop meaningful insights and knowledge. This knowledge then has to be used in decision-making and fed back to an export of company's innovation efforts and strategic planning (Souchon *et al.*, 2003; Wagasuki *et al.*, 2008). In effect, CI's analysis phase is where intelligence is created; that is, information is converted into actionable intelligence on which strategic and tactical decisions may be based (Calof & Miller, 1997; Herring, 1998). Much work has been done in the areas of competitive analysis, environmental analysis and competitive theory (Porter, 1980). Reid (1981) emphasises the importance of information processing in export behaviour.

Typical outcomes of the intelligence analysis area for exporters are competitor profiles, product analyses and export strategy. Such export market knowledge may provide a deeper understanding of the relationships between export market information uses and export performance (Toften & Olsen, 2003).

11.4.2.4 Communication

The results of the CI process or project need to be communicated to those with the authority and responsibility to act on the findings. CI needs to be communicated in a usable and actionable or interpreted manner. CI, therefore, goes beyond providing intelligence; it also includes creating user-friendly intelligence that could influence decision-making (Zaltman, Moorman & Deshpandé, 1992). The mode of communication is also an important aspect of communication. According to Weiss (2002) there are a number of options including face-to-face, presentations, telephone calls, emails, and written memos. The choice depends on factors such as time and personality.

Communication is not the final stage of CI. Intelligence that is not used has no value, therefore, the final stage of CI is again the first stage namely planning and focus and the actual use of the intelligence in the decision process. This emphasises the continuous nature of CI. CI requires a decision to be taken. Information passed to management and placed on a shelf without being used to guide business actions is not intelligence (Weiss, 2002).

11.4.2.5 Process and structure

Three aspects provide the contextual influences on the CI process. They are process and structure, organisational culture and awareness and the skills set that is required.

In terms of process and structure, CI requires appropriate policies, procedures and a formal (or informal) infrastructure so employees may contribute effectively to the CI system and gain the benefits from the CI process. There is much support for a formal structure and a systematic approach to CI (Porter, 1980; Ghoshal & Kim, 1986; Ghoshal & Westney, 2006). Such a formal structure includes a database of competitive knowledge and appropriate channels to communicate information and intelligence.

11.4.2.6 Organisational awareness and culture

In order for CI to grow in a sustainable manner and for CI to be implemented and used optimally, there needs to be an appropriate organisational awareness of CI and a culture of competitiveness. There has been support for this culture and awareness construct in the area of market orientation (Pole, Madsen & Dishman, 2000; Slater & Narver, 1995). The company-wide participation in the process of CI is important and this includes all levels of a company from the highest decision-makers to the sales staff. Although decision-makers are the drivers and primary users of CI, Kahaner (1996) intimates that information gathering should be the concern of all the company's personnel. Without proper awareness and attitudes that favour both intelligence and information sharing, it will be a challenge to develop intelligence within a company.

11.4.2.7 Skills

De Pelsmacker, Muller, Viviers, Saayman, Cuyvers and Jegers (2005) added a new contextual aspect namely that having the right skills mix is an imperative for effective CI for exporters. The right skills are especially required for the analysis construct of CI mainly because the process of information gathering often leads to concerns regarding information overload and the quality of information. Information overload is exacerbated by a shortage of skills, particularly in smaller companies, for making sense of and using the information gathered. This shortage often leads to ad hoc information collection when required and decision-making based more on instinct than interpreted information (Calof, 1994). According to Williams (2003), in contrast to Diamantopoulos and Souchon's findings (1999), an oversupply rather than an undersupply of relevant important information creates difficulties. Siriginidi (1996) supports this finding and found that there is a need to train information specialists to reduce the information gap between information needs and sources of information.

11.5   CI use according to size and stages of exports

Many studies have been conducted into the use of CI and especially export marketing intelligence in small- and medium-sized companies (SMEs) and into the CI practices of exporters in various stages of export (Balabanis, Theodosiou & Katsikeas, 2004; Leonidou, 2004; Doole, Grimes, & Demack, 2006; Williams, 2006). Having discussed the importance for exporters to have the right types of information available to enhance export promotion and the use of CI to achieve this, the next part of this chapter will examine the CI practices of small and larger exporters as well as the impact of the stage of exports on the CI practices of exporters. Thereafter, and based on this discussion, recommendations will be made.

11.5.1 CI and size of exporters

Available empirical research indicates that there are widespread differences between SMEs and large exporting companies in both their CI practices and the context within which CI takes place within a company (De Pelsmacker *et al.*, 2005). In particular, large exporting companies exhibit better data collection, analysis and communication skills than smaller companies, which give them an edge in the CI practices over SMEs (Calof & Dishman, 2003). According to Calof & Dishman (2003), CI may be even more important for small companies than for larger ones, since smaller companies cannot absorb market mistakes in the same way that large companies can.

In terms of planning and focus, the types of information required by small and large exporters are by nature similar. Viviers and Calof (2002) found that small- and medium-sized South African exporters regard information related to market access conditions and market intelligence to identify buyers as the most important types of information requested by users. This is confirmed in the literature as described in Table 11.1. Benito, Solberg and Welch (1993) confirm in a survey of 221 Norwegian exporters of various sizes, that the decision-making issues for which information is sought, entry into a new market and developing a distribution network were singled out as the most important. General information about foreign markets was ranked as the most important area of information.

Regarding the collection activity, Groom and David (2001) found that the intelligence gathering activities of small companies is largely informal, despite the fact that the potential returns from CI are greatly valued. Most of the information an exporter might need is accessible in the public domain. Many studies have been conducted into the use of export information in small- and medium-sized companies (SMEs) (Balabanis, Theodosiou & Katsikeas, 2004; Doole, Grimes, & Demack, 2006; Williams, 2006). The information gathering activities of small firms is largely informal. Sources of information that are accessed to gather the required information differ according to the size of an exporter. Smaller exporters with more limited resources might be more likely to use government assistance. Barnea (2006) found in research on small- and medium-sized Israeli exporters that they conduct CI independently, but do expect the government to supply information on global markets through state commercial organisations. This support is more relevant to small- and medium-sized firms because they do not have the resources to develop their own CI capabilities. Previous research has also found that most small firms do not have the resources and/or expertise to track down and analyse the relevant pieces and do not realise or recognise that customers, suppliers and company employees collectively possess most of the competitor information they seek. They continue to rely on outside agents, for instance distributors, freight forwarders and consultants to perform most of the information gathering and processing for them (Doole, Grimes, & Demack, 2006; Williams, 2006). Benito, Solberg and Welch (1993) confirm that customers (external) and sales people (internal) emerged as being of particular importance as sources of information.

Regarding the analysis phase of CI, Calof and Dishman (2003) found that there are few differences between the intelligence practices of smaller and larger companies, with the exception that large companies conduct more formal analyses and make greater use of their employees mainly because they have the resources (Calof, 2003). It can thus be deducted from past research that because an exporter's ability to gather and use information is likely to depend on resource availability (Samiee & Walters, 2000), and thus on size, large exporters have more resources available to allocate to CI activities than do small exporters (Denis & Depelteau, 1985; Hart, Webb & Jones, 1994.)

However, one key advantage for SMEs is the rapid dissemination or communication of information among fewer personnel than is the case in very large firms, and the speed and flexibility with which decisions can be taken (Haley, 1999). Research into the personality characteristics of entrepreneurs has found that many have the attitude that the owner or manager knows the market in which the firm competes and does not need intelligence gathered in a more systematic approach. However, it may be equally important for small firms to have the capability to assess the external business environment properly (Groom & David, 2001).

Regarding the contextual aspect of process and structure, studies on CI practices of exporters of various sizes demonstrate that many large companies are more likely to have CI functions at multiple levels in four strategically significant areas. These are:

(i)   Support for strategic decision-making;

(ii) Early warning of opportunities and threats;

(iii) Competitor assessment; and

(iv) Tracking and support for strategic planning and implementation (Caudron 1994; Attaway 1998).

Larger exporting companies also have a better formal infrastructure for CI (De Pelsmacker *et al.*, 2005). This notion supports previous findings by Bergeron and Hiller (2002) that smaller companies lack the formal infrastructure to conduct CI successfully. However, in contrast to Bergeron and Hiller (2002) who indicated that smaller companies lack employee expertise, research of South African and Flemish exporters (De Pelsmacker *et al.*, 2005) indicates that the involvement and understanding of CI among employees are better in smaller than in larger exporters. This lends some support to the notion of Haley (1999) that smaller companies find it easier to rapidly disseminate information among their staff and the advantage that decisions can be taken with more speed and flexibility, because the owner/manager knows the market in which the company competes. A survey of Spanish exporters found that a formal approach to competitive intelligence that includes a programme of creating awareness and a culture of competitiveness, rather than informal or discontinuous approaches, gives businesses of all sizes competitive advantage and justifies the value of its implementation, but that few exporters implement systematic programmes to benefit from the intelligence effort (Postigo, 2001). Most research into company CI practices focuses on larger (e.g. Fortune 500-level) firms and most management theory is founded upon the systematic analysis of managerial actions in large firms (Haley, 1999). For example, a survey of 85 firms from Business Week's *America's 1,000 Most Valuable Companies* indicate that only 24% of the sample firms had advanced competitor analysis programmes in place, and more than 41% had some competitor analysis function in place (Subramanian & Ishak, 1998). A 1997 study noted that although all of the responding firms had some sort of intelligence gathering function, only 60% had official systems (Futures Group, 1997). The challenge that becomes apparent with regard to smaller companies is that it is difficult to develop and sustain formal CI systems. While SMEs face similar problems and decisions to larger firms, Belich and Dubinsky (1999:53) found that, despite the need to understand foreign markets; smaller firms are less likely to integrate information processing into their corporate systems. On skills, smaller exporters often lack the advantage of expert personnel and extensive resources to implement formal CI systems (Bergeron & Hiller, 2002). A small company may have to obtain training to improve analysis skills or seek outsourced assistance.

11.5.2 CI and stage of exports

When examining the effect that export experience or stage of exports has on the CI activities of exports a few important differences arise.

Previous research has found that companies pass through various stages as they develop their international activities before their foreign activities reach maturity (Viviers, Kroon & Calof, 1996). In each successive stage, the types of information and the nature of assistance required changes (Silverman, Castaldi & Sengupta, 2002). Various authors describe the stages of export. Viviers *et al.* (1996) describe three stages in a study of the export behaviour of South African SMEs: passive exporter, involved exporter and committed exporter. Bilkey and Tesar (1977) identified six export stage profiles in their research on Wisconsin manufacturers:

(i)   Management is not interested in exporting;

(ii)   The company fills unsolicited orders but does not actively pursue export markets;

(iii)   The company's management actively explores exporting (passive exporter);

(iv)   The company starts to experiment with exporting;

(v)   The company becomes an active exporter; and

(vi)   The company becomes a committed exporter.

From a CI planning and focus viewpoint (see section 4.2.1), what is apparent from previous research is that exporters' information needs and the sources of information that exporters use are influenced by their stage of export (Cuyvers, Dumont, Viviers, De Pelsmacker, Muller, Jegers & Saayman, 2008; Souchon & Diamantopoulos, 2000; Viviers & Calof, 2002). Adequate supply information about export is an important factor in completing the current stage in the export process (Weaver & Pak, 1990). This is also highlighted by Leonidou (1995a), who revealed that limited information for locating and analysing foreign markets was the greatest impediment to export. Exporters lacking export experience are likely to have greater information needs in order to deal with export matters, as they cannot rely on past knowledge and experience or internal expertise (Gronhaug & Graham, 1987). They are, therefore, expected to make greater use of information than experienced exporters. Kedia and Chhokar (1986) state that the significant impediments to export activity amongst the companies they studied (machinery manufacturers and food processors) vary according to the respective companies' stage in the export process. While information barriers dominate the decisions as to how and where to export, financial and marketing ones prevail once companies are already exporting. Adequate supply information about exports is an important factor in completing the current stage in the export process (Weaver & Pak, 1990). Leonidou (1995a) also emphasises this and revealed that limited information for locating and analysing foreign markets was the greatest impediment to export.

From an information collection perspective, research has found that exporters that acquire and use export market intelligence serve more global markets than non-users do (Hart *et al.*, 1994; Leonidou, 1997). One explanation for this is that companies pursuing global markets search for additional sources of information (Cavusgil, 1984a). However, owing to the distinct characteristics of different countries and the nature of companies, the extent and amount of information required varies.

A company's inclination to consult wider sources of information is also a function of its internationalisation stage (Cavusgil, 1984a). He found that as companies progress through their internationalisation process the nature of the sources they require and use will change from general market information for the experimental exporters, to industry/business publications and trade show contacts for both the experimental and active exporters. Exporters' need for information also vary according to their export destinations (Bodur & Cavusgil, 1985). As a result, companies employ a wide range of information sources to improve the likelihood of success in their export efforts and these sources of information that exporters use are also influenced by their stage of export (Souchon & Diamantopoulos, 2000; Viviers & Calof, 2002).

Cavusgil (1984b) also found that more internationalised companies are using a wider variety of data sources and have a greater network of sources of information. De Oliveira and Vieira (2006) found that beginner exporters largely make use of government trade promotion organisations to supply the types of information they require emphasising the fact that such exporters' networks are still limited. Cavusgil (1984a) found that as companies progress through their internationalisation process, they would commit more financial and managerial resources to market research, reflecting the need for a more thorough analysis and assessment of potentials in foreign markets. This also means that they would have a greater availability of the required skilled resources to conduct CI effectively.

Regarding the process and structure of CI, previous research into the CI practices of exporters in various stages of exports is limited. Cavusgil (1984a:206-207) found that as exporters become committed, they will find it necessary to develop an internal information system for market research. A study by De Oliveira and Vieira (2006) showed that exporters in the beginner or low intensity stages of the exporting process do not have formalised CI systems in place despite the fact that competition is forcing them to gather and use information about the competitive environment. Although there is little evidence of differences between the CI practices of exporters in various stages of exports, two aspects are notable. One is that the types of assistance that exporters require changes in each successive stage (Bilkey & Tesar, 1977; Czinkota & Johnston, 1985; Silverman *et al.*, 2002) and secondly, as exporters become committed, they will find it necessary to develop an internal information system for market research (Cavusgil, 1984a:206-207). It can, therefore, be said that as exporters gain more experience in the export process, they would require less external assistance and will develop more effective internal CI capabilities.

The link between an exporter's size and experience and an effective CI capability has been established. It is also clear that the more experienced and CI independent an exporter becomes, the less it is dependent on external export promotion assistance.

Regardless of size or stage of exports or the nature of an exporter's CI capability, the types of information that exporters require do not differ significantly. However, exporters do require certain types of information as indicated in Table 11.1 and in this regard, the DSM provides the starting point of key information requirements by providing specific indications of new export markets or opportunities for new products and/or services in existing markets.

11.6 Conclusion

It is apparent that exporters need different types of information and that such information needs to be gathered from a variety of sources using a number of gathering techniques. It is also apparent that information itself does not guarantee export success and a competitive advantage. Information needs to be turned into intelligence through a process of analysis in order for it to become useful. Indeed, decision makers in companies often have the information they need, but they do not use it for a variety of reasons, including the fact that there is often an overload of information and a lack of intelligence. In order to prevent an overload of information that potentially has value, but in its current format is unusable; exporters could consider building a formal CI capability.

From a decision-making perspective, it is true that the same information is often available to competitive firms at the same time. This means that competitive advantage is found in the use of information in decision-making rather than in who does or does not have it. In this regard, CI can play a role in the sense that it is an instrument for exporters to accurately define their information requirements, to gather the right types of information and to subject that information to a process of analysis and interpretation in order to supply intelligence in an actionable format to decision-makers.

In conclusion, research has shown that CI, used in conjunction with the DSM, are indeed valuable export promotion instruments to both small and large exporters and to exporters in various stages of export, as well as EPOs, whether it is conducted internally or with the assistance of external experts. Although the literature base on the effect and benefits of CI for exporters of various sizes and stages of exports is still limited, the examination of the benefits of CI leads to the conclusion that a formal CI system, including a systematic CI process, will have great benefits to all exporters. This is especially relevant during the planning and focus phase where the specific information requirements or types of information that an exporter needs are determined.

References

Attaway, M.C. 1998. A review of issues related to gathering and accessing competitive intelligence. *American Business Review*, 16(1): 125-135.

Balabanis, G., Theodosiou, M. & Katsikeas, C.S. 2004. Export marketing: developments and a research agenda. *International Marketing Review*, 21(4/5): 353-377.

Barnea, A. 2006. Israel study on competitive intelligence. *Competitive Intelligence Magazine,* 9(2): 44-46.

Belich T.J. & Dubinsky, A.J. 1999. Information processing among exporters: an empirical exmination of small firms. *Journal of Marketing Tehory and Practice*, 7(4): 45-59.

Benito, G.R.G. Solberg, C.A. & Welch, L.S. 1993. An exploration of the information behaviour of Norwegian exporters. *International Journal of Information Management,* 13(4): 274-286.

Bergeron, P. & Hiller, C.A. 2002. Competitive intelligence. *Annual Review of Information Science and Technology,* 36(1): 353-390.

Bilkey, W.J. & Tesar, G. 1977. The export behaviour of smaller-sized Wisconsin manufacturing companies. *Journal of International Business Studies*, 193-98, Spring/Summer.

Bodur, M. & Cavusgil, S.T. 1985. Export marketing research orientations of Turkish exporting firms. *European Journal of Marketing*, 19(2): 5-16.

Calof, J.L. 1994. The relationship between firm size and export behaviour revisited. *Journal of International Business Studies*, 2: 367-387.

Calof, J.L. & Breakspear, A. 1999. Competitive intelligence practices of Canadian technology firms. National Research Council/Canadian Institute of Scientific & Technical Information, Ottawa.

Calof, J.L. & Dishman, P. 2003. *The intelligence process: front-end to strategic planning*. Ottawa: University of Ottawa.

Calof, J.L. & Miller, J. 1997. *The status of CI across the globe*. Proceedings of the 12th Annual Conference of the Society of Competitive Intelligence Professionals: 213-223.

Caudron, S. 1994. I spy, you spy. *Industry week, Cleveland*, 243(18): 35.

Cavusgil, S.T. 1984a. Differences among exporting companies based on their degree of internationalization. *Journal of Business Research,* 12: 195-208.

Cavusgil, S.T. 1984b. International marketing research: insights into company practices. *Research in Marketing*, 7: 261-288.

Chetty, S. & Blankenburg-Holm, D. 2000. The role of business networks in the internationalisation of manufacturing firms: a longitudinal case study. *Advances in International Marketing*, 205-222.

Craig, C.S. & Douglas, S.P. 2000. *International Marketing Research*. New York: Prentice Hall.

Crick, D. & Chaudhry, S. 2010. An investigation into UK-based Asian entrepreneurs' perceived competitiveness in overseas markets. *Entrepreneurship and Regional Development*, 22(1): 5-23.

Cuyvers, C, Dumont, M. Viviers, W., De Pelsmacker, P., Muller, M-L., Jegers, M. & Saayman, A. 2008. Export intensity and the competitive intelligence of exporting companies: Evidence from South Africa. *South African Journal of Economic and Management Science*, 11(1): 85-97.

Cuyvers, L., De Pelsmacker, P., Rayp, G. & Roozen, I.T.M. 1995. A decision support model for the planning and assessment of export promotion activities by government export promotion institutions: the Belgian case. *International Journal of Research in Marketing*, 2: 173-186.

Czinkota, M.R. & Johnston, W.J. 1985. Exporting: does sales volume make a difference? *Journal of International Business Studies*, 16(2): 157-161.

Darling, M.S. 1996. Building the knowledge organization. *Business Quarterly*, 61(2): 61-66.

De Oliveira, F.C. & Vieira, D.V. 2006. *The process of Competitive Intelligence: An evaluation of its use in regional exporting companies*. Paper delivered at the 2006 Conference of the International Association for Management of Technology, Beijing, China. [Online.] Available from: http://www.iamot.org/conference/index.php/ocs/10/paper/viewFile/1621/749. Accessed 15 May 2010.

De Pelsmacker, P., Muller, M-L, Viviers, W., Saayman, A Cuyvers, L. & Jegers, M. 2005. Competitive intelligence practices of South African and Belgian exporters. *Marketing Intelligence and Planning*, 23(6): 606-620.

Denis, J-E. & Depelteau, D. 1985. Market knowledge, diversification and export expansion. *Journal of International Business Studies*, 16(3): 77-89.

Deshpandé, R. & Zaltman, G. 1982. Factors affecting the use of market research information: a path analysis. *Journal of Marketing Research,* 19: 14-31.

Diamantopouluos, A. & Souchon, A.L. 1999. Export information acquisition modes: measure development and validation. *International Marketing Review*, 16(2): 143-168.

Doole, I., Grimes, T. & Demack, S. 2006. An exploration of the management practices and processes most closely associated with high levels of export capability in SMEs. *Marketing Intelligence and Planning*, 24(6): 632-647.

Douglas, S. & Craig, C.S. 1983. *International Marketing Research*. Englewood Cliffs, NJ: Prentice Hall.

Douglas, S. & Craig, C.S. 1989. Evolution of global marketing strategy: sale, scope and synergy. *Columbia Journal of World Business,* 24(3): 47-59.

Elbashier, A.M. & Nicholls, J.R. 1983. Export marketing in the Middle East: the importance of cultural differences. *European Journal of Marketing,* 17(1): 68-81.

Elizondo, N. & Glitman, E. 2003. Common mistakes in cross-border CI. *Competitive Intelligence Magazine*, 6(2): 47-48.

Fleisher, C.S. & Bensoussan, B.E. 2003. *Strategic and competitive analysis: methods and approaches to analyzing business competition*. Upper Saddle River, NJ: Prentice Hall.

Fuld, L. 1995. *The new competitor intelligence: the complete resource for finding, analyzing, & using information about your competitors*. New York: Wiley.

Futures Group. 1997. *Ostriches & Eagles*. [Online.] Available from: http://www.tfg.com/pubs/docs. Accessed 5 April 2010.

Garvin, D.A. 1993. Building a learning organization. *Harvard Business Review*, 71(4): 78-91.

Gibb, A.A. & Scott, M. 1986. Understanding small firm growth. In: J.S. Gibb, M. Lewis and T. Faulkner (eds.). *Small firm growth and development*. Hampshire: Gower.

Gilad, B. 1996. Strategic intent and strategic intelligence. In: B. Gilad and J.P. Herring (eds.). *The art and science of business intelligence analysis*. Greenwich: JAI Press.

Goodman, S.K. 1993. Information needs for management decision-making. *Records Management Quarterly*, 27(4): 12-23.

Ghoshal, S. & Kim, S.K. 1986. Building effective intelligence systems for competitive advantage. *Sloan Management Review*, 28(1): 49-58.

Ghoshal, S. & Westney, D.E. 2006. Organizing competitor analysis systems. *Strategic Management Journal*, 12(1): 17-31.

Gronhaug, K. & Graham, J.L. 1987. International Marketing Research revisited. In: S.T. Cavusgil. *Advances in international marketing*. Greenwich, CT: Jai Press.

Groom, J. & David, F. 2001. Competitive intelligence activity among small firms. *SAM Advanced Management Journal*, 66(1): 12-20.

Haley, G.T. 1999. East versus West: strategic marketing management meets the Asian networks. *Journal of Business and Industrial Marketing*, 14(2): 91-101.

Hart, S.J., Webb J.R. & Jones, M.V. 1994. Export marketing research and the effect of export experience in industrial SMEs. *International Marketing Review*, 11(6): 4-22.

Heritage Foundation. 2010. *Economic freedom index*. [Online.] Available from: http://www.heritage.org/index/Country/Tunisia. Accessed 5 April 2010.

Herring, J. 1998. What is intelligence analysis? *Competitive Intelligence Magazine*, 1(2): 13-16.

Herring, J. 1999. Key intelligence topics: a process to identify and define intelligence needs. *Competitive Intelligence Review*, 10(2): 4-14.

Julien, P.A. & Ramangalahy, C. 2003. Competitive strategy and performance of exporting SMEs: an empirical investigation of the impact of their export information search and competencies. *Entrepreneurship Theory and Practice*, 27(3): 227-245.

Kahaner, L. 1996. *Competitive intelligence*. New York: Simon & Schuster.

Kedia, B.L. & Chhokar, J.S. 1986. An empirical investigation of export promotion programmes. *Columbia Journal of World Business*, Winter: 13-20.

Klein, W. 2000. The seven gates of export marketing: key intelligence challenges that exporters must confront before launching a new product. *Competitive Intelligence Magazine*, 3(2): 34-36.

Kohli, A.K. & Jaworski, B.J. 1990. Market orientation: the construct, research propositions, and managerial implications. *Journal of Marketing*, 54(2): 1-18.

Koksal, M.H. 2008. How export marketing research affects company export performance: evidence from Turkish companies. *Marketing Intelligence and Planning*, 26(4): 416-430.

Kotler, P. 1991. *Marketing management: analysis, planning and control*. Cliffs, NJ: Prentice-Hall, Englewood.

Lenz R.T. & Engledow, J.L. 1986a. Environmental analysis units and strategic decision-making: a field study of selected leading-edge corporations. *Strategic Management Journal*, 7(4): 69-89.

Lenz R.T. & Engledow, J.L. 1986b. Environmental analysis: the applicability of current theory. *Strategic Management Journal*, 7(4): 329-346.

Leonidou, L.C. 1995a. The Saudi distribution system: structure, operation and behaviour. *Marketing Intelligence and Planning*, 13(11): 27-35.

Leonidou, L.C. 1997. Finding the right information mix for the export manager. *Long Range Planning*, 30(4): 572-584.

Leonidou, L.C. 2004. An analysis of the barriers hindering small business export development. *Journal of Small Business Management*, 42(3): 279.

Leonidou, L.C. & Adams-Florou, A.S. 1999. Types and sources of export information: insights from small business. *International Small Business Journal*, 17(3): 30-48.

Leonidou, L.C. & Katsikeas, C.S. 1997. Export information sources: the role of organizational and internationalization influences. *Journal of Strategic Marketing*, 5(2): 65-87.

Leonidou, L.C. & Theodosiou, M. 2004. The export marketing information system: an integration of the extant knowledge. *Journal of World Business*, 39(1): 12-36.

Makinen, E.H. 1986. *Acquisition of strategic market information by Finnish firms exporting wood products*. Proceedings of the 15th Annual Conference of the European Marketing Academy, Helsinki, 20-23 May. [Online.] Available from: http://www.lib.unb.ca/Texts/JFE/July97/makinen.html. Accessed 15 March 2010.

Maltz E. & Kohlil, A. 1996. Marketing intelligence dissemination across functional boundaries. *Journal of Marketing Research*, 33(1): 47-61.

Menon, A. & Varadarajan, R. 1992. A model of marketing knowledge use within firms. *Journal of Marketing*, 56: 53-71.

Mohamad, O., Ahmed, Z.U. & Honeycutt, E.D. Jr. 2001. The role of information in export marketing programmes: an analysis by ownership structure. *Multinational Business Review*, 9(2): 57-63.

Moser, C., Nestmann, T. & Wedow, M. 2006. Political risk and export promotion: evidence from Germany. Paper provided by Deutsche Bundesbank, Research Centre. *Discussion paper series 1: Economic Studies*, 36. [Online.] Available from: http://econstor.eu/bitstream/10419/19665/1/200636dkp.pdf. Accessed 18 April 2010.

Pole, J.G., Madsen, E. & Disman, P. 2000. Competitive Intelligence as a construct for organizational change. *Competitive Intelligence Review*, 11(4): 25-31.

Postigo, J. 2001. Competitive intelligence in Spain: a survey of its use by Spanish exporters. *El Profesional de la Informacion*, 10(10): 4-11.

Porter, M.E. 1980. *Competitive strategy: techniques of analyzing industries and competitors*. New York, NY: The Free Press.

Reid, S.D. 1981. The decision-maker and export entry and expansion. *Journal of International Business*, 12: 101-112.

Richey, R.G. & Myers, M.B. 2001. An investigation of market information use in export channel decisions: antecedents and outcomes. *International Journal of Physical Distribution and Logistics Management*, 31(5): 334-353.

Rouach, D. & Santi P. 2001. Competitive intelligence adds value: five intelligence attitudes. *European Management Journal*, 19(5): 552-559.

Saayman, A., Pienaar, J., De Pelsmacker, P., Viviers, W., Cuyvers, L., Muller, M-L. & Jegers, M. 2008. Competitive Intelligence: construct exploration, validation and equivalence. *Aslib Proceedings*, 60(4): 383-411.

Samiee, S. & Walters, P.G.P. 2000. Export education: perceptions of sporadic and regular exporting firms. *International Marketing Review,* 19(1): 80-97.

Sandrey, R. 2003. Non-tariff measures (NTMs) facing export from South African and Southern Africa. *Trade and Industrial Policy strategies (TIPS),* September.

Saxby, C.L., Parker, K.R., Nitse, P.S. & Dishman, P.L. 2002. Environmental scanning and organizational culture. *Marketing Intelligence and Planning,* 20(1): 28-34.

Society of Competitive Intelligence Professionals (SCIP). 2011. What is competitive intelligence? [Online.[Available from: http://www.scip.org/content.cfm?itemnumber=2214&navItemNumber=492. Accessed 28 April 2010.

Silverman, M., Castaldil, R.M. & Sengupta, S. 2002. Increasing the effectiveness of export assistance programs: the case of the California environmental technology industry. *Journal of Global Marketing,* 15(3/4): 173-192.

Siriginidi, S.R. 1996. Business information: its sources and role in globalization. *New Library World,* 97(1): 22-28.

Slater, S.F. & Narver, J.C. 1995. Marketing orientation & the learning organization. *Journal of Marketing,* 59(3): 63-74.

Souchon, A.L. & Diamantopoulos, A. 1996. A conceptual framework of export marketing information use: key issues and research propositions. *Journal of International Marketing,* 4(3): 49-71.

Souchon, A.L. & Diamantopoulos, A. 1997. Use and non-use of export information: some preliminary insights into antecedents and impact on export performance. *Journal of Marketing Management,* 13: 135-151.

Souchon, A.L. & Diamantopoulos, A. 2000. *Enhancing export performance through effective use of information.* Research paper (Sept.), Aston Business School.

Souchon, A.L., Diamantopoulos, A., Holzmueller, H.H., Axinn, C.N., Sinkula, J.M., Simmer, H. & Durden, G.R. 2003. Export information use: a five-country investigation of key determinants. *Journal of International Marketing,* 11(3): 106-127.

Subramanian, R. & Ishak, S. 1998. Competitor analysis practices of US companies: an empirical investigation. *Management International Review,* 38(17): 7.

Toften, K. & Olsen, S.O. 2003. Export market information use, organizational knowledge, and firm performance: a conceptual framework. *International Marketing Review,* 20(1): 95-110.

Toften, K. & Rustad, K. 2005. Attributes of information quality of export market assistance: an exploratory study. *European Journal of Marketing,* 39(5/6): 676-695.

Viviers, W. & Calof, J. 2002. International information seeking behaviour of South African exporters. *South African Journal of Information Management,* 4(3): 10 p.

Viviers, W., Kroon, J. & Calof, J.L. 1996. The export behaviour of South African enterprises: stages and attitudes towards exports. *South African Journal of Business Management,* 27(1/2): 34-41.

Walters, P.G.P. 1983. Export information sources: a study of their usage and utility. *International Marketing Review,* 1(2): 34-43.

Wakasugi, R., Todo, Y., Sato, H., Nishioka, S., Matsuura, T., Ito B. & Tanaka, A. 2008. The Internationalization of Japanese Companies: New Findings Based on Company-Level Data, Discussion papers 08036, Research Institute of Economy, Trade and Industry (RIETI). [Online.] Available from: http://www.rieti.go.jp/jp/publications/dp/10e053.pdf. Accessed 5 June 2011.

Weaver, K.M. & Pak, J. 1990. Export behaviour and attitudes of small- and medium-sized Korean manufacturing firms. *International Small Business Journal*, 8: 59-70.

Weiss, A. 2002. Ask Arthur! Answers to your CI questions. *Competitive Intelligence Magazine,* 5(6): 45.

Williams, J.E.M. 2003. Export information use in small- and medium-sized industrial companies: an application of Diamantopoulos' & Souchon's scale. *International Marketing Review,* 20(1): 44-66.

Williams, J.E.M. 2006. Export marketing information-gathering and processing in small- and medium-sized enterprises. *Marketing Intelligence and Planning*, 24(5): 477-492.

Woods, V.R. & Goolsby, J.R. 1987. Foreign market information preferences of established US exporters. *International Marketing Review,* 4(4): 3-52.

Woods, V.R. & Robertson, K.R. 2000. Evaluating international markets: the importance of information by industry, by country of destination and by type of export transaction. *International Marketing Review*, 17(2): 34-55.

Wright, S. Pickton, D.W. & Callow, J.E. 2002. Competitive Intelligence in UK firms: a typology. *Marketing Intelligence and Planning,* 20(6): 349-360.

Zaltman, G. & Moorman, C. 1988. The importance of personal trust in the use of research. *Journal of Advertising Research*, 28(3): 16-24.

Zaltman, G., Moorman, C. & Deshpandé, R. 1992. Relationships between providers and users of market research: the dynamics of trust within and between organizations. *Journal of Marketing Research*, 32: 318-335.

Chapter 12

Conclusions and agenda for further research

Ludo Cuyvers & Wilma Viviers

In the present volume a decision support model (DSM), which was designed to help export promotion agencies to identify export opportunities in the world at large and to formulate and implement suitable export promotion activities, has been presented and thoroughly assessed. In the course of the years, since the early 1990s when the DSM originated, it was applied several times, both for policy preparation and assistance of export promotion agencies and for purely academic purposes, for the detection of export opportunities of diverse countries, such as Belgium, Thailand, the Philippines and South Africa.

A critical political economy analysis of the use that export promotion organisations have made of the DSM, particularly in Belgium, showed that the export promotion process involves many "players", apart from the export promotion agency, such as the private sector organisations, political and government representatives, powerful exporters, etc. The objective economic and organisational interest of these "players", although overlapping, is not identical, which has occasionally led to interference in (if not boycott of) the DSM research and application process. The process of formulation and implementation of export promotion activities is a very complicated one, the outcome of which depends on the strategic behaviour and interactions of the "players" involved. It is, therefore, difficult to model and analyse using game theory. However, it was shown that even a simple game-theoretical model of the strategic interactions of two major "players" leads to interesting results and begs for extension and further analysis.

Yet, as public resources are scarce (often increasingly so) and as traditional export promotion activities are showing diminishing returns, also taking into account the export promotion activities of the new exporting countries and emerging economies, there is today not much alternative but to extensively use hard statistical data and thorough statistical methods, and to provide a solid scientific foundation for export promotion.

Based on the review of the international market selection literature, which categorised the DSM as a country-level market estimation model, it was concluded that the DSM is the only methodology that includes all possible product-country combinations (markets) in the world as a starting point of the market selection process, making it unique as an analytical tool for export promotion purposes. Moreover, the consecutive filters that are built into the DSM are relying on the most recent, accurate and internationally comparable statistical data at the highest possible level of disaggregation. However, as by their nature, such statistical data only become available with a rather considerable delay; the output of the DSM should always be critically assessed using the various other sources of information available. This combination of the analysis of hard statistical data with other sources of information, including the assessment by privileged witnesses and experts in the field – both at country and product level – is required to optimise the use of the DSM results and will highly improve the usefulness of the DSM output. The DSM seems to be a necessary, but not a sufficient condition for an efficient public export promotion programme.

The results of the DSM to Belgium, which were primarily included as a detailed illustration of how the DSM methodology is actually applied, showed this need abundantly. First of all, important product groups with large export potential are often produced by multinational corporations and normally do not need export promotion. Secondly, a comparison with DSM results for previous years, although somewhat difficult due to changes in the product classification, shows that the export opportunities detected change significantly over time and, therefore, need to be critically assessed and prioritised. The DSM is definitely not a "push button" system, neither in its filtering process, nor in the direct use that can be made of its output. Moreover, in the future, simulations with the DSM based on "shocks" of its decision parameters, instead of comparing results over time, should allow assessing better the robustness of the results.

Evidently, the DSM, although its strength resides in its considering of export opportunities of an exporting country in the world at large, can also be applied at a regional level, worldwide or individual. This was illustrated in the analysis of the export opportunities of South Africa on the African continent. Apart from political considerations, an important reason for restricting the analysis to the African continent is that for reasons of geographical and cultural distance from South Africa, the other African countries are probably offering export opportunities that can easier be tapped than these in faraway markets. Moreover, in the use of the DSM for analysis of export opportunities of a country at a regional level, instead of a global level, more detailed and reliable information on existing trade barriers are available, and the implications of relevant bilateral, multilateral and regional economic agreements for these trade barriers and for international trade of the countries involved can better be ascertained.

Another promising and new avenue which was followed is the application of the DSM methodology to services. This necessitated some important adaptations in the filters of the DSM, in order to fully take into account the nature of the available statistical data. The South African DSM results for services thus detected, revealed important potentials in travel and transport business, as well as in telecommunication, construction, advertising and market research, etc. Apart from the detection of such opportunities per se, the combination of these results for services with these for products is offering an innovative research agenda for the future, also allowing countries to better tap the synergetic effects in the joint export promotion of specific products and related services.

The same arguments hold *mutadis mutandis* for foreign direct investment (FDI), both incoming and outgoing. We are convinced that the basic DSM methodology can be applied to foreign direct investment promotion, which will offer a completely new and unexplored area of research in public choice. By combining the results thus obtained regarding FDI opportunities, with these on export opportunities for products and these for services, a fully integrated approach develops for policy decision-making in the field of international business at large.

Although there is no standard available to compare the number of export opportunities of a country, or the value of potential exports associated with these opportunities, cross-country comparison is possible and leads to some challenging results. In this volume we assessed the DSM results of Belgium, South Africa and Thailand, against each other. However, as the filtering process of the DSM as well as the data used are the same for the three countries, reflecting the global economic situation and recent international trade patterns at a world scale, it will come as no surprise that the results of these countries are similar. Important differences appear once the DSM results, which can be interpreted as showing potential export opportunities, are supplemented with the respective comparative advantage indicators. In this way, actual export opportunities for Belgium, South Africa and Thailand were derived, which in turn were used in an analysis of the potential degree of utilisation of the export opportunities per broad product group and/or importing region in the world. This analysis revealed that Belgium is most adapted to exploit its potential export opportunities in the world market, which should not come too much as a surprise taking into account that a lot of demand in the world still originates in the industrialised countries. It was also shown that Thailand seems to be much better adapted than South Africa to tap into the export potentials in the world. Future research on the export opportunities of other exporting countries will lead to more insight in the patterns of international trade that shape economic development of countries and regions.

Apart from being an instrument to identify export opportunities, export promotion organisations can also use the DSM results in the preparation and assessment of export promotion activities. In Filter 4 of the DSM, the export opportunities detected are grouped according to the respective market shares of the exporting country in the various target markets and according to some general import market characteristics at the level of the respective products. Obviously, export promotion strategies will differ, and hence the export promotion activities required, between, e.g. a yet to tap relatively small export opportunity which shows long-term growth in the past, and a large and relatively stable export opportunity in a country where the exporting country has already achieved a relatively strong market position. Appropriate export promotion strategies at product level can thus be designed, by taking this into account. In the present volume, we have explored this in some detail and attempted to make the strategic considerations based on DSM results as concrete as possible by illustrating the choices made in three detailed case studies of South African export opportunities. If one lesson can be drawn from this exercise it is that the DSM results provide input in this process of concrete strategy formulation, but that much more concrete and detailed information is required for designing an appropriate export promotion strategy. This important input should come from market research, both desk and field research, and from further competitive intelligence on given export opportunities.

Post factum assessment of the export promotion agency's activities has remained an underdeveloped area. One of the major reasons for this unfortunate state of affairs is that often significant time lags are involved between an export promotion activity and its impact. As the DSM identifies existing export opportunities in the world, these can be used as a standard of assessment. Whether the export promotion activities in a given year or a given period, were directed towards the relevant export opportunities, can then be ascertained in various ways. The potentials for such assessment were illustrated in this volume for Belgium in the 1999-2003 period by looking into the correlation between the list of export opportunities and the list of export promotion activities organised. It is striking that not much correlation was found. Most likely, the existing processes of identification, formulation and planning of export promotion activities within the Belgian public export promotion agencies during the period covered, must be held responsible for the poor correlation with the Belgian export opportunities in the world. In the future it would be interesting to do a similar exercise for a more recent period, and also to explore whether time lags are involved between changes in demand in the world and the policy reactions of export promotion agencies.

Last but not least, this volume explores the needs for competitive intelligence of exporters. After export promotion strategies were formulated and implemented by the export promotion agency, using all relevant information, the exporters who follow the export leads, need careful preparation for which the agency, but more importantly private sector organisations and consultants can provide the required input by using the appropriate competitive intelligence techniques. In particular such input will take into account the concrete situation of the individual exporters and the stage of exporting they are in.

Index

www.ingramcontent.com/pod-product-compliance
Lightning Source LLC
Chambersburg PA
CBHW071959220326
41599CB00034BA/6887